VICTIM'S RIGHTS

Other books by Gary North

Marx's Religion of Revolution, 1968 [1989]
An Introduction to Christian Economics, 1973
Unconditional Surrender, 1981
Successful Investing in an Age of Envy, 1981
The Dominion Covenant: Genesis, 1982
Government By Emergency, 1983
The Last Train Out, 1983
Backward, Christian Soldiers?, 1984
75 Bible Questions Your Instructors Pray You Won't Ask, 1984
Coined Freedom: Gold in the Age of the Bureaucrats, 1984
Moses and Pharaoh: Dominion Religion Versus Power Religion, 1985
Negatrends, 1985
The Sinai Strategy, 1986
Conspiracy: A Biblical View, 1986
Unholy Spirits: Occultism and New Age Humanism, 1986
Honest Money, 1986
Fighting Chance, 1986 [with Arthur Robinson]
Dominion and Common Grace, 1987
Inherit the Earth, 1987
The Pirate Economy, 1987
Liberating Planet Earth, 1987
Healer of the Nations, 1987
Is the World Running Down?, 1988
Puritan Economic Experiments, 1988
Political Polytheism: The Myth of Pluralism, 1989
Trespassing for Dear Life, 1989
When Justice Is Aborted, 1989
The Hoax of Higher Criticism, 1989
The Judeo-Christian Tradition, 1990
✳ *Tools of Dominion: The Case Laws of Exodus*, 1990
Millennialism and Social Theory, 1990
Christian Reconstruction, 1990 [with Gary DeMar]

Books edited by Gary North

Foundations of Christian Scholarship, 1976
Tactics of Christian Resistance, 1983
The Theology of Christian Resistance, 1983
Editor, *Journal of Christian Reconstruction* (1974-1981)

VICTIM'S RIGHTS

The Biblical View of Civil Justice

Gary North

Institute for Christian Economics
Tyler, Texas

Copyright ©1990 by Gary North

Published by the Institute for Christian Economics.
P.O. Box 8000, Tyler, Texas 75711

Typesetting by Nhung Pham Nguyen

Printed in the United States of America

Library of Congress Cataloging-in-Publication Data

North, Gary.
   Victim's rights: the biblical view of civil justice / Gary North.
     p. cm.
   Includes bibliographical references and indexes.
   ISBN 0-930464-17-6 (alk. paper): $14.95
   1. Justice – Biblical teaching. 2. Restitution – Biblical teaching. 3. Law (Theology) – Biblical teaching. 4. Justice, Administration of – United States. 5. Victims of crimes – Legal status, laws, etc. – United States. 6. Dominion theology. 7. Bible. O.T. Exodus – Criticism, interpretation, etc. I. Title.
  BS680.J8N67   1990
  241'.622 – dc20   90-44629
                                                                          CIP

This book is dedicated to
Baby Doe
and the 50 million other victims who are aborted annually, worldwide. They, not their executioners, deserve our compassion.

TABLE OF CONTENTS

Preface	ix
Introduction	1
1. The Covenant Lawsuit	15
2. The Death Penalty	34
3. Kidnapping	65
4. The Costs of Private Conflict	85
5. Legitimate Violence	99
6. The Ransom for an Eye	113
7. The Ransom for a Life	137
8. The Principle of Limited Liability	155
9. The Pitfalls of Negligence	167
10. Restitution, Repentance, and Restoration	180
11. Protecting the Victims	193
12. Restoring Full Value	204
13. Restitution and Deterrence	220
14. Guardian of the Oath	233
15. Personal Responsibility and Personal Liberty	242
16. Binding the State	253
17. Emptying the Prisons, Slowly	265
Conclusion	278
APPENDIX: Violent Crime in the United States, 1980	285
Scripture Index	299
General Index	305

PREFACE

A Jacksonville [Texas] man was sentenced by Cherokee County Judicial District Court Judge Morris W. Hassell to 50 years in prison for robbing the Holiday Inn, District Attorney Charles R. Holcomb said Wednesday.

Marvin Hall, 31, also known as Marion Hall, pleaded guilty to a robbery charge in connection with the incident, which occurred a few minutes after midnight Nov. 25, 1989.

In another robbery case, Hassell sentenced James Virgil Walker, 24, to 10 years in prison for robbing Floyd Roach of Rusk of his wallet on Oct. 5, 1989, about a quarter miles from Love's Lookout between Jacksonville and Tyler as the two men were enroute to a Jacksonville club.

Jerry Dale Jones, 26, Jacksonville, was sentenced to 12 years in prison on a charge of burglary of a habitation. Jones took guns, jewelry and an assortment of other items owned by William Patterson in Jacksonville, Holcomb said. Most of the items were recovered, he added.

A 22-year-old Bullard man pleaded guilty to a charge of aggravated sexual assault on a child on Aug. 26, 1986, in Bullard, Assistant District Attorney Elmer Beckworth said. The man was sentenced to eight years and sent to boot camp, a new program that provides counseling and military-type training.[1]

Just a routine news story in a local newspaper, the kind of story that is rarely read by anyone and is instantly forgotten by most of those who do read it. It fills space, in between the ads for beauty aids and new tires. Yet its very undistinguished quality is

---

1. *Tyler Morning Telegraph* (March 19, 1990).

what makes it so remarkable, for it testifies of a society gone mad.

A man robs someone at a motel. He loses up to 50 years of his life. Another man robs the wallet of a drinking partner as they head for a beer-joint across the county line of a "dry" (no liquor) Texas county. He loses a decade of his life. Another man gets a dozen years in jail for burglarizing a home. Most of the stolen goods had been recovered. If all three men serve one-third of their sentences before parole, a conventional experience, then taxpayers of the state of Texas will pay approximately $600,000 (assuming that inflation goes to zero) into the overcrowded Texas prison system to keep them under lock and key.

Meanwhile, a carefully unidentified adult male gets a sentence of eight years for the sexual assault of a child. He will not go to jail; he will be sent to a youth work camp where the men will work all day and receive counselling. It took the court over three years to convict him.

The penal sanctions that a civil law applies to a convicted criminal reveal to the general public what the comparative heinousness of crimes are in the eyes of "society." What, then, do these sentences reveal? That stealing a drinking buddy's wallet is twenty percent more evil than sexually assaulting a child. Committing a robbery at a motel? Clearly, this is six times more heinous than sexually assaulting a child.

Texas is not a unique state, despite the claims to the contrary of both Texans and non-Texans. If its courts' sentences were deemed outrageous in terms of national standards, the United States Supreme Court would intervene, as it regularly does in everything else. But there has been no particular interest by the judicial system in jail sentences that stretch well into the next century for petty crimes.

What can we make of this? I think I am not exaggerating when I say that Americans now suffer from a system of civil justice that can best be described as demonic. Yet they do not perceive themselves as suffering. This nation is supposed to be the most self-consciously Protestant industrial nation on earth. Are such sentences Christianity in action? Do our civil courts reflect the religious commitment of our people?

Obviously, they do. If they did not, voters would change the system. They accept it. So, sometime between the Protestant Reformation and the present, Protestants lost sight of the requirements of civil justice. They have no idea that the Bible speaks to this issue. They have no idea where to look in the Bible for guidance in questions of civil justice. They do not recognize that the Bible says that the civil laws of a society are to testify internationally to the justice of God.

Behold, I have taught you statutes and judgments, even as the LORD my God commanded me, that ye should do so in the land whither ye go to possess it. Keep therefore and do them; for this is your wisdom and your understanding in the sight of the nations, which shall hear all these statutes, and say, Surely this great nation is a wise and understanding people. For what nation is there so great, who hath God so nigh unto them, as the LORD our God is in all things that we call upon him for? And what nation is there so great, that hath statutes and judgments so righteous as all this law, which I set before you this day? (Deut. 4:5-8).

To which the typical Protestant replies, "That's Old Testament stuff!" Indeed, it is. Then he adds: "The New Testament has done away with all that. We're under grace, not law!" Not quite; we are visibly under the jurisdiction of civil judges who are authorized by the electorate to hand out half-century sentences for robbing someone at a motel. God is not mocked. It is never a question of "law vs. no law"; it is a question of *whose* law.

This book explores the biblical legal principles that are supposed to govern such cases as robbing someone at a motel or burglarizing a house. It deals with a lot more than this, but at the very least, it covers these basics. It shows what God says should be done with criminals who commit such crimes. And it also shows what should be done about those silent people who never see justice today: the victims.[2]

This book is a spin-off of my more comprehensive study, *Tools of Dominion: The Case Laws of Exodus* (Institute for Christian Eco-

---

2. There is a small, underfunded, non-profit organization, formed in 1985, which promotes the concept of victim's rights: the National Victim Center, 307 W. Seventh St., Suite 1001, Ft. Worth, TX 76102. There ought to be dozens.

nomics, 1990). That book, a Bible commentary approaching 1,300 pages, is unlikely to be widely read. It is my hope that this shorter work will generate greater interest by the Christian public. Until it does, or a book like it does, we will continue to live in a world devoid of justice, as defined by the One who will at last impose His perfect justice and His eternal sanctions.

INTRODUCTION

Let your light so shine before men, that they may see your good works, and glorify your Father which is in heaven. Think not that I am come to destroy the law, or the prophets: I am not come to destroy, but to fulfil. For verily I say unto you, Till heaven and earth pass, one jot or one tittle shall in no wise pass from the law, till all be fulfilled. Whosoever therefore shall break one of these least commandments, and shall teach men so, he shall be called the least in the kingdom of heaven: but whosoever shall do and teach them, the same shall be called great in the kingdom of heaven (Matt. 5:16-19).

The first sentence of this passage from the Sermon on the Mount is important: "Let your light so shine before men, that they may see your good works, and glorify your Father which is in heaven." This is Jesus' vision of the city on a hill: "Ye are the light of the world. A city that is set on an hill cannot be hid. Neither do men light a candle, and put it under a bushel, but on a candlestick; and it giveth light unto all that are in the house" (Matt. 5:14-15). It is Jesus' confirmation for His people of Israel's original requirement:

Behold, I have taught you statutes and judgments, even as the LORD my God commanded me, that ye should do so in the land whither ye go to possess it. Keep therefore and do them; for this is your wisdom and your understanding in the sight of the nations, which shall hear all these statutes, and say, Surely this great nation is a wise and understanding people. For what nation is there so great, who hath God so nigh unto them, as the LORD our God is in all things that we call upon him for? And what nation is there so great, that hath statutes and judgments so righteous as all this law, which I set before you this day? (Deut. 4:5-8).

What this passage reveals is that *God's Bible-revealed law is a tool of international evangelism*. This fact has been forgotten or ignored by Christians for well over three centuries. The "city on a hill" concept has been redefined by Christians to apply only to personal ethics, family ethics, and church order. It is not supposed to have anything to do with social order. The modern church self-consciously denies what the Bible makes plain, namely, that biblical law is the only God-sanctioned means of bringing permanent social order (Lev. 26; Deut. 28). The Bible teaches this clearly, but modern man sticks his fingers in his ears. He refuses to listen. To admit this would be to admit that the works of his own hands cannot save his soul, heal his institutions, or bring lasting social peace.

This deafness is a sign of God's wrath: He has made modern man judicially blind and deaf, just as He did with the Jews of Jesus' day: "For this people's heart is waxed gross, and their ears are dull of hearing, and their eyes they have closed; lest at any time they should see with their eyes and hear with their ears, and should understand with their heart, and should be converted, and I should heal them" (Matt. 13:15). This was Isaiah's warning, too (Isa. 6:9-10). Jesus then told His disciples that they were not numbered among those who were judicially blind: "But blessed are your eyes, for they see: and your ears, for they hear" (Matt. 13:16).

In our day, however, this blessing has been withdrawn, at least with respect to the church's understanding of (and respect for) God's revealed law. God has given the church over to its sins. The vast majority of God's people today have self-consciously adopted the same view of biblical law that is held by the covenant-breakers. They have abandoned the heritage of the Calvinist Protestant Reformers and the Puritans, who held the civil laws of the Old Testament in high regard — a fact that has been written out of the history books, including most of the specialized monographs written by church historians.[1]

---

1. A notable exception is the remarkable, massively documented book by Henning Graf Reventlow, *The Authority of the Bible and the Rise of the Modern World* (Philadelphia: Fortress Press; London: SCM Press, [1980] 1984).

Ideas have consequences. The American church has been swept by a series of front-page scandals — the mere tip of the iceberg.[2] The pagan world howls with delight. By honoring God's law, Christians evangelize; by self-consciously disobeying it, they "de-evangelize." As Nathan reminded David: "Howbeit, because by this deed thou hast given great occasion to the enemies of the LORD to blaspheme, the child also that is born unto thee shall surely die" (II Sam. 12:14). There are negative sanctions built into God's covenant order; if men will not enforce them, God will. This is how God evangelizes. To which the evangelical church responds: "Mean God, harsh God, naughty, naughty! Go to your room!"

A Harsh God

The position defended by Christian Reconstruction affirms the continuing validity of Old Testament civil laws, including especially the law's negative sanctions, in the New Testament era. Because of this, Christian Reconstruction has been dismissed as a deviant theology, especially by dispensationalists.[3] The Reconstructionists' position on the law is frequently described by its critics as being overly harsh. This accusation — that our position is judicially harsh — rests on a specific though unstated view of the God of the Old Covenant, namely, that God's required civil law system in the Old Testament era was itself judicially harsh,

---

2. I know of one small Calvinist denomination that has this as its unofficial policy for dealing with pastors caught in adultery: the offending man is quietly transferred to a different presbytery. "Get this man away from our wives!" is apparently a major presbyterial motivation. I do not exaggerate. I purchased a portion of my theological library from one of these men. He had resigned voluntarily from the ministry after having been asked to seek employment in a new presbytery.

What non-Calvinists do is not significantly better. Fundamentalist ministers caught in adultery often remain in the same pulpit if they publicly repent. Or they take half the congregation with them in a church split. Everyone knows this, but nothing is done about it. The moral standards of the collapsing humanist culture are dominant within the churches.

3. H. Wayne House and Thomas Ice, *Dominion Theology: Blessing or Curse?* (Portland, Oregon: Multnomah Press, 1988); Hal Lindsey, *The Road to Holocaust* (New York: Bantam, 1989). For a detailed response to both books, see Greg L. Bahnsen and Kenneth L. Gentry, *House Divided: The Break-Up of Dispensational Theology* (Tyler, Texas: Institute for Christian Economics, 1989).

but fortunately for us, Jesus has abolished it, or at least drastically softened its harsh aspects. Jesus, in other words, is meek and mild, but His Father in heaven is mean and harsh. Fortunately for us, we are assured, Jesus has persuaded His Father to change His mind about the penalties of the law. God the Father insisted on civil justice; fortunately for us, Jesus insists only on love.[4] "No creed but the Bible, no law but love!" has been the battle cry of fundamentalist antinomians throughout the twentieth century.

It is not only the fundamentalists who have been promoters of this antinomian view of God's law and sanctions in history. It has been the whole Church, with the exception of the Calvinist Protestant Reformers – William Tyndale is a good example,[5] but so are Bucer[6] and Calvin[7] – and the seventeenth-century Puritans. They alone were willing to affirm a positive view of Old Testament law. Since then, it has been all downhill: from the Newtonian revolution – Newton, it should be noted, was in private a dedicated alchemist and an anti-Trinitarian mystic[8] – through natural law theory and Scottish Common Sense rationalism[9] to modern neo-orthodoxy and neo-evangelicalism. *God's people have hated His law.* In response, He has steadily removed

---

4. See Lindsey, *Road to Holocaust*, p. 158.

5. See especially his Prologue to his translation of Jonah (1531) and his Prologue to Romans (1534). Cf. Reventlow, *Authority of the Bible*, pp. 106-7.

6. Bucer, *De regno Christi* (1550); Reventlow, pp. 83-86.

7. John Calvin, *The Covenant Enforced*, edited by James B. Jordan (Tyler, Texas: Institute for Christian Economics, 1990).

8. See especially J. E. McGuire and P. M. Rattansi, "Newton and the Pipes of Pan," *Notes and Queries of the Royal Society of London*, XXI (1966), pp. 108-43. See also Betty J. T. Dobbs, *The Foundations of Newton's Alchemy; Or, "The Hunting of the Green Lyon"* (Cambridge: Cambridge University Press, 1977); Keith Thomas, *Religion and the Decline of Magic* (New York: Scribner's, 1971), pp. 226, 292, 352, 644; John Maynard Keynes, "Newton the Man," in *Newton Tercentennary Celebrations* (Cambridge: Cambridge University Press, 1947); Frances A. Yates, *Collected Essays*, vol. 3, *Ideas and Ideals in the North European Renaissance* (London: Routledge & Kegan Paul, 1984), p. 121. On Newton's anti-Trinitarianism, see Gale E. Christianson, *In the Presence of the Creation: Isaac Newton and His Times* (New York: Free Press, 1984), pp. 470, 564.

9. S. A. Grave, *The Scottish Philosophy of Common Sense* (Oxford: Clarendon Press, 1960). See also Sydney E. Ahlstrom, "The Scottish Philosophy and American Theology," *Church History*, XXIV (1955), pp. 257-72.

them from power and influence for the last three centuries.

Historical Judgments and the Final Judgment

Christians today hate the idea that God holds individuals personally responsible for obeying His revealed law, and so they also deny that God holds society collectively responsible for obeying His law. They deny the possibility of the following:

> And it shall be, if thou do at all forget the LORD thy God, and walk after other gods, and serve them, and worship them, I testify against you this day that ye shall surely perish. As the nations which the LORD destroyeth before your face, so shall ye perish; because ye would not be obedient unto the voice of the LORD your God (Deut. 8:19-20).

Such preliminary historical negative judgments are intended by God to remind men of His final judgment at the end of history. Covenant-breaking man hates the thought of the latter, so he denies the possibility of the former. Things happen randomly, not covenantally, he prefers to believe. In preference to a belief in the final judgment, self-proclaimed autonomous man will believe in the sovereignty of anything else, from creeping things (Rom. 1:22-23) to impersonal random forces that produce creeping things out of lifeless chemicals (Darwinism). He much prefers to believe in the cosmic death of the universe rather than the eternal resurrection of all men, some to eternal joy in the presence of God, and the rest to God's eternal torturing.[10]

The doctrine of final judgment affects every other theological doctrine, although modern theologians in all camps are almost perversely unwilling to admit this possibility or even debate it. It also affects social theory, which social theorists have been equally unwilling to discuss. *There can be no society without a doctrine of final judgment.* This doctrine is an inescapable concept. The question is never, "Final judgment or no final judgment?" The question is: "Who will administer this final judgment?" There are also two secondary questions: "Who speaks representatively in history for this judge? Who administers his preliminary, representative judgments?"

---

10. Gary North, *Is the World Running Down? Crisis in the Christian Worldview* (Tyler, Texas: Institute for Christian Economics, 1988), ch. 2.

The social question of questions in man's history is this one, although it is seldom asked formally: *"Heaven or hell on earth?"* It has to be one or the other in every society, progressively revealed over time.[11] There is no neutral third position.[12] It is this crucial question which political pluralists devote their lives either to avoiding or denying.[13]

Harsh for Whom?

I have written this book in order to challenge the arguments of the critics of Old Testament law. My goal here is simple to describe though not so simple to execute: to demonstrate that the negative penalties of the Old Testament case laws were not harsh but just, not a threat to society but rather the necessary judicial foundation of civic freedom. I do not attempt to prove here that most of the Old Testament's civil laws are still binding today. That argument has been made elsewhere,[14] and will continue to be refined as God's Church continues to move toward the final judgment. Instead, I examine a specific group of Old Testament case laws that in one way or another upheld the interests of victims of criminal acts. It is my argument throughout this book that *the Old Testament was harsh on criminals because it was "soft on victims."*

God's Old Testament laws, both ecclesiastical and civil, protected the victims' interests. These laws were harsh on criminals

---

11. Amillennialists teach that Satan's kingdom will be progressively dominant in history. In this sense, they are "pre-mils without earthly hope." Premillennialists deny the progressive character of this development. They see Christian progress as discontinuous; prior to the Second Coming and Jesus' establishment of an earthly millennium, covenant-breaking men are said to be progressively dominant in society. After Jesus returns, Christians are said to be dominant. But there is no neutrality with respect to historical development; one kingdom is steadily overcoming the efforts of the other throughout history, all sides agree.

12. I am writing a book on this subject, *Heaven or Hell on Earth: The Sociology of Final Judgment*.

13. Gary North, *Political Polytheism: The Myth of Pluralism* (Tyler, Texas: Institute for Christian Economics, 1989).

14. Greg L. Bahnsen, *Theonomy in Christian Ethics* (2nd ed.; Phillipsburg, New Jersey: Presbyterian & Reformed, 1984); Bahnsen, *By This Standard: The Authority of God's Law Today* (Tyler, Texas: Institute for Christian Economics, 1985).

by today's standards, although they were mild compared to the civil laws of ancient Near Eastern laws generally or to Islamic justice today, and incredibly mild compared to the screaming, merciless, eternal agony of the lake of fire that is in store for everyone who rejects Jesus Christ as his personal savior (Rev. 20:14-15). (It never ceases to amaze me that Christians who say they believe in eternal punishment get all in a dither about the supposed injustice of a New Covenant era application of this or that Old Testament law. What specific Old Testament punishment matches eternal torture by a wrathful, jealous God? It is not surprising that evangelicals today are steadily abandoning the doctrine of eternal judgment in the lake of fire; such a view conflicts with their denial of the legitimacy of Old Testament civil sanctions today.)

Subsidizing the Criminal

In the modern world, we have experienced a huge increase in criminal activity.[15] This has been the inevitable result of the West's steady abandonment of biblical penal sanctions. Western society has been in revolt against God's penal sanctions for many centuries. From the beginning, the West substituted public torture followed by capital punishment by an executioner in place of the Old Testament's requirement of execution by public stoning. Second, it substituted imprisonment for restitution to victims. Third, in the 1820's, the United States began to substitute the centralized state prison systems for local jails and public flogging, and these new institutions became the penal models for the whole Western world.[16] Fourth, civil courts substituted life imprisonment for capital punishment. Fifth, judges substituted parole for life imprisonment. By the early 1970's, for example, the median time served in prison for homicide in the State of Massachusetts was under three years.[17] Step by step, the West began to subsidize the criminals at the expense of the victims, and all in the name of compassion.

---

15. See the Appendix, "Violent Crime in the United States, 1980."

16. David J. Rothman, *The Discovery of the Asylum: Social Order and Disorder in the New Republic* (Boston: Little, Brown, 1971).

17. James Q. Wilson, *Thinking About Crime* (New York: Basic Books, 1975), p. 186.

Humanist man's god is man himself, especially collective mankind, who is supposedly incarnate in the State. Crimes against individuals are understood by humanists as essentially crimes against mankind, which in turn are perceived as crimes against the State. We hear the phrase, "He has paid his debt to society" after some murderer or brutal thief has spent three or four years in jail. But what about his victim and the victim's heirs? What has he paid to them? Nothing. Similarly, we read editorials about some foreign nation's "crimes against humanity." When we examine these crimes more carefully, they turn out to be crimes against the liberal's vision of the messianic State — crimes committed by this or that foreign dictator who is: 1) perceived as not being a liberal, a socialist, or a Communist, and 2) who also has lost a major war or has recently been deposed.

But what about specific penalties for specific crimes against specific victims? What about a system of restitution that helps both victim and criminal to recover? Silence. Why? Because such specifics point too clearly to the idea of God's final judgment and covenant-breaking man's desperate need for someone to make adequate restitution for him. This, above all, is what covenant-breaking man does not want to think about. Because he refuses to acknowledge the restitution payment offered to God in his behalf,[18] he denies that God will ever impose negative sanctions, in the next world surely, and therefore in this world, too.

Destroying Social Order

As the intellectuals' concern about crimes against humanity has increased, their concern about crimes against God has decreased.[19] We seldom hear discussions of crimes against the very fabric of communal life. One exception to this rule is Harvard University's political scientist James Q. Wilson: "Predatory crime does not merely victimize individuals, it impedes and, in the extreme case, even prevents the formation and maintenance of

---

18. On the differences between common grace and special (soul-saving) grace, see Gary North, *Dominion and Common Grace*, (Tyler, Texas: Institute for Christian Economics, 1987).

19. See, for example, Leonard W. Levy, *Treason Against God: A History of the Offense of Blasphemy* (New York: Schocken, 1981).

community. By disrupting the delicate nexus of ties, formal and informal, by which we are linked with our neighbors, crime atomizes society and makes of its members mere individual calculators estimating their own advantage, especially their own chances for survival amidst their fellows."[20]

The Old Testament's law-order, *when enforced by the judges*, overcame these criminal tendencies toward social atomization. Old Testament criminal law was designed by God to protect the community by defending the rights of innocent victims. Today, we have seen the rise of the messianic State, whose self-appointed task is to heal society through a program of salvation by legislation. Humanism substitutes the concept of salvation by man's law for salvation by God's grace. It also substitutes its own sanctions for the Bible's sanctions. It promises to redeem (rehabilitate) criminals, but then neglects to defend their victims. Until quite recently, it focused exclusively on rehabilitation rather than restitution, not understanding that *without restitution there can be no rehabilitation, socially or psychologically*. Without Jesus Christ's restitution payment to God for the sins of man, there could never have been rehabilitation cosmically, for even with it, the whole world came under a curse (Gen. 3:18). Society's institutions of justice are supposed to reflect the judicial terms of this cosmic redemption. When they do not, we can confidently expect God's historical negative sanctions to reform the institutions (Deut. 28:15-68).

The Negative Function of Biblical Civil Law

The function of civil law, according to the Bible, is not to save men's souls but to restrain their evil public behavior. Biblical law points to God and His judgment, and so can become a means of special saving grace (Rom. 7:7-12), but the function of all biblical civil law is negative, not positive. Biblical civil law imposes negative sanctions only. It denies the presupposition that man can be saved by law, let alone by legislation. The builders of the modern messianic State have forgotten this, and as a result, we are now engulfed in wave after wave of tyrannical legislation: the never-ending quest to redeem man by remaking his social and economic

---

20. Wilson, *Thinking About Crime*, p. 21.

environment. We are also engulfed in wave after wave of crime, with only the demographics of an aging population serving as a mitigating factor in the industrialized West: a high percentage of crimes are committed by unmarried young men.

What is needed is a return to a legal order that treats all men as responsible moral agents – responsible primarily before God and secondarily before other men. The State should treat criminals as deviants who must be restrained by force, and victims as people with legal rights that must be defended. Biblical law rests on this view of man.

Sanctions: An Inescapable Concept

Undergirding every social order there is a deeply religious view of what constitutes the good society. Behind every view of the good society there is a concept of the bad society, and every society rests on the proposition that negative sanctions must be brought against those whose acts threaten the good society and promote the bad society. It is therefore impossible to conceive of a society without sanctions. It is equally impossible to speak of the State as an agency of society without speaking of legitimate sanctions. *Sanctions are inescapable social concepts.* It is never a question of "sanctions vs. no sanctions." It is always a question of "Which sanctions?"

This leads us to an important conclusion: any attempt to deny the legitimacy of the sanctions specified in the Bible, both Old and New Testaments, is necessarily an attempt to substitute a different set of sanctions. This leads to another conclusion, one which has been vigorously denied by Protestant Christians for at least three centuries, and by other Christians since the second century, A.D.: *any attempt to substitute civil sanctions different from those required by the Bible is necessarily also an attempt to establish or defend an anti-Christian civil order, meaning an anti-Christian society.* This is another way of saying that *there is no neutrality* – not in philosophy, religion, or social theory. There is no social order that can be accurately described as neutral with respect to the claims of Jesus Christ, and the claims of Christ mean the laws of Christ governing every area of life. Jesus said: "If ye love me, keep my commandments" (John 14:15). Jesus also said: "He that is not with me is against me; and he that gathereth not with me scattereth abroad" (Matt. 12:30). By systematically applying this inescapable biblical principle of non-neutrality in several areas of social theory and policy,[21] and by presenting Bible-based evidence for it, verse by verse, the Christian Reconstructionists have earned the hostility of American humanism,[22] conservatism,[23] fundamentalism,[24] traditional pentecostalism,[25] conservative Lutheranism,[26] Calvinistic Presbyterianism,[27] and neo-evangelicalism.[28] (Other groups would be equally outraged, except they have yet to hear about us.)

The New Schizophrenia

If the critics are correct, then this book will reveal just how far Christian Reconstructionists are from the truth, and how close the humanists are to the truth. Either the Word of God establishes the judicial standards for society or else the word of man does. *There is no third position.* This is the reason why those Christians who insist that the Christian Reconstructionists are wrong about the legitimacy of biblical civil law are so frequently (i.e., always) found to be supporters of this or that humanist social program, baptizing it in the name of Christianity. They have no explicitly

---

21. See, for example, the ten-volume set I edited, the Biblical Blueprints Series, published by Dominion Press, Ft. Worth, Texas, 1986-87.

22. Frederick Edwords and Stephen McCabe, "Getting Out God's Vote: Pat Robertson and the Evangelicals," *The Humanist* (May/June 1987). The article links Christian Reconstructionism with Robertson's political ambitions.

23. Anson Shupe, "Prophets of a Biblical America," *Wall Street Journal* (April 12, 1989), editorial page.

24. House and Ice, *Dominion Theology*; Lindsey, *Road to Holocaust*.

25. The Assemblies of God passed a resolution in 1987 declaring "Dominion Theology" a heresy.

26. "Reconstruction and Post-Millennialism: Mixing Law and Gospel – Constructing an Earthly Kingdom," *Christian News* (Oct. 10, 1988), p. 10.

27. Meredith G. Kline, "Comments on an Old-New Error," *Westminster Theological Journal*, XLI (Fall 1978), a critical review of Greg Bahnsen's *Theonomy in Christian Ethics*.

28. Douglas E. Chismar and David A. Rausch, "Regarding Theonomy: An Essay of Concern," *Journal of the Evangelical Theological Society*, vol. 27 (September 1984); Rodney Clapp, "Democracy as Heresy," *Christianity Today* (Feb. 20, 1987).

Bible-based alternatives, no uniquely Christian "third way." They are in the difficult position of trying to fight the deeply political religion of humanism without appealing to biblical law, and trying to refute Christian Reconstruction without becoming mouthpieces for humanism. They want to be regarded as Christian social commentators — not just social commentators who happen to be Christians — yet they categorically refuse to accept as judicially binding any biblical book that appears in the canon of Scripture before the Gospel of Matthew.

Since 1980, more and more conservative Christians have been speaking out on social issues. This used to be a near-monopoly of Social Gospel liberals[29] and neo-evangelical not-yet-completely-liberals.[30] Conservative evangelicals are even writing whole books on social issues. Francis Schaeffer's later books seem to have legitimized such publishing efforts within conservative evangelicalism. Like Schaeffer's books, these recent books are very peculiar intellectual exercises. They adopt an odd outline: a "no biblical law" chapter, followed by a "Christian relevance" chapter, followed by a "no biblical law" chapter, etc. Schaeffer used something very similar to this approach in *A Christian Manifesto* (1981).[31] Charles Colson's *Kingdoms in Conflict* (1987) develops this approach into a fine art.[32] So does Carl Henry's *Twilight of a Great Civilization* (1988).

Reading these published defenses of an "unspecific middle" position is like imagining a single fleet-footed man playing a lonely game of table tennis. He serves: "Wham! — no Old Testament law!" Then there is a frantic rush to get to the other side of the

---

29. C. Gregg Singer, *The Unholy Alliance* (New Rochelle, New York: Arlington House 1975).

30. Ronald H. Nash, *The New Evangelicalism* (Grand Rapids, Michigan: Zondervan, 1963); Richard Quebedeaux, *The Worldly Evangelicals* ((New York: Harper & Row, 1978).

31. For a detailed analysis of the schizophrenia of *A Christian Manifesto*, see Gary North and David Chilton, "Apologetics and Strategy," *Christianity and Civilization 3* (1983), pp. 116-31.

32. Charles Colson (with Ellen Santille Vaughn), *Kingdoms in Conflict* (New York: William Morrow; Grand Rapids: Zondervan, 1987). Morrow is a secular publishing house; Zondervan is fundamentalist.

table to return the shot: "Wham! Uniquely Christian social relevance!" The ball goes faster and faster, back and forth, until the man at last drops from exhaustion. The outcome of the game is resolved only by the unwillingness or inability of the player to continue. It has nothing to do with the strength of either position. The astounding thing is that each author seems utterly oblivious to the fact that he is "playing both sides of the table." Each time he hits the ball, he acts as though he expects someone else on the other side to return it. It is as if the author writes two separate manuscripts, one pro-biblical law and one against, as a kind of academic exercise, and then some inebriated editor mistakenly assembles them into a single volume. Amazingly, these books sell! And the reviewers seem blissfully unaware of the intellectual schizophrenia they are reviewing. I suspect that they are suffering from the same bizarre affliction.[33]

Conclusion

There is today a near-universal agreement within the Christian community that the case laws of the Old Testament do not *and should not* apply to today's societies. We are assured that there are no biblical blueprints for "secular" social institutions. This position is generally defended in the name of religious pluralism. It has been the dominant political idea within even the most conservative Christian circles in America for well over a century.[34] Is this position true? It rests squarely on the concept of religious neutrality in social theory. Can it be true if the Bible is true?

It is the reader's moral responsibility to determine for himself which approach seems the most biblical in the search for appropriate civil sanctions: 1) going to the Bible; 2) going to Harvard University and the Harvard Law School or one of their humanist-

---

33. Gary North, "The Intellectual Schizophrenia of the New Christian Right," *Christianity and Civilization*, 1 (1982), pp. 1-40; Kevin Craig, "Social Apologetics," *ibid.*, pp. 41-76.

34. Gary Scott Smith, *The Seeds of Secularization: Calvinism, Culture, and Pluralism in America, 1870-1915* (Grand Rapids, Michigan: Christian University Press, 1985). With the exception of Bob Jones University, I am unaware of any officially Bible-based, Ph.D. granting university. Still, the publishing company's name has a nice ring to it. The firm is a subdivision of William B. Eerdmans Company.

accredited clones; 3) going to the Chamber of Commerce. There are millions of professionally naive Christians today who insist that they are not doing the second or third just because they refuse to do the first. They are self-deceived.

1
THE COVENANT LAWSUIT

And he that smiteth his father, or his mother, shall be surely put to death (Ex. 21:15).

And he that curseth his father, or his mother, shall surely be put to death (Ex. 21:17).

The theocentric principle here is obvious: God the Father must not be attacked by His children. Parents are God's covenantal agents in the family, which is a hierarchical, oath-bound covenantal institution. They are God's covenantal *representatives* in the family. To strike an earthly parent is the covenantal equivalent of striking at God. It is an act of moral rebellion so great that the death penalty is invoked.

The doctrine of hierarchy, which includes the doctrine of representation,[1] is point two of the biblical covenant model. The Book of Exodus, the second book in the Pentateuch, is primarily concerned with point two of the covenant, for the Pentateuch is itself structured in terms of the biblical covenant's five-point structure.[2] It is appropriate that questions relating to representation should be the focus of several of the case laws of Exodus.

The covenant's representation principle is built into the creation. We know that the visible creation testifies to the existence of the invisible God. "For the invisible things of him from the creation of the world are clearly seen, being understood by the

---

1. Ray R. Sutton, *That You May Prosper: Dominion By Covenant* (Tyler, Texas: Institute for Christian Economics, 1987), pp. 46-47.

2. Gary North, *The Dominion Covenant: Genesis* (2nd ed.; Tyler, Texas: Institute for Christian Economics, 1987), pp. x-xiv.

things that are made, even his eternal power and Godhead; so that they are without excuse" (Rom. 1:20). Men, as creatures, cannot strike at God directly. They must act through intermediaries. Men strike some aspect of God's creation in their attempt to strike at God. A crime is committed in history against God-created men and the God-created environment, but always in the creation's capacity as reflecting God. Men are creatures, so they must use the creation as the only available means of any attempted attack on God. As Cornelius Van Til once wrote, the child must sit on the father's lap in order to slap his face.

Biblically and covenantally speaking, the earthly victim of a crime is always the secondary victim; *God is always the primary victim*. Ours is a theocentric universe, not anthropocentric. This means, additionally, that the criminal acts in his own interests secondarily; when committing a biblically prohibited act, he acts primarily as Satan's representative, just as Adam did. This judicial principle — the doctrine of covenantal representation — is not intuitively apparent to those who are not trained to think theocentrically and covenantally. We must learn to think theocentrically and representatively (covenantally) when we think about crime and punishment.

Christians and Jews should therefore begin any consideration of the principles of biblical jurisprudence with this fundamental legal principle: *God is always the primary victim of every sin and every crime*. This leads to a crucial conclusion: *the victims of any crime or unlawful attack become the legal representatives of God*. The victim of a crime is authorized by God, the Author of history, to initiate a covenant lawsuit against the suspected criminal. He and he alone is so authorized. While it is legitimate to speak of primary and secondary earthly victims of crime, we must always bear in mind that the primary cosmic victim is always God.

Because of the somewhat intricate nature of my arguments in this chapter, I think it is best if I state my conclusion in advance, so that the reader will be better able to assess the cogency of my argumentation. The conclusion that I have come to after having studied in detail this and other biblical case laws is that the following judicial principle is dominant in the Bible: *if the victim of a crime fails to initiate this covenant lawsuit, then the other covenantal agents of God must honor this decision* — the civil magistrate, the church officer, and the head of a household. They are not authorized in this instance to step in and prosecute in God's name as God-ordained covenantal judges. They are unquestionably judges.[3] But because of the principle of victim's rights, they are prohibited from prosecuting if the victim decides to forego bringing the lawsuit, *unless they can show that they themselves have become victims because of the original victim's failure to prosecute.*

This does not mean that the civil government cannot lawfully prosecute a criminal who has either bribed or threatened a victim or a witness to withhold evidence from the court. Such an act is defined in modern jurisprudence as obstructing justice; it places the judges at a disadvantage in pursuing their God-given assignment. It reduces their ability to protect the public. The criminal would walk out of the court as a free man when he should be placed under restraints or even executed. If allowed to go free without suffering sanctions, he would place other citizens under a greater statistical probability of fraud or violence. For example, the public is entitled to information from victims regarding felonies committed by repeat offenders. Thus, the court has a legitimate right to impose sanctions against criminals who use the threat of violence against a victim, and on both the victim and the criminal if the latter has paid the victim to keep quiet regarding a felony that would otherwise have led to the lawful execution of the criminal if convicted.

What we must understand is that in biblical jurisprudence, *it is the victim whose rights must always be upheld*, not simply because he was harmed by the criminal, but also because *he served as God's surrogate when he became the victim.* God is the primary victim, and His rights must be upheld first and foremost. His specified judicial sanctions must be enforced by His designated covenantal representatives. His case laws provide mankind with the proper guidelines of how His honor is to be upheld in various cases.

There is another Bible-sanctioned office to consider, the office

---

3. Gary North, *When Justice Is Aborted: Biblical Standards for Non-Violent Resistance* (Ft. Worth, Texas: Dominion Press, 1989), ch. 2.

of *witness*. The witness is authorized to bring relevant information to one of these covenantal judges, so that the judge can initiate the covenant lawsuit against the suspected violator.[4] The witness plays a very important role in the prosecution of God's covenant lawsuits. Without at least two witnesses, it is illegal to execute anyone (Deut. 17:6). Also, the affirming witnesses in a capital lawsuit must be the first people to cast stones (Deut. 17:7).

The Biblical Hierarchical Structure

Adam was allowed to do anything he wanted in the garden, except eat from the forbidden tree. There was a specific sanction attached to that crime, a capital sanction. This reveals a fundamental biblical judicial principle: *anything is permitted unless it is explicitly prohibited by law, or prohibited by an extension of a case law's principle*. This principle places the individual under public law, but it also relies on self-government as the primary policing device. It creates the bottom-up appeals court character of biblical society. Men are judicially free to act however they please unless society, through its various covenantal courts, has been authorized by God's Bible-revealed law to restrict certain specified kinds of behavior.

The bottom-up appeals court structure of the biblical hierarchy is in opposition to the principle of top-down bureaucratic control. Under the latter hierarchical system, in theory nothing is permitted except what has been commanded. The decision-making private individual is tightly restricted; the centralized State is expanded. This is the governing principle of all socialist economic planning. It assumes the omniscience and omnicompetence of distant central planners.[5]

---

4. The hostility of siblings against "tattletales" in a family is easily explainable: youthful law-breakers resent judgment. They resent witnesses whose action brings the dreaded sanctions. But what about parents? Parents who side with the critics of "tattletales" are thereby attempting to escape their God-given role as judges. They are saying, in principle, "We don't want to know about it. We don't want to serve as judges, despite our position as God's designated representative agents in this family."

5. Gary North, *Marx's Religion of Revolution: Regeneration Through Chaos* (Tyler, Texas: Institute for Christian Economics, [1968] 1989), Appendix A: "Socialist Economic Calculation."

What a free society needs is predictable law.[6] The maximum sanction for any crime must be specified in written law or at least in traditional legal precedent. The criminal must know the maximum negative consequences of conviction. He is under law, but so are his judges. The State as well as the criminal are restrained under biblical law. The State is placed under tight judicial restraints, and first and foremost of these restraints is the requirement that crimes and their respective sanctions be announced in advance. There must be no *ex post facto* statutes or sanctions. This reduces the arbitrary authority of judges to apply sanctions or increase sanctions beyond what is specified in the law code. They sometimes possess the authority to reduce the specified sanctions, as this chapter argues, but never to increase them. This restriction drastically reduces the growth of arbitrary civil power. (By adhering to this biblical principle of responsible freedom under specified law, the West made possible the development of modern capitalism and its accompanying high per capita wealth.)

The limits on the biblical State's ability to impose arbitrary sanctions are derived from three case-law principles. First, the God-given authority of the victim to refuse to prosecute, and also his authority to reduce the applicable sanctions upon conviction of the criminal, restrict the power of the civil magistrate. Second, the maximum sanction allowed by existing law keeps the State under restraint. Third, the *pleonasm of execution* — "dying, he shall die" — inhibits the authority of the judges to subsidize outrageous crimes by imposing reduced sanctions in specific cases: where the State has lawfully initiated the covenant lawsuit because there is no earthly victim who could initiate it. To deny any of these principles is to promote the advent of the messianic State.

To describe the working of these three case-law principles, we need to begin with the maximum civil sanction: execution. Because public execution is the maximum civil sanction allowed by God's law, it has the most critics.

Capital Punishment: Yesterday and Today

One of the complaints against the continuing legitimacy of

---

6. F. A. Hayek, *The Constitution of Liberty* (University of Chicago Press, 1960).

biblical law is that the death penalty is too rigorous to be applied as a sanction against most of the capital crimes specified by the Old Testament. Therefore, conclude the Mosaic law's critics, execution is no longer a valid civil sanction today, except in the case of murder.[7] This line of argumentation leads to the peculiar conclusion that in the Old Covenant era, covenantally faithful people were expected by God to be a lot more rigorous about prosecuting criminals, and were therefore expected to be more willing to see God's civil sanctions enforced. This rigorous "Old Testament attitude" toward criminals is no longer valid, it is said, because of the coming of the New Covenant. But if Christians are to be less rigorous regarding crime and its appropriate civil sanctions, then God also must have adopted a more lenient attitude, which is supposedly reflected in His New Covenant law. A major problem with this line of reasoning is the fact that God's New Covenant standards seem to be more rigorous, e.g., the prohibition of easy divorce (Matt. 19:7-9).[8] With greater maturity and greater revelation, Christians are supposed to be less lenient about sin. After all, more is expected from him to whom more has been given (Luke 12:47-48). The New Testament gives Christians greater revelation and assigns us far more responsibility than was the case in the Old Covenant era. Christ's resurrection is behind us. The Holy Spirit has come.

It could be argued, of course, that because greater mercy has been shown to us, we should extend greater mercy. With respect to the judicial principle of victim's rights, I quite agree. The victim should be more merciful, so long as his mercy does not subsidize further evil. He must judge the character of the criminal. But this does not answer the question of designated capital crimes. Is it the State's responsibility to adopt the principle of reduced New Covenant sanctions, despite the explicit revelation of the Old Covenant case laws? Should the State adopt a judicial principle different from that which prevailed in the Old Covenant? I answer no. Furthermore, I also answer that civil judges in Old Covenant

---

7. For example, see John Murray, *Principles of Conduct* (Grand Rapids, Michigan: Eerdmans, 1957), p. 118.

8. See below: "Divorce by Covenantal Death."

Israel had the God-given authority to reduce the severity of the specified sanctions under certain circumstances. I develop the evidence for this conclusion in this chapter.

Critics of capital punishment also argue that righteous and sensitive jury members today are unwilling to hand down "guilty" verdicts against offenders in many cases, since the death penalty is much too harsh. If the death penalty is kept on the statute books, critics argue, serious criminal behavior is therefore indirectly subsidized by victims' unwillingness to prosecute and juries' unwillingness to convict. Thus, conclude the critics, we should ignore the Old Testament's capital sanction in all but the case of premeditated murder. Some Christian critics would even abandon capital punishment in this instance, following the lead of secular humanist criminologists and jurists.

It is my belief that in the twentieth century, there are three affirmations the denial of which best indicates the presence of Christian heresy. Heresy is easy to conceal in a world of endless qualifications and maneuvering. But three affirmations go right to the heart of the neo-evangelical and neo-orthodox rejection of biblical revelation. The first is the inerrancy of the Bible, as delivered in the original manuscripts. The second is the doctrine of eternal punishment. The third is the doctrine of capital punishment, as specified in the Old Testament case laws (unless modified by a specific New Testament revelation). I think the third is related to the second: God's merciless torturing of His covenant-breaking enemies, and the State's merciless delivery of capital crime-committing offenders into the court of the eternally torturing Judge. Therefore, the affirmation of the legitimacy of case-law specified capital punishment is an initial step back on the road to Christian orthodoxy.

The Rebellious Son

One of the Christian antinomians' most effective arguments today against the revealed law of God is the law which requires the execution of the rebellious son. This brings us to the passages under consideration in this chapter: the execution of a son who strikes his father (Ex. 21:15) or assaults his parents verbally (Ex.

21:17). Both of these passages contain the phrase, "he shall surely be put to death." Literally, the Hebrew phrase reads: "dying, he shall surely die" — a *pleonasm*. There is no question that biblical law specifies execution as the appropriate penalty for *adult* rebellious sons.[9] Biblical law's critics see this as a grave defect in the case law system, almost as if God made a horrendous mistake in the Old Testament, which He somehow rectified in the New Testament. If capital punishment is automatic upon conviction, say the critics of capital punishment, then the parents will probably refuse to take him before the judges. They will swallow their injured pride and tolerate evil in their midst. So runs the argument against a specific capital punishment specified in the Mosaic law. It is a representative argument that is subsequently used against virtually all of the biblical case laws to which the capital sanction is attached.

The obvious preliminary response to this line of reasoning is this: Were parents in the Old Covenant significantly different from parents today? Were they more willing to see their sons executed? There is something inherently unconvincing about the critics' line of argumentation. It assumes too great a discontinuity between the emotional make-up of righteous people in the Old Testament and righteous people today. Furthermore, if the biblically required sanction of execution is too harsh today, was God too harsh in ancient Israel? What has changed? God's character? Men's character? Men's emotions? Social circumstances? The critics become conveniently vague at this point. They prefer not to speculate about the reason or reasons for the supposed change. But the questions do not go away.

Until we have surveyed the evidence that undergirds the biblical concept of victim's rights, we must defer considering the judicial problem of executing the rebellious son who strikes his parent. This sanction can be understood properly only in terms of the Bible's concept of victim's rights. We will return to it in Chapter 2 (pp. 51-53). But as we consider the question of victim's rights, we need to keep in mind this question: *Is execution really what these texts require in every instance of the stated infractions, striking and cursing parents?*

---

9. The sons are drunkards (Deut. 21:20).

I am devoting much of this chapter to a detailed consideration of the key phrase, "shall surely be put to death." It requires a lengthy excursion in order to deal with some things not intuitively obvious from the text. The conclusion that I reach will prove useful in interpreting the next verse in Exodus, one which specifies capital punishment for kidnappers. The same problem of interpretation occurs throughout Exodus, Leviticus, and Numbers, though not Deuteronomy, since the phrase "he shall surely die" does not occur in Deuteronomy.

I begin my discussion by considering the theological basis of all prosecutions by any court, or the covenant lawsuit.

Who Will Bring the Covenant Lawsuit?

Adam and Eve had to serve as witnesses and judges in the garden. There was no escape from these two offices. The serpent had forced their hand. They had heard Satan's temptation, namely, that they could be as God if they disobeyed God (Gen. 3:5). They had become witnesses. They could not escape from their knowledge of the serpent's words. He had spoken in their presence.[10] They could stand with God and God's law by obeying God's word concerning Himself, the forbidden fruit, and the promised sentence of execution, or they could stand with Satan and his word concerning God, the forbidden fruit, and the promised execution. But when called upon by God to testify in His court, they would be required to testify, either against themselves if they stood with Satan or against Satan if they stood with God.[11] They both sought to escape self-incrimination. Adam blamed Eve, and

---

10. This assumes that Adam was at Eve's side when the serpent spoke. If he was not, then only Eve heard him speak. She should then have gone to Adam for confirmation, and he would have had to ask the serpent to repeat his claim. As I argue in my study of the incident, in order for Satan to gain the biblically specified pair of witnesses against God, they both had to act against God's law. I think that Adam was next to Eve when the serpent spoke. Adam let her act in his name. He allowed her to test the serpent's claim.

11. This is the theological foundation of the idea of the subpoena. The State has a legitimate right to compel the appearance of an individual in court, as well as compel his truthful testimony. This right is denied by some libertarians. Cf. Murray N. Rothbard, *For a New Liberty: The Libertarian Manifesto* (rev. ed.; New York: Collier, 1978), p. 87.

Eve blamed the serpent. Still, there was no available judicial escape. Their fig leaves testified against them. They knew they were guilty, and their wardrobes testified to their sense of guilt.

They also had to serve as judges. They could issue a condemnation of God by eating the forbidden fruit, or they could issue a condemnation of Satan, either by eating of the tree of life, or by eating from any tree except the forbidden one, or by not eating anything at all. But they could not avoid serving as judges. They had to *decide*. They had to *act*. They had to *render judgment*.[12]

The two offices, witness and judge, were inherent in their position as God's authorized representatives on earth (Gen. 1:26-28). Because of Satan's rebellion and his temptation of them, they were forced to decide: *Against whom would they bring the required covenant lawsuit: God or Satan?* They brought it against God. They served as Satan's agents. They implicitly claimed to be the victims of God's discriminatory restrictions against them, for God had denied them access to the forbidden fruit, and He had obviously lied to them concerning His power to enforce His will. They must have regarded His promised sanctions as a lie. Why else would anyone commit automatic suicide for a bite of forbidden fruit? They brought their covenant lawsuit against God *in absentia* by partaking of the forbidden fruit in the presence of Satan, thereby indulging in a satanic sacrament, an unholy communion service. They ate a ritual meal in the presence of the prince of demons. This is what Paul warns against: eating at the table of demons (I Cor. 10:21).

From the day that the serpent tempted Adam and Eve by testifying falsely concerning God's revealed word, there has been a designated victim of all criminal behavior: God. Satan needed to recruit human accomplices in his war against God. He needed two witnesses, the required number to prosecute anyone successfully for a capital crime (Deut. 17:6). But the moment that Adam and Eve brought their false testimony into God's court, they became subject to the penalty for perjury: suffering the same punishment to which the falsely accused victim was subject (Deut. 19:16-19). If their testimony had been true, then God must have

---

12. North, *Dominion Covenant: Genesis*, Appendix E: "Witnesses and Judges."

lied about who is truly sovereign over the universe. He would have given false testimony against the true god, man. God would have been guilty of calling man to worship a false god, which is a capital offense (Deut. 13:6-9). He would also have been guilty of false prophesying, another capital offense (Deut. 13:1-5). Adam and Eve had sought to indict God for a capital offense; they were subsequently executed by God. So are all their heirs who persist in refusing to renounce the judicial accusations of their parents, who represented them in God's court.

In His grace, God offered them a judicial covering, a temporary stay of execution, which was symbolized by the animal skins (Gen. 3:21). This symbolic covering required the slaying of an animal. God offered them time on earth to repent. He offered them a way to make restitution to Him: the blood sacrifice of specified animals. He did this because He looked forward in time to the death of His Son on the cross, the only possible restitution payment large enough to cover the sin of Adam and his heirs.

His Son's representative death is the basis of all of God's gifts to mankind in history. *Grace is an unearned gift*, meaning a gift earned by Christ at Calvary and given by God to all men in history. Christ's restitution payment serves as the basis of *common grace* to covenant-breakers in history and *special grace* to covenant-keepers in history and eternity.[13] The words of Christ on the cross are the basis of common grace in history: "Then said Jesus, Father, forgive them; for they know not what they do" (Luke 23:34). Ignorance of the law is no excuse, but Jesus Christ grants grace to the ignorant anyway. He paid God's price; He suffered God's sanctions; so He has the right to grant temporal (common) forgiveness on no terms at all, and eternal (special) forgiveness on His own terms.

Criminal and Victim as Covenantal Representatives

Adam and Eve served as Satan's representatives when they had communion with him, thereby bringing a covenant lawsuit

---

13. Gary North, *Dominion and Common Grace: The Biblical Basis of Progress* (Tyler, Texas: Institute for Christian Economics, 1987).

against God. Had they refused to take Satan's advice, they would have served as God's representatives against Satan. The point is, *representation is an inescapable concept.* The issue is never this one: "To serve or not to serve as the covenantal representative of a supernatural being." The question is rather: "Which supernatural being shall I represent covenantally?" There is no escape from this decision and its consequences.

What does the word *covenant* mean biblically? God has created a legal relationship to man, one which is based on a legal *bond.* There is no personal relationship between God and man apart from this legal bond. The covenant structure has five parts:

1. Transcendence yet presence of God
2. Hierarchy (representative authority)
3. Ethics (law)
4. Oath (judgment and sanctions)
5. Succession (inheritance and continuity)

By combining the first letters, we get an acronym: THEOS, the Greek word for God. God's three covenantal institutions are governed in terms of this five-point structure. These institutions of God-authorized government are: church, State, and family. The covenant structure is an inescapable concept.[14]

When a man sins, he thereby brings a covenantal lawsuit against God. His action violates all five points of the covenant. First, he denies that God is who He says He is: the Law-giver and eternal Judge. Second, he declares himself no longer under God's hierarchical authority. Third, he says that God's ethical standards do not apply to him. Fourth, he denies that God can or will apply His sanctions, either in history or eternity. Fifth, he asserts that covenant-breakers shall inherit the earth.

Let us consider in greater detail point two: hierarchy. By rebelling against God, he thereby places himself under the hierarchical authority of Satan. *He becomes Satan's representative.* This is why Christ spoke to Peter so harshly when Peter denied that Christ would soon go to His death: "Get thee behind me, Satan" (Matt. 16:23a). Men's actions are always representative. This is

---

14. Sutton, *That You May Prosper, op. cit.*

why God judges between the saved and lost, between sheep and goats, on judgment day (Matt. 25:32). The eternal life-and-death question on that great and terrible day will be: *Which sovereign did you represent and serve on earth, God or Satan?*

It is clear that Adam and Eve sinned directly against God. More specifically, they sinned against the God who walked in the garden (Gen. 3:8). This is the character of all sin: a denial of God's word, His authority, His ethical character, His sanctions, and His ability to disinherit covenant-breakers. *Sin is a representative denial of God's covenant*: His transcendence, His authority, His law, His judgment, and His inheritance. Man sins against God covenantally. He would steal the very throne of God if he could. "For thou hast said in thine heart, I will ascend into heaven, I will exalt my throne above the stars of God: I will sit also upon the mount of the congregation, in the sides of the north: I will ascend above the heights of the clouds; I will be like the most High" (Isa. 14:13-14). What will be the result of this attempted theft of God's glory? "Yet thou shalt be brought down to hell, to the sides of the pit" (Isa. 14:15).

Divorce by Covenantal Death

I have argued that *sin is always a representative act*. It is the act of bringing a covenantal lawsuit against God. A crime is a special kind of sin: a publicly verifiable act against God's civil law. It is an act of defiance against God's civil covenant with either an individual or some aspect of the environment as God's representative agent.

We can see the principle of victim's rights more clearly by focusing on marital divorce as a covenant lawsuit. Jesus sets forth this law regarding divorce: "It hath been said, Whosoever shall put away his wife, let him give her a writing of divorcement: But I say unto you, That whosoever shall put away his wife, saving for the cause of fornication, causeth her to commit adultery: and whosoever shall marry her that is divorced committeth adultery" (Matt. 5:31-32).

In this chapter, I do not want to cover all the theological ground that Ray Sutton covers in his book, *Second Chance: Biblical*

Blueprints for Divorce and Remarriage.[15] I agree with his argument that divorce is above all a covenantal act, and that any crime listed in the Old Testament as a capital offense constitutes legal grounds for divorce today. Jesus did not abrogate the Old Testament case laws that governed divorce and remarriage, except to make them more rigorous. The principle of New Testament divorce is the same as it was in the Old Testament: *divorce by covenantal execution*. There may also be physical execution involved, but in both Old and New Testament law, *covenantal execution is primary*; eternal execution in God's heavenly court is of greater consequence than physical execution by the civil government's court (Matt. 10:28). Biblically speaking, physical execution is simply the God-ordained legal consequence of specific forms of covenantal execution. This has also been argued by R. J. Rushdoony[16] and Greg Bahnsen[17] with respect to divorce. I do not try to prove this argument in this chapter; I begin with the assumption that it is biblically correct. Those who disagree should consult these other sources.

This line of reasoning from the Old Testament's case laws raises an important practical and legal issue. When a spouse commits an act that produces covenantal death — judicial death in the eyes of God — and when this is proven in one or both of God's authorized earthly courts, ecclesiastical and civil, either by the injured spouse or by other witnesses, the covenantally dead person becomes subject to covenantal sanctions. In a systematically biblical civil government, the maximum penalty attached to many of these crimes would be death. This would lead to divorce by physical execution because there has *already been* divorce by covenantal execution.

John 8

The standard response from those who reject such a "harsh"

---

15. Ft. Worth, Texas: Dominion Press, 1987.

16. R. J. Rushdoony, *The Institutes of Biblical Law* (Nutley, New Jersey: Craig Press, 1973), pp. 401-15.

17. Greg L. Bahnsen, *Theonomy in Christian Ethics* (2nd ed.; Phillipsburg, New Jersey: Presbyterian & Reformed, 1984), pp. 105-16.

The Covenant Lawsuit

(i.e., God-established) penalty is an appeal to John 8, the case of the woman who was taken in adultery. I believe that this passage was in the original Bible text. Biblical "higher critics" and many orthodox Christians deny this, since most of the older Greek manuscripts do not include John 7:53-8:11.[18] Most modern translations of the Bible provide a marginal note to this effect. But if this passage is not in the Bible, then surely the Old Testament's capital sanction against adultery has not been altered. If John 8 is not in the biblical canon, then there is no other passage that supports the case for an alteration of the capital sanction against adulterers except Joseph's forgiving of Mary, which we will examine in detail later.[19]

John 8 deals with a woman who was discovered in the very act of adultery (v. 4). Her accusers (witnesses) brought her before Jesus, challenging Him to render judgment. This was clearly an attempted trap on their part, for Jesus was neither a civil nor an ecclesiastical official. The woman's accusers were also judicially corrupt. They were law-breaking deceivers, for they were being highly selective: her partner was not brought before Jesus. (Might he have been one of their ecclesiastical or professional associates?)

Jesus challenged them: "He that is without sin among you, let him first cast a stone at her" (v. 7b). Then He stooped down and wrote something in the dirt (v. 8) – the only instance recorded in the New Testament of His writing anything. (Might He have written the names of women who were well known – biblically speaking – by the woman's accusers?) We do not know what He wrote. We do know that her accusers immediately decided to leave. Discretion was the better part of valor, in their view. They did not continue to press charges against her. Thus, *without the presence of two witnesses, she could not be legally convicted of a capital crime, according to Old Covenant law* (Deut. 17:6). The witnesses had

---

18. Cf. Gary North, *The Hoax of Higher Criticism* (Tyler, Texas: Institute for Christian Economics, 1989).

19. The loss of this supposed defense of a New Testament alteration in the adultery sanction would be a bitter pill to swallow for neo-evangelicals, far too many of whom are prone to accept the hoax of higher criticism, and virtually all of whom spend their intellectual careers seeking exegetical ways around the Old Testament case laws and their sanctions.

to cast the first stones (Deut. 17:7), but they all had departed. So, Jesus asked her an obviously rhetorical question: "Woman, where are those thine accusers? Hath no man condemned thee? She said, No man, Lord. And Jesus said unto her, Neither do I condemn thee: go, and sin no more" (vv. 10b-11).

Jesus knew she was guilty as initially accused. He told her to go and sin no more, making clear to her that He knew she was guilty. But adultery is a civil matter. *Without witnesses, she could not be lawfully convicted.* She acknowledged Him as Lord in her own words; He warned her not to do this thing again.

There are millions of short-sighted, instinctively law-breaking and covenant-denying Christians who argue that this incident proves that adultery is no longer a capital crime. They invariably point to Jesus' words, "He that is without sin among you, let him first cast a stone at her." They challenge those who affirm the law: "You see, we [meaning *you*] are not to judge anyone unless we [meaning *you*] have no sin." This interpretation of Christ's words is utter lunacy. Its implications are preposterous. If pressed, these "he who is without sin" interpreters will admit that the New Testament does allow the State to enforce penalties against criminals (Rom. 13:1-7). But then their whole argument collapses. He who is sinful *must* cast the first stone, for all people have sinned and come short of the glory of God (Rom. 3:23). If their argument is taken seriously, then John 8 prohibits all capital punishment, and probably all punishment by anyone, any time. If true, this principle of interpretation would make all covenantal sanctions impossible to enforce: family, church, and State. It would mean the end of all human government. It cannot possibly mean this.

In the Old Testament, God established the death penalty for various crimes. Were Old Covenant judges and witnesses without sin? Obviously not. So, what did Jesus really mean?

This Particular Sin

The most obvious explanation is that He meant "He that is without *this particular* sin, let him cast the first stone." Then He started writing something in the dirt. The witnesses immediately departed. The biblical judicial principle is this: those who have committed a particular crime, but who have not been tried and convicted by a lawful court, or who have not privately offered to make restitution, and who have therefore not been forgiven by the victim, are not fit to serve as witnesses or judges of those who are accused of having committed the same crime. This is a reasonable interpretation, and a reasonable view of justice. It does not necessitate the scrapping of all civil law, all capital sanctions, and the sanction of death for men who commit adultery with other men's wives.

When Jesus told her to go and sin no more, did He really expect her to be able to avoid all sin for the rest of her life? Of course not. But what He did expect her to be able to do was to avoid the sin of adultery. He did not have *sin in general* in mind in this passage when He used the word *sin*, but rather the *particular sin of adultery*. Thus, it is totally misleading for people to use this passage as a proof text that Jesus established a new civil penalty, or even no penalty at all, for the civil crime of adultery. He did not abandon the Mosaic law in John 8. On the contrary, He followed the Mosaic law's procedural requirements to the letter. *She was publicly innocent in terms of the procedural requirements of the Mosaic law.* Thus, He did not execute His historical wrath upon her in His capacity as perfect humanity. Only the witnesses were allowed to do that, and they had departed. He would deal with her later as God, the perfect Witness, on judgment day in His court; until then, she was granted time to repent and reform her ways. So are all the rest of us.

Obvious, isn't it? Yet for several generations, pietists and antinomians (those who reject biblical law) have persuaded Christians that John 8 represents some remarkable break with the Old Testament. Christians who hate God's law also hate the New Testament, so they do whatever they can to distort it and misinterpret it, even when their misinterpretations lead to obviously preposterous conclusions. They do not worry about preposterous conclusions; they worry instead about a sovereign God who threatens individuals and society with judgments in history for sin. They are in principle adulterers themselves, and they are looking for an escape from God's authorized civil sanctions against adultery, should they someday fall into this sin. They are looking for loopholes – civil, ecclesiastical, and psychological.

Witnesses as Unauthorized Prosecutors

There is another aspect of this incident that must be considered. Jesus dealt directly with the sins of the witnesses. He did not focus on questions of legal procedure. He did not point out that they should have gone immediately to a civil court. He did not ask them rhetorically, "Who made me a judge over you?" He did not remind them that the other guilty party was missing. It is clear that His main concern was not with the procedural details of the incident; He preferred instead to deal positively with the sinful condition of the accused woman. She was the focus of His concern, not her accusers. He acted to remove them from His presence, so that He might restore her to moral and judicial wholeness. This was His tactic in all of His public confrontations with His accusers. He did this with Israel in A.D. 70. He removed Israel from His presence, so that He might restore the gentiles to moral and judicial wholeness. (When He has accomplished this, He will then redeem Israel: Romans 11.)

He could also have asked these two questions: "Where is the victim?" "Why is the victim not here to press charges?" More to the point, He could have asked: "By what authority have you, the witnesses, substituted your judgment for the victim's? Who made you the authorized prosecutors of this covenant lawsuit? On whose behalf are you acting?" He did not ask these questions, not because they were irrelevant to the situation, but because they were secondary to His main concern: dealing positively with the sin of the woman.

Did the Mosaic law give to witnesses an independent authority to prosecute the covenant lawsuit as agents solely of the State? If so, then the State has the right to prosecute despite the decision of the victim not to prosecute. This would clearly compromise the judicial principle of victim's rights. I am arguing in this chapter that *the State possesses no independent authority to prosecute if the victim voluntarily decides not to prosecute*, an argument based heavily on Joseph's decision as a just man to put Mary away privately. (See below: "The Victim's Decision, [pp. 46-48].") The victim's decision is final until God intervenes directly — sickness, calamity, death, or at His Second Coming — to bring His own covenant lawsuit. Thus, the witnesses in John 8 were violating yet another principle of the Mosaic law. The whole incident was one of utter lawlessness and rebellion, which is the characteristic feature of every challenge to the God-given authority of Jesus Christ.

Conclusion

Fundamental to the concept of biblical jurisprudence is the idea of the covenant lawsuit. Ultimately, God brings this lawsuit against all mankind. He brings it against each person for each sinful act. Only the substitute sacrifice by Jesus Christ at the cross allows God to overlook these sins in individuals: eternally for His covenant people, and in history for covenant-breakers.

The victim initiates God's covenant lawsuit against the person who injured him. He acts as God's authorized agent. The goal of the victim is restitution in history: to the victim, but also representatively to God.

The victim has the legal authority not to press charges. He is allowed to show mercy in history to the criminal. Jesus did this at Calvary. The civil government has no independent authority to bring this lawsuit unless it can show that the victim is incompetent or unable to make this decision (a minor, a feeble-minded person, or deceased). One other exception: if the State can prove that the criminal is threatening the victim, thereby making the victim into an accomplice to thwart God's civil justice. Otherwise, there should be no restrictions against settling out of court.

2

THE DEATH PENALTY

Then said Jesus, Father, forgive them; for they know not what they do (Luke 23:34a).

As the cosmic lawgiver, God has the right to set the penalties for crimes. Biblical law provides society with God's specified penalties. What is crucial to understand is that the biblical principle of *God as the victim who names the penalty* leads to a derivative principle: the earthly victim of the prohibited act is also allowed to name the penalty to be imposed on the criminal, so long as it does not exceed the limits specified by the Bible.

There is one exception to this rule, argue some biblical scholars: if the specified penalty is death, and if a particular phrase appears in the text, then the State must enforce whenever it unilaterally prosecutes and convicts the criminal. The phrase is: "surely he shall die" or "dying, he shall die." This phrase, which biblical scholars call a *pleonasm*, initially appears to be an identifying mark of infractions of God's law that inescapably require the death penalty. I argue that this is an incorrect interpretation of the use of the pleonasm, but I could be wrong. This is why we need to explore the usage of this pleonasm in the section below, "Dying, He Shall Die." First, however, we must consider the principle of victim's rights.

We know that sanctions against non-capital crimes are to be imposed by the civil government at the discretion of the victim. He can refuse to accept any restitution payment or a reduced restitution payment. He can lawfully cancel the debt owed to him (Matt. 18:23-35). I argue that this principle of forgiveness also applies to capital crimes in which there is an identifiable human victim who is capable of bringing a covenant civil lawsuit against the criminal. We see this judicial principle in action at the crucifixion. Jesus requested that the Father not immediately destroy His executioners. "Then said Jesus, Father, forgive them; for they know not what they do" (Luke 23:34a). He extended additional time to them. This was His unmerited favor or gift to them, just as God had extended life to Adam, Eve, and Cain. As both the primary victim (God) and the secondary victim (perfect man), Jesus Christ possessed the right to extend temporal mercy to His enemies, even for this capital crime. His divinity authorized this extension of mercy. So did His perfect humanity, for He was the victim of a rigged trial. I argue that as the victim, He could lawfully extend mercy only before He physically died.

The question is: Are victims allowed to extend mercy in cases where the State appears to be required by the presence of the pleonasm, "surely he shall die," to execute the convicted criminal? We know that in his capacity as a lawful prosecutor of God's covenant lawsuit, the earthly victim does possess the right — the legal authorization from God — to extend mercy to a convicted criminal for any crime other than a capital crime. He can lawfully forgive the restitution payment owed to him. Why not also in the case of a capital crime?

The State as God's Prosecutor

In order to answer this question, we need to understand that the victim is not the only one who can lawfully initiate a covenant lawsuit against a suspected criminal. God has more than one covenantal agent in society. Witnesses can bring incriminating information to an authorized agent of covenantal government, and this agent can lawfully institute covenant lawsuit proceedings against any criminal, *but only if there is no earthly victim of the crime who is capable of bringing charges.*[1] If there is an identifiable earthly victim, then he alone becomes the exclusive agent who is author-

---

1. For a list of capital crimes and an identification of those cases in which the State is authorized to initiate the covenant lawsuit, see the subhead at the end of this chapter: "Addendum: Cases to Which the Pleonasm Is Attached."

ized to initiate a covenant lawsuit against the suspected criminal. This restriction on State's authority to initiate a covenant lawsuit is an implication of the doctrine of victim's rights. The victim possesses the right to forgive. The State is not authorized to ignore or supersede this right.

The interests of the community are upheld by identifying the criminal or member of the criminal class. Remember, God is the primary victim of crime; He has authorized *representatives* to defend the integrity of His name. If a community refuses to do this – if church, State, and family governments break down – God threatens to bring His negative sanctions through other agencies: war, pestilence, and famine (Deut. 28:15-68). This is why an unsolved murder in a field required a public blood sacrifice by the nearest city's civil magistrates, not the priests (Deut. 21:1-9).[2]

A Legal Claim

Who acts as God's authorized agent in the bringing of a covenantal civil lawsuit? The victim, the witnesses, or those who are authorized agents of the civil government. If the initiator of the lawsuit is the victim, he is not acting primarily on his own behalf, but as an agent of God because of his position as the victimized intermediary between the criminal and God, the ultimate victim. He is acting secondarily in his own behalf, for any restitution payment will go to him. Similarly, witnesses who bring evidence to the State for use in prosecuting the covenant lawsuit are acting as representative agents of God through the civil government. They do not act on their own behalf, for they have *no legal claim* on the resources of the person who is being charged with the crime, should he be convicted. Witnesses are not victims. They are acting in the name of God as authorized and oath-bound agents of the State when they testify in a civil court. *Where there is no direct legal claim, there is no direct covenantal relationship.* Thus, witnesses are acting as indirect agents of God as participants in the civil commonwealth.

Because crimes are always crimes against God, the State has a law-enforcement role to play, for the State possesses God's

---

2. Clearly, the Book of Hebrews has annulled this practice today.

authorized monopoly of the sword: the imposition of physical sanctions. The State in turn implicitly delegates the office of witness to those who view a crime or who have information relevant to the State's prosecution of a covenant lawsuit. (This is the judicial basis of what in English common law is known as "citizen's arrest," although it is seldom invoked today.) This is why the State can lawfully compel honest testimony from a witness: the witness is under the authority of the State. It is in fact unlawful to withhold evidence of a crime when subpoenaed. While the State may offer a reward for the capture and conviction of a criminal (a positive sanction: blessing), this is at the discretion of the State. The witness who seeks an announced reward has a claim on the State, not on the criminal.

The most important example in history of a reward-seeking witness is Judas Iscariot, who collected 30 pieces of silver from the Jewish court to witness against Jesus Christ. He later returned the money, not because it is inherently wrong to accept money as an honest witness, but because he knew he had been a false witness in a rigged, dishonest trial. The Jewish leaders self-righteously replied, "What is that to us?" (Matt. 27:4b). They felt no sense of guilt, so why should he? They also recognized the tainted nature of the money, which was the price of blood, and as true Pharisees, they refused to accept his repayment (Matt. 27:6). Committing murder by rigging a court was irrelevant in their view, a means to a legitimate end; getting paid for false witness-bearing, however, was seen by them as a sin. This is the essence of Pharisaism, the classic historical example of Pharisaism in action. They were happy to serve as the most corrupt court in man's history, but they judiciously refused to accept money for their efforts. (What is not recognized by most Christian commentators is that the testimony of a witness in a Jewish court was invalidated, at least by the law of the Pharisees, if he had received payment for testifying.)[3]

What is my conclusion? Only that witnesses have no legal claim on the criminal. The authorized agents of God in the prose-

---

3. *Bekhoroth* 4:6, in *The Mishnah*, edited by Herbert Danby (New York: Oxford University Press, [1933] 1987), p. 534.

cution of a covenant lawsuit are officers of one of the three courts — church, State, and family — and the victim of the crime.

The Right of Refusal

If the authorized biblical penalty is economic restitution, then the victim whose covenant lawsuit is successfully prosecuted by the civil government has the right to refuse payment, or the right to take less than what biblical law authorizes. Like the creditor who has the right to take less in repayment, or to extend the debtor more time to repay, or even to forgive the debt, so is the victim of a criminal who has been convicted in a court of law. The nineteenth-century Jewish commentator S. R. Hirsch remarked that the victim of a theft "can renounce altogether his right to repayment by the sale of the malefactor, and content himself with a signed promise to pay as soon as the circumstances of the thief improve."[4]

What if the victim refuses to prosecute? I see no warrant in most cases for the State then to prosecute. The court can lawfully serve as the agent of the victim in certain exceptional cases. Two examples would be victims who are orphaned minors or mental incompetents. Nevertheless, under normal circumstances, a decision not to prosecute by a victim who is legally competent to initiate a covenant lawsuit is a binding decision. He thereby loses his legal claim on any future restitution payments by the convicted criminal. If he is willing to suffer this loss, then the State must honor his or her decision. The individual, not the State, is the victim; the principle of victim's rights is binding on the State. Only if the criminal act in some way also injured the State or society could the State then prosecute, but only on its own behalf.[5]

The case of Judah and Tamar is representative. Judah refused to prosecute Tamar for whoredom when she brought tangible

---

4. Samson Raphael Hirsch, *The Pentateuch Translated and Explained*, translated by Isaac Levy, 5 vols., *Exodus* (3rd ed.; London: Honig & Sons, 1967), p. 295: at Exodus 21:6.

5. Treason that also involves theft would be an example. The victim of the theft might not prosecute, but the State could, for treason is an act of attempted murder against the society.

evidence that he was the guilty party and that she had merely been claiming her legal right to the levirate marriage (Gen. 38:26). On the other hand, the victim also escapes the threat of a counter-lawsuit from the accused if the latter should be declared innocent by the court. Again, the case of Judah and Tamar is representative. Judah did not want to be convicted of false witness-bearing, for he had committed the crime with her, and he was therefore not authorized to bring accusations against her in his own name. As the head of both his family and the local civil government, he dropped all charges.

Civil Sanctions

Old Testament law specifies that criminals are subject to several types of civil sanctions: corporal punishment – lashings, but with no more than forty lashes (Deut. 25:3) and the slicing of a woman's hand in one instance (Deut. 25:12)[6] – economic restitution, banishment, and the death penalty.

The punishment of lashing is curious. No crime in the Bible is specifically said to require lashing. The language of the King James Version indicates an exception to this rule: the required scourging of a bondmaid who is betrothed to one man and who then commits fornication with another man (Lev. 19:20). However, the Hebrew word translated as "scourge" does not necessarily mean physical scourging; it is better translated as "punishment," or even "inquiry." Nevertheless, the lack of any reference to specific crimes with which this physical sanction is associated does not mean that no public crime is subject to lashing, or else there would be no prohibition against imposing more than forty lashes. This is a sanction to be imposed at the discretion of the judges in cases where there is *no identifiable victim who has suffered either economic loss or physical or verbal abuse.* Presumably, this sanction is appropriate for such acts as public nudity by adults, prostitution, public drunkenness, repeated disturbances of the peace,

---

6. The language of the King James makes it appear that the woman's hand is to be cut off. This is incorrect: it is permanently injured, but not cut off: James B. Jordan, *The Law of the Covenant: An Exposition of Exodus 21-23* (Tyler, Texas: Institute for Christian Economics, 1984), pp. 118-19.

and public acts prohibited by God, but for which no identifiable victim can be found. The victim of such "victimless crimes" — God — is entitled to restitution: lashes. *Eternal punishment is the model: God is repaid through the suffering of the criminal.* In the Old Testament era, if the restitution payment to the victim was larger than the criminal or his kinsman-redeemer could afford to pay, the criminal was sold into slavery. The purchase price went to the victim. This was the only way that a Hebrew could become an involuntary lifetime slave in Israel, and even in this instance, it was lifetime slavery only if he could not earn enough to meet the restitution payment or if his kinsman-redeemer refused to pay. Non-criminal Hebrew debt slaves were to be released in the seventh, "sabbatical" year (Deut. 15); voluntary jubilee year slaves were to be released in the year of jubilee (Lev. 25:39-41).[7] The criminal became a slave to another person because he had been a slave to sin — specifically, he had committed a criminal act that had seriously damaged someone else's property or body.

Identifying the Primary Victim

Some crimes are so great that God authorizes the death penalty. This means the criminal's immediate deliverance into God's court. This in turn leads to his subsequent delivery into permanent slavery in hell and the lake of fire unless he repents prior to his physical execution by the civil government. This removal of temporal life is restitution to God for a criminal's major transgression of God's covenant laws. *The death penalty points clearly to God's position as the primary victim.* It also points to His status as eternal Judge.

In cases of murder, the State becomes the delegated representative of God. The deceased obviously cannot initiate the covenant lawsuit. The State therefore initiates it on behalf of both the deceased and God. No restitution payment is possible to the deceased; thus, God must judge the criminal directly in His court. The State is required to deliver the criminal's soul immediately into the hands of God, who is the primary victim and also the

---

7. Gary North, *Tools of Dominion: The Case Laws of Exodus* (Tyler, Texas: Institute for Christian Economics, 1990), pp. 125-31.

legal representative of the deceased victim. The State must not allow a murderer to escape immediate entry into God's court – physical execution – by the payment of a fine: "Moreover ye shall take no satisfaction for the life of a murderer, which is guilty of death: but he shall be surely put to death" (Num. 35:31).

Christ's resurrection is the basis of man's escape from God's immediate and direct imposition of the death penalty, both the first death (physical death) and the eternal second death (Rev. 20:14). Because Jesus Christ rose from the dead, His previous grant of temporary forgiveness to Rome and Israel received God's sanction. It was also on the basis of this resurrection that God granted a stay of execution to Adam and Eve. But judgment eventually comes in history: Adam and Eve died, and Israel and Rome fell. The question then arises: Does the resurrection of Jesus Christ also serve as the basis of a man's legitimate escape from the death penalty from a civil court? If so, in which cases and on what judicial basis?

"Dying, He Must Die"

We need to deal with a problem of interpretation that confronts us over and over in Old Testament case laws. It is a phrase that occurs in many passages.[8] A person convicted of a specified crime "shall surely be put to death." As mentioned earlier, the Hebrew phrase is what scholars call a pleonasm: "dying, he shall surely die." It is emphatic language. We find it in Exodus 21:12: "He that smiteth a man, so that he die, shall be surely put to death." James Jordan commented in 1984: "The emphasis means that the death penalty cannot be set aside by any payment of money."[9] But because of a series of problems in interpretation, he subsequently changed his mind about the meaning of this pleonasm.[10]

What Is the Problem?

Why should the interpretation of this pleonasm of execution

---

8. These verses are displayed under the subhead at the end of this chapter: "Addendum: Cases to Which the Pleonasm Is Attached."

9. Jordan, *Law of the Covenant*, p. 96n.

10. They are not the same objections that I raise in this chapter.

be such a problem? Because the same phrase appears in the case of crimes that we normally would not think would involve automatic capital punishment. These include crimes that have no immediate human victims: sabbath-breaking (Ex. 31:14-15) and bestiality (Ex. 22:19; Lev. 20:15-16). These also include crimes in which no one dies: assaulting parents physically (Ex. 21:15) or verbally (Ex. 21:17), adultery that involves another man's wife (Lev. 20:10), blasphemy against God (Lev. 24:16), and wizardry and witchcraft (Lev. 20:27). One crime to which this pleonasm is attached is often regarded by modern societies as a capital crime: kidnapping (Ex. 21:16).[11]

To survey the nature of the exegetical problem, let us consider in greater detail the case of adultery that involves a man with another man's wife: "And the man that committeth adultery with another man's wife, even he that committeth adultery with his neighbour's wife, the adulterer and the adulteress shall surely be put to death" (Lev. 20:10). The pleonasm of execution appears here: "shall surely be put to death." Capital punishment for both of the adulterers can legitimately be imposed at the insistence of the victim, the woman's husband. Why? *Because the government of the covenantal family was broken by adultery.* The injured party, meaning the head of the household, is the lawful covenantal representative of God. He is authorized to bring charges against the adulterers as the injured party and also as the head of the family unit. Because the Bible specifies adultery as a civil crime, he also brings this lawsuit in civil court.

The victimized husband can lawfully file the covenant lawsuit in up to three covenantal courts: family, church, and State. A covenant lawsuit is first presented by the victimized husband to the suspected partner, and then (at the discretion of the victimized husband) it is presented in the appropriate court or courts. The institutional church has a legitimate role to play if either of the marriage partners is a member. It pronounces the sentence of covenantal death against the offending party. Thus, adultery can sometimes affect all three covenantal institutions. The victim declares that the covenantal bond of marriage has been broken, and

---

11. See Chapter 3: "Kidnapping."

that the adulterers have now come under God's wrath. If the suspected adulterous male partner is married, his wife can also file appropriate lawsuits against her husband. Biblical law makes it clear, however, that *the husband of the adulterous wife has primary authority to specify the penalty.* It is his covenantal household office as the head of the family that has been attacked by the adulterers. If he decides on the death penalty for his wife, as we shall see, her criminal consort cannot escape her fate. As the officer of his family's government, the victimized husband specifies the penalty; the wife of the adulterer cannot stay the hand of the civil magistrate.

Two questions arise. Can the husband legally grant mercy to the wife if she is convicted, that is, can he specify a lesser punishment? Furthermore, if he can, and if he does this, must he show equal mercy to the convicted man?

No Respect for Persons

The example of Jesus on the cross indicates that the victim can lawfully spare the criminal. He asked His Father to forgive them, meaning Jews and Romans (Luke 23:34). He spared both of the "adulterers," Israel and her consort, Rome. Israel again and again in Old Testament history committed spiritual adultery with foreign gods and nations, yet God always spared the nation until A.D. 70.[12] The Book of Hosea centers on this theme of the husband's forgiveness of an adulterous wife. Romans 11 indicates that professing Israel will someday be re-grafted into the church through mass conversion,[13] so God has still withheld the death penalty from Israel as a covenantal people (though not necessarily as the modern political unit that we call the state of Israel).

What is the problem here? The pleonasm appears in Leviticus 20:10, "dying, they shall die." If the language of inescapable death is accepted at face value, then the husband of the adulteress

---

12. David Chilton, *The Days of Vengeance: An Exposition of the Book of Revelation* (Ft. Worth: Dominion Press, 1987).

13. This postmillennial position has been defended by such Calvinist commentators on Romans 11 as Charles Hodge, Robert Haldane, and John Murray. The Larger Catechism of the Westminster Confession of Faith also teaches it: Answer 191.

cannot lawfully request a reduced penalty, such as the forfeiture of her dowry to him, rather than insist on her execution. But is he so restricted? God spared Israel time after time. It would seem reasonable that the injured husband might prefer a lesser penalty, just as God did with Israel. Maybe he still loves her. Maybe this is her first transgression. He feels deeply injured, but not enough to have her executed. Perhaps she is a good mother. Perhaps he wants to keep her as his wife. Perhaps not. What if he wants a divorce? This would be granted by the State. He could also require her to transfer her dowry to him.

By showing mercy to his wife, he must also show mercy to her consort. In the case of adultery involving another man's wife, the two adulterers must receive the same negative sanction. The judges are not permitted to show partiality to persons in rendering official judgment. The victimized husband who decides to prosecute is acting as a judge, for if the adulterers are convicted, he specifies the penalty. If he wants total vengeance against the man, he must also demand the same penalty for his wife. If he shows leniency to her, he must show the same leniency to him. Why? Because in our capacity as God-ordained judges, men are not to show partiality, or as the Bible says, "respect of persons" (Deut. 1:17; 16:19; II Sam. 14:14; Acts 10:34). When Joseph decided as a just man to put Mary away privately, he necessarily also decided not to seek civil justice against any suspected consort.

The Bible does not directly discuss the question of leniency by the victim. The pleonasm "dying, they shall die" is attached to this crime of adultery (Lev. 20:10). Nevertheless, I am arguing that the victim can specify a lesser penalty for the adulterers. If I am correct, then in such cases, the criminals do not "surely die" at the hands of the court. But if they are not automatically executed upon conviction, then what does the presence of the pleonasm mean? Why is it found in some biblical texts specifying capital punishment, but not in all of them? The pleonasm is there for emphasis, the lexicographers say.[14] Then what exactly does it emphasize? Not the absolute necessity of the death penalty in

---

14. *Genesius' Hebrew Grammar* (Oxford, [1910] 1974), sect. 113n, p. 342; cited by Jordan, *The Death Penalty in the Mosaic Law* (Tyler, Texas: Biblical Horizons, 1988), p. 9.

every case in which it appears, if I am correct in my reasoning. It does not apply in cases where the victim shows leniency. The victim decides.

The Victimized Wife

The Old Testament specifies the death penalty for wives who commit adultery. It does not specify the death penalty for a husband who commits adultery. Is this an oversight? Or does this indicate that God does respect persons, leaving victimized wives more vulnerable than victimized husbands? Does the Mosaic law in fact show respect for persons, discriminating against victimized wives?

The answer is found in the nature of the lawsuit. The victimized husband brings the lawsuit in his capacity as head of his household. The family is one of God's three covenantal governments. It is marked by a covenantal oath. Thus, the death penalty as the maximum for an adulterous wife places the decision in the hands of a covenant head. It is not that the Bible discriminates against victimized wives. It simply places the primary authority for prosecuting the covenant lawsuit in the hands of the covenantal head of the household.

If the adulterous wife could be executed at the discretion of the wife of her adulterous consort, then the primary authority to impose the penalty would be removed from the head of the household and transferred to the subordinate member of another household. The victimized husband who had decided to keep his wife would lose her if the wife of her consort prosecuted, saw her husband convicted, and asked for the death penalty. Since the court is not allowed to discriminate, it would also have to execute the adulterous wife. Thus, the adulterous wife's husband would lose control over the sanction.

The victimized wife can lawfully sue for divorce. The judges are authorized to grant this. Even if the husband of the adulterous wife does not insist on a divorce, the victimized wife is allowed to gain legal separation. Why, if there must be equality of negative sanctions placed on both adulterers? *Because the judges' announcement of the divorce is not the imposition of a negative sanction; it is simply a legal announcement of a broken marriage*. The marriage was covenantally broken by her husband's act of adultery; the wife is simply declaring her formal acceptance of her new legal status as an unmarried woman. She asks the court to make this declaration public. Biblical law always protects the innocent party. She is not compelled to re-adopt her husband back into the marriage. But she cannot lawfully insist on physical execution of her adulterous husband. The wife of an adulterous husband has only secondary rights as a victim because in this two-party sin, she is the secondary earthly victim. She is not the head of her household. She cannot lawfully seek the execution of the victimized husband's wife by insisting on the execution of her husband.

The Bible is silent regarding the execution of an adulterous husband who commits adultery with an unmarried woman. It is clear, however, that his wife is the primary earthly victim. It seems to me that the wife, as the primary earthly victim, then gains the legal authority to prosecute the two adulterers to the limit of the law. She can require the execution of both partners if they are convicted of adultery by a civil court.

If I am correct about this, then we now know why there is no civil sanction against prostitution specified in the Old Testament, except for the required execution of the daughter of a priest who becomes a prostitute. "And the daughter of any priest, if she profane herself by playing the whore, she profaneth her father: she shall be burnt with fire" (Lev. 21:9). If the victimized wife can have her convicted husband executed for having committed adultery with a prostitute, then the prostitute is required to share his fate. Thus, there is no need for an explicit civil sanction against prostitution. The victimized wife decides. If this view is correct, then the threat of the capital sanction would tend to confine prostitution to unmarried persons. It would therefore reduce prostitution's assault on marriage.

The Victim's Decision

What would it take to get a victim to accept a reduced penalty? The criminal would make a public confession of guilt and repentance, and then offer to pay restitution to the victim. This might work. Then again, it might not. *The key to the criminal's escape from death is the decision of the victim.* The victim cannot lawfully demand a penalty greater than the one specified in the case law, but he can accept something less.

In a later essay, James Jordan took another look at the pleonasm, "surely he shall die."[15] He cites Numbers 35:30-31: "Whoso killeth any person, the murderer shall be put to death by the mouth of witnesses: but one witness shall not testify against any person to cause him to die. Moreover ye shall take no satisfaction for the life of a murderer, which is guilty of death: but he shall surely be put to death." The law specifically says that there can be no substitute payment. The question then arises: Which is more authoritative, the pleonasm's language or the automatic penalty attached to murder? Is murder unique? Is it only in murder cases that the State must invariably impose the death penalty? Or is the death penalty the inescapable consequence of the pleonasm? Does the presence of the pleonasm indicate the idea of "accept no substitutes" wherever it occurs, or is it merely emphasis? If merely emphasis, what exactly does it emphasize?

If adultery always requires the death penalty (Lev. 20:10), Jordan asks, then why did Joseph decide to put Mary away quietly rather than prosecuting her (Matt. 1:19)? My answer: *victim's rights.* The primary earthly victim always has the legal right not to prosecute. This was Joseph's decision. The civil government was not to intervene, nor was the priestly government. Similarly, the decision to forgive was also Christ's decision at the cross, although He had earlier warned the Jewish leaders that He would eventually bring judgment on them (Luke 21), which He did in A.D. 70.

Joseph forgave Mary. This was clearly a decision made under the terms of Old Covenant law. The New Covenant had not yet been established. Thus, when the text identifies Joseph as a just man, its frame of reference is the Old Covenant law. *Joseph was not violating any principle of the Mosaic law when he showed mercy to Mary and refused to prosecute.* He chose to put her away quietly in order to avoid having to bring a civil covenant lawsuit against

---

15. Jordan, *Death Penalty*, p. 9.

her. In his capacity as the betrothed husband, Joseph decided to break off the betrothal. Only if Mary's family had protested — unlikely, given the apparent circumstances of her pregnancy and the capital sanction involved (Deut. 22:20-21) — would he have been required to pursue his accusation in a civil or ecclesiastical court in order to defend his decision to break the betrothal.

The first question then is this: If the victim does decide to prosecute, and the person is convicted, can the victim then specify a lesser penalty? I think the answer is yes. I offer this explanation: the principle of victim's rights still applies, but in the case of murder, the victim cannot volunteer to accept a reduced penalty; thus, the State must impose the maximum penalty. This leads me to a general principle: *When the State becomes the prosecuting agent of case laws where this pleonasm occurs, it must enforce the death penalty on conviction.* There are no exceptions.

The second question is this: If the victim decides not to prosecute, can any other court intervene and prosecute in God's name? The case of Joseph and Mary indicates that Joseph's decision would have been authoritative and final. Her pregnancy would have been visible to all, yet if he had chosen not to prosecute, she could remain free of concern about any other court bringing charges against her. Had she actually been an adulteress, and had her consort been married, then the victimized wife could bring charges against them, but she could gain only a divorce: the court's declaration of a broken marriage. She could not require civil penalties against Mary, and therefore also not against her husband. Joseph, not the victimized wife, was the primary earthly victim and therefore the one who possessed the option of freeing his betrothed wife from any civil penalties.

What Does the Pleonasm Emphasize?

I think the pleonasm identifies *crimes that are the highest on God's list of abominations.* The normal penalty for these crimes is death; anything less than this which the victim specifies is a manifestation of great mercy. By upholding the principle of victim's rights, biblical law also creates incentives for criminals to deal less harshly with victims during the actual crime. If the victim is not brutal-ized, he may decide to show leniency if the criminal is later convicted. This protects the victim. Biblical law is designed to protect the victim.

Must civil judges impose the *maximum penalty* allowed by biblical law when the State is the victim, or when by law the State is God's designated agent to protect the community by upholding God's rights and enforcing His sanctions? Not always. The principle of victim's rights governs the imposition of civil sanctions. Judges have the God-given authority to impose a reduced penalty according to circumstances. The only exceptions to this rule are those cases in which the pleonasm occurs; the judges cannot reduce the sanctions in such cases. This is the meaning of the pleonasm: *the elimination of judicial discretion in imposing sanctions when the State initiates the lawsuit.*

Consider two alternative lines of reasoning. First, if we argue that the judges must impose the *maximum* penalty in *all* cases that specify the death penalty, irrespective of the presence of the pleonasm, then the emphasis aspect of the pleonasm disappears judicially. If all capital crimes require the death penalty, of what purpose is the pleonasm? This would indicate that the pleonasm has some function other than judicial emphasis. I cannot imagine what this other function might be. The presence of the pleonasm must indicate *the legitimacy of judicial discretion in cases where the pleonasm is missing.* By requiring judges to impose the maximum penalty in all cases, judicial discretion disappears. The judicial principle of victim's rights would therefore disappear.

Second, if we argue that the judges can in *all* cases legitimately impose a *lesser* penalty, then the emphasis aspect of the pleonasm also disappears judicially. Cases that are governed by the pleonasm would then become indistinguishable from those that are not. The pleonasm would lose its force.

My conclusion is this: if the pleonasm of execution is understood to have any judicial effect in distinguishing capital cases, and if the principle of victim's rights is also to be honored in all cases, then the pleonasm should be interpreted as *eliminating judicial discretion in applying sanctions in all cases in which prosecution has been lawfully initiated by the civil government.* The judges must not reduce the sanction of execution in any case in which 1) the State lawfully initiates the lawsuit, and 2) the sanction is marked by the pleonasm.

Thus, the pleonasm applies *only* to a unique set of capital crimes: where there is no identifiable or surviving human or institutional victim who could specify a reduced sanction. The victim is God alone. The State therefore is authorized to initiate the covenant lawsuit. *There is no earthly victim who has the authority to reduce the sanction.* The community through the civil government is called upon to execute the convicted criminal. In short, in the so-called "victimless crimes" in which the pleonasm of execution applies, civil judges have no choice in deciding on the appropriate sanction. The sanction is always execution. *"Dying, he shall die" binds the judges in capital crimes where the State acts as the covenant lawsuit's prosecutor without the presence of an intermediary or representative human victim.*

The pleonasm is not a denial of the principle of victim's rights because God, as the primary cosmic victim, has specified the appropriate sanction. This sanction must be imposed by the State in the absence of any secondary victim — a victim who is always authorized to speak in God's name. In the absence of such a representative, the pleonasm takes effect. The pleonasm must therefore *not* be understood as a limitation on the judicial principle of victim's rights. It limits the discretion of civil judges in those cases where there is no identifiable or surviving earthly victim, but it does not limit the discretion of the victim. Biblical law allows the victim, as God's representative, to reduce the penalty.

Rabbinic Law

Rabbinic law also recognizes the legitimacy of the victim's option of reducing or forgiving a criminal, as S. R. Hirsch's previous comments indicate, but not in capital crimes. While he did not refer to the pleonasm, Hirsch summarized the principle of Jewish law with respect to capital crimes. "The whole idea of the right to grant clemency or mercy was entirely absent in the Jewish Code of Law. Justice and judgment is [sic] the perogative [sic] of God not Man. When the very precisely defined Law of

God, — giving Man no scope for his own judgment or arbitrary discretion — ordains death for a criminal, the carrying out of this sentence is not an act of harshness to be commuted for any consideration whatsoever, it is itself the most considerate atonement, atonement for the community, atonement for the land, atonement for the criminal. . . ."[16]

The Christian cannot legitimately speak of atonement through a criminal's execution in this post-Calvary era, but he can and should speak of delivering the criminal directly into God's court, thereby placing him under God's sanctions rather than placing the community under God's sanctions for its unwillingness to obey God's law. The community that allows a criminal convicted of a capital crime to live is like a community that offers sanctuary to someone who is supposed to be tried in God's court. The community is required by God to extradite him. It cannot legitimately offer the evil-doer sanctuary. The text of Exodus 21:14 is clear: ". . . thou shalt take him from mine altar, that he may die." If a criminal is not to be granted sanctuary from a human civil court at the very altar of God, then surely a human civil court cannot legitimately grant him sanctuary by refusing to extradite him to God's heavenly court by executing him.

Taking a Rebellious Son to Court

In Chapter 1 (pp. 21-22), I raised the question of the parents' willingness to take a rebellious son to court. Would they do this if the death penalty were inescapable upon his conviction? Prob-

---

16. Hirsch, *Exodus*, p. 306: at Exodus 21:14. Hirsch immediately abandons this rigorous judicial principle in his discussion of kidnapping. The Talmud sets up so many extra stipulations regarding the definition of kidnapping that it is virtually impossible to execute a kidnapper under Jewish law. Hirsch says that the kidnapper is to be executed only "if he has made the man feel that he is being treated as an object, a thing" (p. 306). This sounds more like Immanuel Kant than the God of the Bible. Jewish lawyer and Talmudic scholar George Horowitz comments on the Talmudic view of kidnapping: "That the Rabbis considered the death penalty too severe for this wrong to society and the individual, seems quite plain from the foregoing rules. But they were bound by the express command of Scripture; hence they devised such requirements as made conviction virtually impossible. There is no record, moreover, that a regular court ever convicted a person of Manstealing." Horowitz, *The Spirit of Jewish Law* (New York: Central Book Co., [1953] 1963), pp. 197-98.

ably not. The key question then is this: Is the death penalty absolutely required by the pleonasm of execution? The point I have tried to make in this exposition is that *this pleonasm applies only in cases where the State is authorized to initiate the prosecution*, i.e., in cases where there is no earthly victim who can bring charges. This is not the situation in cases involving a rebellious son. Parents can and must bring their son before the civil authorities and complain about his conduct. God requires them to bring him to the civil court. The judges would then enforce a penalty specified by the parents, although they might first recommend an appropriate penalty. The son would obey his parents far more readily in the future, since he would know that the parents could take him back and insist on escalating penalties up to the death penalty if he committed similar infractions again. This fear would reinforce the parents' authority in the home.

What if they refuse to bring a formal charge against their rebellious son? Then they have implicitly subsidized evil behavior. They have implicitly *sanctioned* it. They know that they are risking the possibility that he will become an incorrigible adult. If he does, they will lose him anyway. Better to bring him before the civil court early. Better to obey God. Better to avoid God's sanctions against the family for the parents' refusal to obey. The son may learn fear of the civil court even though he has no fear of the family court.

If they bring him several times, the court will undoubtedly recommend increased sanctions. He has been identified as an incorrigible youth. The day that he commits a crime against someone outside his family, the court will be able to demonstrate to the victim that leniency is no solution, that this man is a habitual criminal. Thus, by allowing parents to insist on the death penalty, but by also allowing them to be lenient, God encourages parents to identify rebellious sons before the latter become incorrigible criminals. The court can take steps to enforce parentally recommended sanctions before it is too late.

This law, Rushdoony perceptively argues, is a law against the development of a professional criminal class. "But the godly exercise of capital punishment cleanses the land of evil and protects the righteous. In calling for the death of incorrigible juvenile delinquents, which means, therefore, in terms of case law, the death of incorrigible adult delinquents; the law declares, 'so shalt thou put evil away from among you; and all Israel shall hear, and fear' (Deut. 21:21)."[17]

What is true of this case law is true of all the other capital cases in which this pleonasm occurs and in which the victim is the specified agent who brings the covenant lawsuit. The victim has the option of specifying the penalty. If the case is one in which the State lawfully prosecutes in God's name, then the pleonasm is binding. Execution is mandatory.

Noah's Covenant and Execution

Dispensational authors H. Wayne House and Thomas Ice present a weak case for their speculations regarding the pre-New Covenant legal order as it applied to the nations. They insist that "Nowhere in the nations is capital punishment obligatorily extended beyond the penalty for taking human life. . . ."[18] They assert, though do not prove, that *none* of the Mosaic law's sanctions ever applied directly or even was intended in principle to apply to the nations, except the capital sanction for murder. This unique sanction is binding on all men always, they argue, so its authority came from Noah to Moses; it in no way went from Moses to the nations.

This is a clever attempt to escape the suggestion that in the New Covenant era, Christians have a responsibility to pressure civil governments to impose specific sanctions against specific crimes on the basis of biblical revelation. Such a view of "Noahic biblical law," if correct, would allow Christians to avoid personal responsibility in civil affairs, since they could not speak authoritatively in the name of the Lord when it comes to specifying civil crimes or penalties. The price of such a theological position regarding biblical law is, predictably, the cultural, political, and judicial irrelevance of Christianity. This is why dispensationalism

---

17. Rushdoony, *Institutes of Biblical Law*; pp. 77-78; cf. p. 188.
18. H. Wayne House and Thomas Ice, *Dominion Theology: Blessing or Curse?* (Portland, Oregon: Multnomah Press, 1988), p. 90.

is in principle culturally retreatist and culturally irrelevant, and why no dispensationalist in over a century and a half has published a book on Christian social ethics during the so-called "Church Age."

House and Ice go on to say that "in Israel this penalty [execution] was exacted for various crimes. . . ."[19] If they mean merely that in Israel, the maximum sanction of execution could be required by the victim in several capital crimes, then they are correct. If they mean that in those cases where the State lawfully prosecuted in God's name as His designated representative, and where the pleonasm "dying, he shall surely die" was attached to the biblical sanction, then they are also correct. If this is all they mean, however, then they have not said anything very significant. They have not shown that God restricted these judicial principles to Old Covenant Israel.

The judicial principle of a *maximum allowable sanction for any given crime* was also in principle God's requirement for the nations. Without this God-imposed judicial restriction, the State can lawfully become all-powerful, messianic, and therefore demonic. There will always be sanctions imposed by civil government. The only question is: Whose law establishes the specified judicial limits of State-imposed sanctions, God's or self-proclaimed autonomous man's?

To answer, as House and Ice do, that it depends upon when and where you live in God's world, is to abandon the concept of universal biblical ethics and therefore also to abandon the principle of universally restricted civil governments. Any attempted distinction between the Old Covenant nations and Mosaic Israel which is based on a theory of differing judicial sanctions for the same civil crimes is misguided. Civil sanctions are always specified by God because *God always wants limits on the State and always wants to see victims protected.* In other words, He always wants judicial limits on the pretensions of autonomous man. God killed nations under the Old Covenant, just as He kills New Covenant nations, because they failed to apply His civil sanctions in history. If this was not the message which Jonah brought to Nineveh, what was?

---

19. *Idem.*

The Death Penalty

The principle of victim-imposed sanctions is also God's requirement for all nations in this New Covenant era, now that the death, resurrection, and ascension of Jesus Christ, plus the sending of the Holy Spirit and the creation of the church, have extended *God's now-resurrected law-order* to the nations. The New Covenant is truly new; its Bible-specified laws and sanctions have been *universalized definitively in history* by the earthly ministry of Jesus Christ. The resurrection is behind us. Surely the sanctions of God's law for the nations are no less binding today than before Christ arose from the dead and incorporated His church! Yet House and Ice insist that the Mosaic sanctions are even less binding, for the Mosaic law does not even bind national Israel any longer, and so the law has no visible geographical example and testimony, as it had in the Old Covenant era (Deut. 4:5-8).

House and Ice do their dispensational best to create a false dichotomy between the God-required social laws of nations and the Mosaic social laws of Israel. They also try to create a dichotomy between New Covenant social laws and the Mosaic social laws. They want to place all Christians under the penal sanctions of the Noahic covenant (as the Calvinist ethicist John Murray sought to do before them),[20] both in the Old Covenant era and

---

20. Murray wrote: "It is conceivable that the progress of revelation would remove the necessity for the penal sanction [in the case of murder]. This is the case with the death penalty for adultery. And the same holds true for many other penal sanctions of the Mosaic economy. Does the same principle apply to the death penalty for murder?" John Murray, *Principles of Conduct*, p. 118. He goes on to argue that the sanction of execution is still valid because "murder is the capital sin." *Idem.* I find it interesting that dispensationalist antinomians House and Ice should have come to the same judicial conclusion that Calvinist Murray reached. Whether this ought to embarrass House and Ice more than it ought to embarrass Professor Murray's Calvinist disciples is a question I like to ask myself, but do not have the time or energy to answer.

I think Ray Sutton's assessment of Murray's theological motivation is plausible. Murray did not share Scottish Presbyterianism's rigorous view of the sabbath: for example, making illegal all public transportation services on Sunday. In the U.S., however, he was regarded as a rigorous sabbatarian. He did not give examinations on Mondays, since students would be tempted to study on Sunday. The pleonasm is attached to the sabbath laws (Ex. 21:34), which indicates that the Scottish view of the sabbath is an embarrassingly watered-down version of the Old Testament's sabbatarianism. Thus, in order to avoid having to adopt a view of the sabbath like the one I offer in *The Sinai Strategy* – that the locus of sovereignty of sabbath

in the New Covenant era.[21]

Noah's Covenant: Low Content

Why this preference by modern conservative theologians for Noah's covenant? Because in Noah's covenant *only one civil infraction* is specified: murder; and *only one penal sanction*: execution (Gen. 9:5). This absence of judicial specifics allows the civil government to specify as criminal whatever behavior it disapproves of, and also allows it to impose whatever sanctions it wants to, without any mandatory reference to any other biblical law or sanction. This political perspective is basically an application of pre-Darwinian humanism's social contract or social compact theory of the State, pioneered by Thomas Hobbes in *Leviathan* (1651) and developed by John Locke (1690) and Rousseau (1762). This older viewpoint was originally a secularized version of, and reaction against, the Puritans' biblical covenant theory of civil government.[22] It imputes primary sovereignty to the people rather than to God and His revealed law.[23]

What is judiciously not discussed by the defenders of the "Noahic covenant theory of the State" is that *the older social contract theory relied completely on the concept of natural law, and in Locke's case, natural rights.* This epistemologically naive view of civil law has been refuted from two sides: by Darwinism's view of the evolving universe and by Van Til's presuppositional apologetic. Without the doctrine of natural law or some version of natural rights theory

---

enforcement has been shifted in the New Covenant era, and therefore all of its civil and ecclesiastical sanctions have been removed — Murray preferred to defend the abolition of all capital sanctions in New Testament times, except the one for murder. Thus, he could retain a watered-down version of sabbatarianism, yet not be forced to admit that the O.T. sabbath's sanctions had been uniquely singled out by God for a drastic modification in the New Covenant era. The cost of this theological strategy was very high: his adoption of an essentially dispensational view of biblical law — the House-Ice view of Noah's one-law, one-sanction covenant as God's covenant for the nations.

21. "The Noahic covenant is perpetual. It serves as a basis of God's relationship and the standards imposed upon the nations." House and Ice, *op. cit.*, p. 127.

22. A. D. Lindsey, *The Modern Democratic State* (New York: Oxford University Press, [1943] 1959), ch. 5.

23. Rousseau's version of the sovereignty of the General Will might best be described as the Cole Porter theory of the State: "Anything Goes."

to govern their theory of the State, *defenders of the "Noahic covenant" theory have implicitly granted judicially unlimited power to the modern State*, no matter how much they protest against such a development. They may be political conservatives personally; it makes no difference. Their personal political preferences become just that: personal preferences. Their personal political preferences are self-consciously and explicitly unconnected with any biblical-theological system of social ethics and political theory.[24]

Such a view of Noah's low-content covenant grants enormous authority to self-proclaimed autonomous man and his representative, the messianic State. The power-seeking covenant-breaker is as pleased with such a view of the State as the responsibility-fleeing Christian pietist is. This is why there is now and always has been *an implicit judicial alliance between antinomian Christians and humanist statists*. Here is an ideal way to silence Christians in all judicial matters except murder: insist that "The Bible doesn't offer a blueprint for civil law!" With this judicial affirmation, antinomian, responsibility-fleeing Christians sound the retreat, and secular humanists and other covenant-breaking power-seekers sound the attack. The victim is in principle victimized ever further by this view of Noah's drastically restricted covenant, and the messianic State is unchained by it. *All this is accomplished in the name of a "higher" view of theistic ethics than the Mosaic law supposedly offered to the Israelites.*

This supposed dichotomy between Noah's covenantal sanctions and Moses' covenantal sanctions, and also between Moses' covenantal sanctions and Jesus' covenantal sanctions, cannot survive a careful examination of the biblical principle of victim's rights, which is also the principle of the judicially limited State. The biblical judicial principle is this: victims of criminal acts possess the God-granted legal right to specify no penalty or any penalty up to the maximum limit allowed by God's Bible-revealed law. Neither the State nor the humanistic sociologist is entitled

---

24. I studied systematic theology under John Murray. In private, he was an anti-New Deal conservative. In public, he was politically mute. Both Wayne House and Tommy Ice are political conservatives. In terms of a developed social and political theory, however, they are equally mute.

by God to increase or reduce this victim-specified penalty. But in order to keep the principle of victim's rights from becoming tyrannical, God's law specifies maximum penalties. Men must be restrained by law, including victims. To argue that there ever was, ever is, or ever will be a time when men are not under God's specified judicial sanctions is to argue that they are under sanctions imposed by autonomous man, meaning the self-proclaimed autonomous State. In short, to argue this is inescapably to argue also that God has in history authorized either the tyranny of the unchained State or else the implicit subsidizing of criminal behavior through the State's unwillingness to impose God's specified sanctions. In either case, victims lose. This is what antinomians of all varieties refuse even to discuss, let alone answer biblically.

There will always be sanctions. The relevant questions are: Which sanctions? What laws? Who judges? There will always be *judicial chains*, either attached to Satan (Rev. 20:1-2), his demonic host (II Pet. 2:4; Jude 6), and his covenantal earthly representatives, or else attached to the righteous victims of Satan's covenantal representatives (Acts 12:7; 21:33). The modern antinomian Christian and the modern power-seeking statist want to break God's judicial chain, His revealed law. The result is the victimization of the judicially innocent and the expansion of the messianic State.

Conclusion

All sins are against God and God's law. All sinners are criminals in the hand of a temporarily merciful Victim. God sits on His throne as final Judge and even temporal Judge (e.g., He slew Ananias and Sapphira: Acts 5:5, 10). But to sin against God, men usually must sin against something in the creation.[25] The Bible provides case laws that define those sins against any aspect of the creation which constitute civil, familial, or ecclesiastical infractions. Where a sin does constitute an infraction, *the victim must represent God by becoming a plaintiff against the sinner.* He upholds the integrity of the injured party and also seeks restitution. In some

---

25. An exception could be mental sins, yet in a sense even these are sins against the creation: a misuse of man's gift of reason.

The Death Penalty

cases, restitution is made only to the victim; in other cases, it must also be made to God through a payment to His church (Lev. 6:1-7).

The Bible provides five remedies for criminal behavior: 1) flogging (up to 40 lashes), 2) the slashing of a woman's hand; 3) economic restitution, which can be large enough to require 4) up to a lifetime of bondage; and 5) execution. The goals of these penalties include: 1) upholding God's interests by enforcing His law (civil worship);[26] 2) penalizing criminal behavior, sometimes by removing the criminal from this world (vengeance); 3) warning all people of the eternal judgment to come (evangelism); 4) protecting civil order (deterrence); and 5) protecting the interests of victims (justice). Ultimately, all of these goals can be summarized in one phrase: *upholding God's covenant.*

Notice that there is no mention of imprisonment. Hirsch wrote a century and a half ago: "Punishments of imprisonment, with all the intendant despair and moral degradation that dwell behind prison bars, with all the worry and distress that it entails for wife and child, are unknown in Torah jurisprudence. Where its power holds sway, prison for criminals does not exist. It only knows of remand custody, and even this, according to the whole prescribed legal procedure, and especially through the absolute rejection of all circumstantial evidence, can only be of the shortest duration."[27]

The law upholds the victim's interests. The criminal is to make restitution to his victim. The victim has the right to extend mercy, but that is his decision, not the judge's. Judges are to serve as agents of the victim, who is God's primary earthly representative in criminal affairs. The primary goal of criminal justice theory should be to discover and enforce civil penalties that uphold victim's rights within the guidelines established by Scripture.

When the victim refuses to prosecute, the other covenantal courts are required by God to honor this decision. The criminal

---

26. If civil magistrates are ministers, as Paul says they are (Rom. 13:4), then there is an element of worship in their enforcement of God's law. Sanctions are imposed in God's name.

27. Hirsch, *Exodus*, p. 294; at Exodus 21:6.

is not to be prosecuted by any covenantal court without the cooperation of the victim. When the State is the victim, or when a victim cannot be identified (e.g., a speeding violation), the judges are allowed to impose penalties up to the limit of God's Bible-revealed civil law, or when a penalty is not specified by the Bible, up to the limit of the written statute.[28] They can also impose reduced penalties, except where the pleonasm occurs. Where the pleonasm occurs, and where the State is not itself the victim, the judges must act as God's agents and impose the penalty that the pleonasm requires. This is the judicial function of the pleonasm of execution: *a restriction on leniency by civil judges when punishing "victimless crimes."* The judges must execute the convicted criminal without mercy. God requires him to be delivered speedily into His court.

Those who reject my thesis regarding the pleonasm must solve some very difficult problems. First, on what legal basis other than victim's rights did Joseph, said by the text to be a just man, fail to prosecute Mary either in a priestly court or a civil court? Had the law's sanction been changed by God before the birth of Jesus Christ? What is the evidence for such a view of the law's sanctions? Second, on what legal basis other than victim's rights did Jesus announce the temporal forgiveness of those who had crucified Him? Third, on what legal basis other than victim's rights had God refused to execute Israel for her adulteries? Put differently, what was the judicial basis of the Book of Hosea? Fourth, on what legal basis other than victim's rights did God divorce Israel when He transferred His kingdom to the church (Matt. 21:43), yet also allow her to survive another generation after the crucifixion of Jesus Christ and the incorporation of the church by the Holy Spirit? Not until critics provide consistent, well-developed, Bible-supported answers to these and related judi-

---

28. The Bible does not specify the amount of a proper fine for a speeding violation. It lays down the general principle of protecting potential victims. The civil authorities must then decide what the fine should be by balancing the risks to people as pedestrians vs. the benefits to people as drivers. Fines should vary according to speed and also according to geographical safety considerations such as school zones. See North, *Tools of Dominion*, ch. 11: "Criminal Law and Restoration," under the subhead, "Fines Should Compensate Victims," pp. 395-96.

cial questions should they abandon the principle of victim's rights.

Addendum: Cases to Which the Pleonasm Is Attached

I have put in bold face those case laws in which the State in Old Testament Israel was required to initiate the prosecution, and therefore those cases in which the convicted criminal had to be put to death.

He that smiteth a man, so that he die, shall be surely put to death (Ex. 21:12).

And he that smiteth his father, or his mother, shall be surely put to death (Ex. 21:15).

And he that stealeth a man, and selleth him, or if he be found in his hand, he shall surely be put to death (Ex. 21:16).

And he that curseth his father, or his mother, shall surely be put to death (Ex. 21:17).

Whosoever lieth with a beast shall surely be put to death (Ex. 22:19).

Ye shall keep the sabbath therefore; for it is holy unto you: every one that defileth it shall surely be put to death: for whosoever doeth any work therein, that soul shall be cut off from among his people (Ex. 31:14).

Six days may work be done; but in the seventh is the sabbath of rest, holy to the LORD: whosoever doeth any work in the sabbath day, he shall surely be put to death (Ex. 31:15).

Again, thou shalt say to the children of Israel, Whosoever he be of the children of Israel, or of the strangers that sojourn in Israel, that giveth any of his seed unto Molech; he shall surely be put to death: the people of the land shall stone him with stones (Lev. 20:2).

For every one that curseth his father or his mother shall be surely put to death: he hath cursed his father or his mother; his blood shall be upon him (Lev. 20:9).

And the man that committeth adultery with another man's wife, even he that committeth adultery with his neighbour's wife, the adulterer and the adulteress shall surely be put to death (Lev. 20:10).

And the man that lieth with his father's wife hath uncovered his father's nakedness: both of them shall surely be put to death; their blood shall be upon them (Lev. 20:11).

And if a man lie with his daughter-in-law, both of them shall surely be put to death: they have wrought confusion; their blood shall be upon them (Lev. 20:12).

If a man also lie with mankind, as he lieth with a woman, both of them have committed an abomination: they shall surely be put to death; their blood shall be upon them (Lev. 20:13).

And if a man lie with a beast, he shall surely be put to death: and ye shall slay the beast (Lev. 20:15).

And if a woman approach unto any beast, and lie down thereto, thou shalt kill the woman, and the beast: they shall surely be put to death; their blood shall be upon them (Lev. 20:16).

A man also or woman that hath a familiar spirit, or that is a wizard, shall surely be put to death: they shall stone them with stones: their blood shall be upon them (Lev. 20:27).

And he that blasphemeth the name of the LORD, **he shall surely be put to death, and all the congregation shall certainly stone him: as well the stranger, as he that is born in the land, when he blasphemeth the name of the** LORD, **shall be put to death** (Lev. 24:16).

And he that killeth any man shall surely be put to death (Lev. 24:17).

I the LORD have said, I will surely do it unto all this evil congregation, that are gathered together against me: in this wilderness they shall be consumed, and there they shall die (Num. 14:35).

For the LORD had said of them, They shall surely die in the wilderness. And there was not left a man of them, save Caleb the son of Jephunneh, and Joshua the son of Nun (Num. 26:65).

And if he smite him with an instrument of iron, so that he die, he is a murderer: the murderer shall surely be put to death. And if he smite him with throwing a stone, wherewith he may die, and he die, he is a murderer: the murderer shall surely be put to death. Or if he smite him with an hand weapon of wood, wherewith he may die, and he die, he is a

The Death Penalty

murderer: the murderer shall surely be put to death (Num. 35:16-18).

But if he thrust him of hatred, or hurl at him by laying of wait, that he die; Or in enmity smite him with his hand, that he die: he that smote him shall surely be put to death; for he is a murderer: the revenger of blood shall slay the murderer, when he meeteth him (Num. 35:20-21).

Moreover ye shall take no satisfaction for the life of a murderer, which is guilty of death: but he shall be surely put to death (Num. 35:31).

No instances of the pleonasm appear in the Book of Deuteronomy. I do not think that this has any biblical-theological significance. The biblical hermeneutical principle of the continuity of a God-revealed law is that unless a law or its sanction is repealed by a subsequent biblical revelation, it is still judicially binding. The pleonasms did not have to be repeated in Deuteronomy in order for them to be binding in the land. God's laws in Exodus, Leviticus, and Numbers were not exclusively "wilderness laws," with the laws of Deuteronomy alone to serve as the law of Israel in the land. In any case, the severity of God's sanctions tends to increase over time as men's maturity increases. This is a basic principle of biblical jurisprudence: *men's knowledge of God increases over time, and so does their personal and corporate responsibility.* "The lord of that servant will come in a day when he looketh not for him, and at an hour when he is not aware, and will cut him in sunder, and will appoint him his portion with the unbelievers. And that servant, which knew his lord's will, and prepared not himself, neither did according to his will, shall be beaten with many stripes. But he that knew not, and did commit things worthy of stripes, shall be beaten with few stripes. For unto whomsoever much is given, of him shall be much required: and to whom men have committed much, of him they will ask the more" (Luke 12:46-48). Because they were required by God to exercise greater responsibility in the Promised Land, as testified to by the ending of the miraculous agricultural subsidy of the manna (Josh. 5:12), the law's civil sanctions did not decrease in rigor; if anything, they increased. The pleonasm was still judicially binding in Canaan.

The equivalent phrase in Deuteronomy is, "so shalt thou put [purge] evil away from you" (Deut. 17:7; 19:19; 21:21; 22:21, 24; 24:7).

3

KIDNAPPING

And he that stealeth a man, and selleth him, or if he be found in his hand, he shall surely be put to death (Ex. 21:16).

In Chapter 2, I set forth my thesis that the pleonasm, "he shall surely be put to death," is binding on the civil authorities when the State initiates the prosecution of the covenant lawsuit, but it does not bind the victim when he initiates the prosecution. We must examine the implications of this principle in the case of kidnapping, a crime that is bound by the terms of the pleonasm.

Before getting to this problem, however, we must search for the theocentric principle that governs the crime of kidnapping. James Jordan quite properly lists kidnapping under the general heading of *violence*. The nature of violence biblically is that it represents an attempted assault on God, an attempt to murder God by murdering His image.[1] He lists other aspects of violence: the desire of sinful men to play god, the desire to achieve autonomous vengeance, and sado-masochism.[2] Violence should be understood as a sinner's rebellious attempt to achieve dominion by power.[3] It is a form of *revolution*. The preaching of the gospel is intended to reduce violence.

Ultimately, this crime and its civil penalty should be understood in terms of the assumption of a *theocentric* universe. Jordan's assessment is valid: "The death penalty is appropriate because

---
1. James B. Jordan, *The Law of the Covenant: An Exposition of Exodus 21-23* (Tyler, Texas: Institute for Christian Economics, 1984), p. 93.
2. *Ibid.*, pp. 93-96.
3. *Ibid.*, p. 95.

kidnapping is an assault on the very person of the image of God, and as such is a radical manifestation of man's desire to murder God. Like rape, it is a deep violation of personhood and manifests a deep-rooted contempt for God and his image."[4]

Nevertheless, the crime of kidnapping goes beyond the question of the image of God in man. Kidnapping is more than an assault against God's image in man. It is not simply man's blood that is inviolate (Gen. 9:6); it is also his life's *calling*. It is not simply his image that commands respect from other men; it is also his *God-ordained assignment in life*. Perhaps it would be better to argue that man's imaging also includes the calling. God is revealed in Genesis 1 as a God who works and who judges. Man images this God. Kidnapping is therefore an assault on both of these aspects of man's imaging.

Who is the true owner of the kidnapper's victim? God is. God owns the whole world (Ps. 50:10). Nevertheless, stealing a privately owned animal is not a capital crime (Ex. 22:1). Why the special case of a man? The answer is found in man's special position: subordinate under God and possessing authority over the creation. Man is made in God's image (Gen. 1:27; 9:6). By interfering with a man's God-given calling before God, the kidnapper disrupts God's revealed administrative structure for subduing the earth. Each man must work out his salvation — or, presumably, work out his damnation — with fear and trembling (Phil. 2:12). The kidnapper asserts his presumed autonomy and illegitimate authority over the victim, as if he were God, as if he possessed a lawful right to determine what another man's responsibilities on earth ought to be.

The Death Penalty

The Bible recognizes that there are two potential criminals involved in kidnapping: the actual kidnapper and the person to whom he sells the victim. The international slave trade did exist. (White slavery — kidnapping of white girls who are then sold into the Middle East or other foreign areas — still appears to exist.) The passage deals with both types of criminals: "And he that

---
4. *Ibid.*, p. 104.

stealeth a man, and selleth him, or if he be found in his hand, he shall surely be put to death." Both the kidnapper and the recipient of the stolen victim are subject to the death penalty.[5] Slave traders were at risk.

The obvious problem with a universally mandatory death penalty is that a crime whose effects are less permanent than murder bears the same permanent penalty that murder does. Consider the case of kidnapping. The kidnapper has a strong incentive to kill the victim if he thinks that the authorities are closing in on him. The victim may later identify him as the kidnapper; better to kill the source of the incriminating evidence. After all, the penalty for murder is the same as the penalty for kidnapping. A person can only be killed once by the civil government. Jordan recognizes this problem.[6] So do humanist legal theorists.

Then why does the Bible specify the death penalty for kidnapping? Isn't this dangerous for the victim? Other ancient Near Eastern law codes — if we can accurately call them codes[7] — did not impose such a harsh penalty. The code of Hammurabi specified the death penalty for kidnapping only when an aristocrat kidnapped the young son of another aristocrat.[8] What lies behind the rigorous biblical penalty?

The Bible does not limit the death penalty to cases involving physical harm to the victim. The person who is kidnapped in order to be sold as a slave is not said to have been harmed. If

---

5. Dale Patrick, *Old Testament Law* (Atlanta, Georgia: John Knox Press, 1985), p. 74.

6. James B. Jordan, *The Death Penalty in the Mosaic Law* (Tyler, Texas: Biblical Horizons, 1988), p. 17.

7. Shalom Paul cites the 1963 warning of his teacher, E. A. Speiser, regarding the famous Code of Hammurabi: "The handful of jurists . . . seem agreed that what we have before us is not properly a code or a digest but 'a series of amendments to the common law of Babylon' (Driver and Miles, *Babylonian Laws* I, p. 41)." Shalom Paul, *Studies in the Book of the Covenant in the Light of Cuneiform and Biblical Law* (Leiden: E. J. Brill, 1970), p. 3n. But Yehezkel Kaufman insists that Deuteronomy "is unquestionably intended to be a law code in the ancient Near Eastern sense." *The Religion of Israel* (Chicago: University of Chicago Press, 1960), p. 46.

8. Hammurabi Code, paragraph 14: *Ancient Near Eastern Texts Relating to the Old Testament*, edited by James B. Pritchard (3rd ed.; Princeton, New Jersey: Princeton University Press, 1969), p. 166.

anything, the kidnapper who intends to sell the victim into servitude has an economic incentive not to harm the victim, since an injury would presumably reduce the market value of "the property." Yet the kidnapper potentially faces the most fearful penalty that society can inflict. Why such a concern for this crime?

Sacrilege

To steal from God involves sacrilege. Rushdoony has made an interesting study on the meaning and implications of sacrilege, and his general comments apply in the case of kidnapping. "*Theft is basic to the word, and sacrilege is theft directed against God. It is apparent from this that the idea of sacrilege is present throughout Scripture. . . .* The concept of sacrilege rests on God's sovereignty and the fact that He has an absolute ownership over all things: men and the universe are God's property. The covenant people are *doubly* God's property: *first*, by virtue of His creation, and, *second*, by virtue of His redemption. For this reason, sin is more than personal and more than man-centered. It is a theological offense."[9] So serious is the crime of sacrilege that it is compared by Paul to adultery and idolatry (Rom. 2:22), both of which were capital crimes in the Old Testament.[10] (The code of Hammurabi specified the death penalty for those who stole the property of either church or State, and also for those who received the stolen goods.)[11]

Because sacrilege is theft, it requires restitution.[12] Since sacrilege is theft against God, it requires restitution to God. In this case, the crime is so great that the maximum restitution is the death of the criminal. No lower payment can suffice if the State prosecutes and convicts in God's name. The implied assertion of autonomy by the criminal, who seeks to play God, represents a

---

9. R. J. Rushdoony, *Law and Society*, vol. II of *Institutes of Biblical Law* (Vallecito, California: Ross House Books, 1982), p. 28.

10. *Ibid.*, p. 31.

11. CH, paragraph 6; *Ancient Near Eastern Texts*, p. 166. There was an exception: if the person stole an ox or a sheep from church or State, he paid thirty-fold restitution; it was ten-fold restitution if the animal had belonged to a private citizen: CH, paragraph 8, *idem*.

12. Rushdoony, *Law and Society*, p. 33.

form of idolatry, worshipping another God. The kidnapper steals God's property — a person made in His image — and seeks to profit from the asset. This is the essence of the crime of Adam, to be as God (Gen. 3:5).

Future Deterrence

The death penalty is final. Its beneficial effects for society are twofold: it restrains the judgment of God on society, and it provides a deterrence effect — deterring the criminal from future crime (he dies), deterring other criminals from committing similar crimes (fear of death), and deterring God from bringing His covenant judgments on the community for its failure to uphold covenant law (fear of God's wrath). Capital punishment is God's way of telling criminals, whether convicted criminals or potential criminals, that they have gone too far by committing certain crimes. It also warns the community that God's law is to be respected. Obviously, there is no element of rehabilitation for the convicted criminal in the imposition of the death penalty. The State speeds the convicted criminal's march toward final judgment. The State delivers the sinner into the presence of the final and perfect Judge.[13]

If we interpret the presence of the pleonasm as making the death penalty mandatory, irrespective of the wishes of the victim, then we create a problem for the victim. *A mandatory death penalty may actually increase the risk to the victim, once the criminal act has taken place.* First, the victim may have seen the criminal. His positive identification of the kidnapper and his testimony against him can convict him. Second, should the criminal begin to suspect that he is about to be caught by the authorities, he may choose to kill the victim and dispose of the body. By disposing of the evidence of the crime, the victim loses his life, while the criminal reduces his risk of being detected. This is a good reason to suppose that

---

13. One reason why the torture of a convicted criminal prior to his execution is immoral is that it symbolically arrogates to the State what God reserves exclusively for Himself: the legal authority to torture people for eternity. It is a right that God exercises exclusively. By torturing a person prior to his execution, the State asserts that its punishments are on a par with God's, that the State's penalties are to be feared as much or more than God's. On the State as torturer, see Edward Peters, *Torture* (London: Basil Blackwell, 1985), ch. 5.

the death penalty for kidnapping is a maximum allowable penalty, one which a victim can impose but need not impose on a convicted kidnapper.

What if the kidnapper has stolen more than one adult person? What if one adult victim asks the court to impose the death penalty, but the other victim asks for leniency? Or, if the kidnapper has stolen more than one minor, what if the parent or legal guardian of one asks for the death penalty, but the parent or legal guardian of the other recommends leniency? The victim who demands execution is sovereign. The extension of mercy is not mandatory. The pleonasm of execution is attached to this law. The presence of the pleonasm indicates that capital punishment is the normal sanction. Anything less than execution is abnormal: a unique sign of leniency by the victim. The victim who specifies execution is adhering to God's written law. He is upholding the sanctity of the sanction against sacrilege. His decision is final.

Can the State prosecute if the victim declines? Only if the State is itself a victim. It seems reasonable to allow the State to recover the costs of searching for the victim. The kidnapper has stolen from the State by his criminal act. If the State successfully prosecutes a kidnapper, judges can impose a double restitution penalty payment for the costs incurred. But the judges cannot lawfully impose the capital sanction. They must uphold the principle of victim's rights.

Confession Before Conviction

There is the possibility that in other circumstances, the threat of the death penalty may reduce the risk to the victim. A criminal in the Bible is allowed to go to the authorities before he has been caught and make a 20 percent restitution payment, plus the capital value of the stolen property or unpaid vow (Lev. 6:1-7). The kidnap victim in the Old Testament presumably would have been sold as a servant. The market price of this sort of servant could have been calculated in the Old Testament.[14] The judges could also have used the Bible's fixed price system for a servant killed

---

14. Writes the early nineteenth-century Jewish commentator S. R. Hirsch: "The value of any human life can not be expressed in pounds, shillings and pence. But

by a goring ox: 30 shekels of silver (Ex. 21:32). Or perhaps the prices listed for human vows to the temple could have been used by the judges (Lev. 27:3-7). The Bible always offers opportunities for repentance. By allowing the kidnapper to escape the threat of the death penalty by surrendering to the authorities, biblical law reduces the threat to the kidnap victims in those cases where a kidnapper repents before he is arrested.

Ransom

But what about the modern form of kidnapping, where the kidnapper demands a ransom? The same principle operates: the repenting but as yet unarrested kidnapper offers to the victim the value of the ransom demanded, plus one-fifth. In most cases, this would mean a lifetime of servitude to repay the debt. Servitude for the kidnapper is better for the victim and society than what the modern criminal justice system imposes. The modern criminal justice system would probably impose a life sentence in jail for the criminal, at the expense of taxpayers, with parole possible (likely) in a few years. The kidnap victim gets nothing.

There was a motion picture in 1956 called *Ransom*. The hero of the film is a rich businessman. His son is kidnapped, and the kidnappers demand a huge ransom. The police tell him that kidnap victims wind up dead about half the time, whether a ransom is paid or not. The father decides not to pay. He goes to his bank and gets the money demanded by the kidnappers. He then calls in the local television station, which broadcasts his announcement. In front of him on a desk is the money, in cash. He says to all those listening that if his son is murdered, he

---

atonement-money has to be paid in certain cases. This 'atonement-money' the token value of his own life, in the case of a free man, is estimated at the amount he would fetch if sold in the market as a slave. There is no other way of fixing the amount of human life in terms of hard cash." Samson Raphael Hirsch, *The Pentateuch Translated and Explained*, translated by Isaac Levy, 5 vols., *Exodus* (3rd ed.; London: Honig & Sons, 1967), p. 323; at Exodus 21:32. This ignores another valid means of estimating a kidnapped man's hard-cash value: the ransom payment demanded by the kidnapper (what economists call "reservation value"). Another problem with Hirsch's restricted means of estimating a person's value is that today there is no lawful slave market operating. He must have known that this would complicate things for the judges.

intends to pay every cent of the money to anyone who will tell him the name of the person who kidnapped his son. He offers to pay the accomplices to the crime. He reminds the kidnapper of the risk of relying on the reliability of his accomplices. He then points to the money and declares to the kidnapper, "This is as close to this money as you'll ever get." When he returns home, his neighbors are outraged. They throw rocks through his window. He had not shown filial piety. He deserves to be an outcast. But at the end of the movie, his son is returned to him. The kidnapper was fearful of being turned in for the reward.

What the movie's hero did was to place a greater priority on *bringing the criminal to justice* than he placed on public acceptance of his act. (The statistical risk to his son, he had been told, was the same, whether he paid the ransom or not.) By using the ransom money in a unique way — as a reward that would increase the likelihood of someone's becoming an informant — the father increased the odds in favor of his son's survival. (The majority of crimes are probably solved as a result of informants.)[15] He relied on the threat of punishment more than he did on the good will of the criminal in honoring the terms of the transaction, his son's life for a cash payment. He turned to the law for protection, not to the criminal's sense of honor.

In 1973, the grandson of J. Paul Getty, one of the world's richest men, was kidnapped in Italy. The kidnapping received worldwide attention. The kidnappers demanded over a million dollars as the ransom.[16] Getty publicly refused to pay. He said that if he did, this would place his fourteen other grandchildren in jeopardy. By not paying, he said, he was telling all other potential kidnappers that it was useless to kidnap any of his relatives. The kidnappers cut off the youth's ear and sent it to his mother. Still the grandfather refused. Privately, he lent $850,000 to the boy's father to pay the ransom — at 4 percent, of course. Getty never missed an opportunity for profit.[17] The gamble paid

---

15. Edward Powell, "The Coming Crisis in Criminal Investigation," *Journal of Christian Reconstruction*, II (Winter 1975-76), pp. 81-83.

16. The price of gold was then about $100 an ounce.

17. Fellow billionaire industrialist Armand Hammer refers to him as "that tight

off: the kidnappers released him.[18] No other Getty relatives became victims.[19]

Equal Penalties or Equal Results?

The Bible does not forbid the victim's family to pay a ransom, but the threat of the death penalty makes the risk of conviction so great that few potential kidnappers would take the risk, except for a very high return. The average citizen therefore receives additional but indirect protection because of this biblical law. The penalty to the convicted kidnapper is so high that the money which the middle-class victim's relatives could raise to pay the ransom probably would not compensate most potential kidnappers for the tremendous risk involved. Presumably, kidnappers will avoid kidnapping poorer people.

In effect, *the threat of the death penalty increases the likelihood that members of very rich families or senior employees of very rich corporations will be the primary victims of kidnappers.* Also, in cases of politically motivated kidnappings, the famous or politically powerful could become the victims. They seem to be discriminated against economically by biblical law: high penalties make it more profitable for kidnappers to single their families out for attack. On the other hand, these people possess greater economic resources, making it more likely that they can more easily afford to protect themselves and their relatives.

From the point of view of economic analysis, the stiff penalty for kidnapping protects society at large, though not always the actual victim of the crime, and it protects the average citizen

---

old weasel." Armand Hammer (with Neil Lyndon), *Hammer* (New York: Putnam's, 1987), p. 386. Hammer did respect him as an entrepreneur, however.

18. The grandson later suffered a stroke as a result of alcohol and drug abuse, and is paralyzed and blind. *Time* (March 17, 1986), p. 80.

19. I have instructed my wife never to pay a ransom for me under any conditions. I have also told her that I will not pay a ransom for her or any of our children. The goal is to reduce the risk of kidnapping before it takes place, not to increase the likelihood of the victim's survival. The evil of kidnapping should not be rewarded. It should be made devastatingly unprofitable. The same should be true for terrorist kidnappings. The policy of the state of Israel regarding terrorist kidnappings is correct: a kidnapper-for-victims exchange before any victim is harmed, but no compromise thereafter.

more than it protects the rich. The law applies to all kidnappers equally; it has varying effects on different people and groups within the society. Because the Bible requires *equality before the law*, it produces *different results*. To equalize the results — equal risk for rich families and poor families — the Bible would have to impose the death penalty only for kidnappers of rich people. (This, as we have seen, is what Hammurabi's Code did: it imposed the death penalty only on those who kidnapped the sons of aristocrats.) The economic payoff would have to be made lower in the case of a kidnapper who steals a poor person. Therefore, in order to put poor families at risk as high as that borne by rich families, the law would have to discriminate between kidnappers of the poor and kidnappers of the rich. But *the kidnapper sins primarily against God*, so the death penalty can be specified by the victim in both cases. God is not a respecter of persons, meaning those convicted of a capital crime. The question is not the economic status of the victims, but the nature of the crime (sacrilege) and the sanctions specified by the victims (victim's rights). Thus, a consistent application of this law in every case of kidnapping increases the risk of being kidnapped for the rich.

Equality

This brings up a very important question relating to the word "equality." When men demand equality, what do they really want? If they demand *equality before the law* — "Equal penalties for identical crimes, irrespective of persons!" — then they are simultaneously demanding *unequal economic results*. This is not true only in the case of the variation of risk for different economic groups when a society demands the death penalty for all kidnappers. This is true of the economy in general. When men demand *equal economic results*, they are simultaneously demanding *inequality before the law*. Hayek's analysis is correct: "From the fact that people are very different it follows that, if we treat them equally, the result must be inequality in their actual position, and that the only way to place them in an equal position would be to treat them differently. Equality before the law and material equality are therefore not only different but are in conflict with each other; and we can achieve either the one or the other, but not both at the same time. The equality before the law which freedom requires leads to material inequality. Our argument will be that, though where the state must use coercion for other reasons, it should treat all people alike, the desire of making people more alike in their condition cannot be accepted in a free society as a justification for further and discriminatory coercion."[20]

Biblical law is clear: *equality before the civil law is the God-sanctioned concept of equality*. Equality of results does not apply to the sanctions that God imposes after a person dies, either positive sanctions or negative sanctions. The principle of *positive sanctions* is specified in I Corinthians 3:11-15: "For other foundation can no man lay than that is laid, which is Jesus Christ. Now if any man build upon this foundation gold, silver, precious stones, wood, hay, stubble; Every man's work shall be made manifest: for the day shall declare it, because it shall be revealed by fire; and the fire shall try every man's work of what sort it is. If any man's work abide which he hath built thereupon, he shall receive a reward. If any man's work shall be burned, he shall suffer loss: but he himself shall be saved; yet so as by fire." The principle of *negative sanctions* is specified in Luke 12:47-48: "And that servant, which knew his lord's will, and prepared not himself, neither did according to his will, shall be beaten with many stripes. But he that knew not, and did commit things worthy of stripes, shall be beaten with few stripes. For unto whomsoever much is given, of him shall be much required: and to whom men have committed much, of him they will ask the more."

Time Perspective

The establishment of the death penalty is necessary to increase risk to the potential kidnapper — risk that is proportional to the magnitude of his proposed crime. By calculating in advance the permanent nature of the penalty (death), the criminal is forced to come to grips with the future. The criminal presumably is present-oriented.[21] Certainly, he ignores the eternal consequences

---

20. F. A. Hayek, *The Constitution of Liberty* (University of Chicago Press, 1960), p. 87.
21. Edward C. Banfield, "Present-Orientedness and Crime"; Gerald P. O'Driscoll,

of his acts. He generally lives for the moment. His long-term fate is total destruction on the day of judgment. He discounts this, refusing to act in terms of this knowledge. That day seems too far away chronologically, and God is not visible. "Perhaps God is not going to enforce the promised penalty. Maybe God doesn't even exist," the criminal thinks to himself. Therefore, God sets the civil government's penalty so high that even a present-oriented criminal will feel the restraining pressure of extreme risk, even if his psychological rate of discount is very high. The severity of the earthly punishment testifies to the severity of the eternal punishment. It serves as an "earnest" or down payment on eternity.

The Bible teaches us that history is linear. History has a beginning and an end. The Bible also teaches us that our thoughts, as well as our deeds, have consequences in history and also in eternity beyond the grave (Matt. 5:28). It tells men to redeem (buy back) their time (Eph. 5:16), to work while there is still light (John 9:4). If God-fearing people must be educated and motivated for them to believe such doctrines, then we have to come to grips with the reality of a world in which members of a criminal class reject all these doctrines. More than this: members of a professional criminal class self-consciously live in terms of *a rival set of attitudes* toward time, personal responsibility, and the consequences of human action.

The possibility of the death penalty for kidnapping forces the potential kidnapper to count the cost of his transgression. Remember, *a person's perception of total cost (including risk) is affected directly by his perception of time.* If men discount the future greatly, as Esau did with respect to his birthright, then they will accept low cash bids for future income.[22] Present-oriented men discount future benefits and future curses alike; the distant future is of very little concern to them. As Harvard political scientist Edward Banfield comments: "At the present-oriented end of the scale, the lower-class individual lives from moment to moment. If he has any

---

"Professor Banfield on Time Horizon: What Has He Taught Us About Crime?" in Randy E. Barnett and John Hegel III (eds.), *Assessing the Criminal: Restitution, Retribution, and the Legal Process* (Cambridge, Massachusetts: Ballinger, 1977).

22. North, *Dominion Covenant: Genesis*, pp. 126-28, 182-83.

awareness of a future, it is of something fixed, fated, beyond his control: things happen *to* him, he does not *make* them happen. Impulse governs his behavior, either because he cannot discipline himself to sacrifice a present for a future satisfaction or because he has no sense of the future. He is therefore radically improvident: whatever he cannot use immediately he considers valueless. His bodily needs (especially for sex) and his taste for 'action' take precedence over everything else — and certainly over any work routine."[23]

A law-order must recognize present-oriented people for what they are. The kidnapper may be somewhat more future-oriented than the lower-class man. He makes plans, counts costs, and takes risks. But he discounts the long-term consequences of his acts. He does not care about the effects on the victim, his family, or the community. It is this *radical lack of concern for the lives and callings of other men* that makes him a menace to society. To catch his attention, to convince him of the seriousness of his crime, the Bible stipulates the death penalty. Richard Posner, an economist and also a judge for the U.S. Court of Appeals, acknowledges the validity of relationship between a criminal's time perspective and the need for capital punishment, but only in a footnote: "Notice that if criminals' discount rates are very high, capital punishment may be an inescapable method of punishing very serious crimes."[24]

The total discontinuity involved in the execution of the kidnapper favors *continuity in the lives of the innocent*. It is the innocent people of society who deserve continuity, not the kidnappers. The decision to prosecute, or to specify a penalty other than death, is in the hands of the victim or his survivors. The victim is allowed by biblical law to bargain with the kidnapper in order to obtain his freedom. (The kidnapper would have no way to get even with a victim who subsequently changed his mind and called for the death penalty.)

---

23. Edward Banfield, *The Heavenly City Revisited* (Boston: Little, Brown, 1973), p. 61.

24. Richard Posner, *Economic Analysis of Law* (Boston: Little, Brown, 1986), p. 212n.

Kidnapping and the Slave Trade

The abolition of slavery has made kidnapping less profitable financially. Before slavery was abolished by law, the slave market offered a profit to kidnappers because *they could capitalize the entire working lifetime of the victim*. There were numerous buyers who were willing to bid against each other for the lifetime output of kidnap victims. Today, only families, major corporations, and civil governments are willing and able to buy back a victim, and very often not primarily because of the victim's earning power.

The slave trade existed for many centuries because of the ready market for its victims. The purchase of slaves by slave-buyers created the market price of the slaves, from ancient Greece until the not-so-ancient 1960's. As recently as 1960, in the words of Britain's Lord Shackleton, African Muslims on pilgrimages sold slaves on arrival, "using them as living traveller's cheques."[25] Slavery was officially outlawed in Saudi Arabia in 1962 and by Oman in 1970.[26] Nevertheless, though African slavery declined sharply in the 1960's, "slave-trading continued to flourish in Mauritania, Mali, Niger, and Chad, along the drought-stricken southern fringe of the Sahara."[27] As recently as 1981, the United Nations Human Rights Commission reported that there were 100,000 slaves in Mauritania. Other estimates place the total number of slaves at 250,000 among the nomadic tribes of the drought-ridden Sahel in North Africa.[28] The slave-owners are Moors (Islamic), while the slaves are blacks from Senegal. There are no open slave markets because the trade is officially illegal. The biggest part of the trade is in children. They belong to the owners of the mothers.[29]

A steady economic demand for slaves created the demand for

---

25. Cited by David Brion Davis, *Slavery and Human Progress* (New York: Oxford University Press, 1984), p. 317.

26. *Ibid.*, p. 319.

27. *Idem.*

28. Roger Sawyer, *Slavery in the Twentieth Century* (London: Routledge & Kegan Paul, 1986), p. 14.

29. Bernard D. Nossiter, "U.N. Group Gets Report on Slaves in Mauritania," *New York Times* (Aug. 21, 1981).

new victims. The *slave traders*, so hated and despised in the eighteenth and nineteenth centuries by "respectable" English-speaking society, including most slave owners, and equally despised by slave-owning writers in the ancient world,[30] were, from a strictly economic point of view, nothing less than *the paid agents of the buyers.* They were performing specialized work as purchasing agents for slave-buyers. The Arab and native African kidnappers were, to that extent, merely the specialized collection agents of the slave-buyers. They were economic middlemen, entrepreneurs. The entrepreneur necessarily serves the wants of consumers.

In every free market transaction, the potential consumers of any economic good or service are competing with other consumers for control over all scarce economic resources. They compete directly and indirectly for the final output of the economy. The outcome of this competition establishes prices, quality standards, and costs related directly to the production of all economic goods. The middlemen (entrepreneurs) simply serve those consumers whose competing bids are expected to produce the highest profits. *Consumers ultimately determine prices and therefore also costs.*[31] This economic process was no less true of the slave trade. It is one of the peculiar aspects of "the peculiar institution" of American Negro slavery that the "final consumers" refused to recognize their own personal responsibility, as economic actors and political voters, for the operations of the entire slave-delivery system.

What we should recognize here is the relationship between the abolition of compulsory slavery and the reduction of involuntary servitude for citizens in general. By making illegal the *market* for imported slaves, Western nations reduced the demand for imported slaves in the early 1800's. This in turn reduced the risk of being kidnapped for the average African.[32] A policy of State-enforced coercion against slave-buying reduced the profit-seeking

---

30. Thomas Wiedemann, *Greek and Roman Slavery* (Baltimore, Maryland: Johns Hopkins University Press, 1981), pp. 6, 106-7.

31. Murray N. Rothbard, *Man, Economy, and State* (New York: New York University Press, [1962] 1979), pp. 301-8.

32. This falling demand for imported slaves was offset by an increase in demand for legal, domestically produced slaves. This transformed some plantations into

private coercive activity of kidnapping Africans thousands of miles away.

This policy worked only because 1) the British navy enforced its regulations against the slave traders, 2) a majority of citizens in the recipient nations were steadily educated to reject the idea of the legitimacy of involuntary servitude, and 3) slavery's defenders were defeated on the battlefield, in the case of the American South in the 1860's. The economic lesson: disregarding the needs and preferences of slave-holders (the final users) by outlawing slavery led to the reduction of the entire slave trade. The profitability of the international slave trade was reduced. We learn that there are cases where State coercion is valid, when that coercion is directed against private coercers. The anti-slave trade legislation recognized the complicity of slave-owners (final users) in the coercive international slave trade. The market for slaves was not a free market, for the supply side of the equation was based on coercion.

Monopoly Returns and Reduced Crime

There is a curious myth that laws against evil acts do not reduce the total number of these acts that criminals commit. Some critics even go so far as to argue that the very presence of the law subsidizes evil, in the case of laws against the sale of illegal drugs or laws against prostitution. Somehow, passing a law makes the prohibited market more profitable, and therefore the law leads to greater output of the prohibited substances or services. This is a very odd argument when it comes from people who defend the efficiency and productivity of laissez-faire economics.

A fundamental principle of economics is this: the division of labor is limited by the extent of the market. This was articulated

---

slave-breeding centers, especially in the Virginia tidewater region, where soil-eroding agricultural techniques had reduced the land's output, and therefore had reduced the regional market value of the human tools who produced the output. This region began to export slaves to buyers who cultivated the fresher soils of Louisiana and Mississippi. See Alfred H. Conrad and John R. Meyer, "The Economics of Slavery in the Ante-Bellum South," *Journal of Political Economy*, LXVI (April 1958); reprinted in Robert W. Fogel and Stanley L. Engerman (eds.), *The Reinterpretation of American Economic History* (New York: Harper & Row, 1971), ch. 25.

by Adam Smith in Chapter 3 of *Wealth of Nations* (1776). Another basic principle is this one: the greater the division of labor, the greater the output per unit of resource input — in short, the greater the efficiency of the market. When the market increases in size, it makes possible an increase in cost-effective production. Advertising and mass-production techniques lower the cost of production and therefore increase the total quantity of goods and services demanded. This is well understood by all economists.

Nevertheless, there are some people who still believe that laws against so-called "victimless crimes" — sins that they do not regard as major transgressions, I suspect — actually increase the profitability of crime. On the contrary, such laws increase the risk of the prohibited activities, both to sellers and consumers. Prices rise; the market shrinks; per unit costs rise; efficiency drops. What such laws do is create monopoly returns for a few criminals. But the critics of such laws conveniently forget that *monopoly returns are always the product of reduced output.* This, in fact, is the conventional definition of a monopoly. Thus, civil laws do reduce the extent of the specified criminal behavior.[33] They confine such behavior to certain criminal subclasses within the society. Biblically speaking, such laws place *boundaries* around such behavior.

There is no doubt that nineteenth-century laws against the slave trade drastically reduced the profitability of the international slave trade. These laws increased the risks for slavers, reduced their profits, and narrowed their markets. The result was a drop in output (slavery) per unit of resource input.

Household Evangelism

Apart from the one exception provided by the jubilee law, the Old Testament recognized the legitimacy of involuntary slavery of foreigners only when the slaves were female captives taken after a battle (Deut. 20:10-11, 14). To fight a war for the *purpose* of taking slaves would have been illegitimate, for this was (and is) the foreign policy of empires. It is true that the jubilee law did

---

33. Cf. James M. Buchanan, "A Defense of Organized Crime?" in Ralph Andreano and John J. Siegfried (eds.), *The Economics of Crime* (New York: Wiley, 1980), pp. 395-409.

allow both the importation of pagan slaves and the purchase of children from resident aliens, but the purpose of this practice was primarily covenantal: bringing slaves of demon-possessed cultures into servitude under Israelite families that were in turn under God.

Once the New Testament gospel became an international phenomenon that spread outward from local churches rather than from a central sanctuary in Jerusalem, there was no longer any need to bring potential converts into the land through purchase. Jesus completely fulfilled the terms of the jubilee law, including the kingdom-oriented goals of the imported slave law. He transferred the kingdom from the land of Israel to the church international: "Therefore say I unto you, The kingdom of God shall be taken from you, and given to a nation bringing forth the fruits thereof" (Matt. 21:43).[34] He abolished the jubilee's land tenure laws, as well as the slave-holding laws associated with the land of Israel as the exclusive place of temple sacrifice and worship.

Adoption

Nevertheless, in principle there remains a modern Christian practice that resembles the Old Testament jubilee slave law. It is the practice of adoption. Christians pay lawyers to arrange for the adoption of infants whose pagan parents do not want them. This is true household adoption rather than permanent slavery, but biblical law requires children to support parents in their old age, so the arrangement is not purely altruistic. The practice of adoption is governed by civil law in order to reduce the creation of a market for profit,[35] therefore discouraging the kidnapping of in-

---

34. Gary North, *Healer of the Nations: Biblical Blueprints for International Relations* (Ft. Worth, Texas: Dominion Press, 1987), Introduction.

35. Actually, the adoption laws have created a profitable market for babies, but only state-licensed lawyers and adoption agencies are legally allowed to reap these profits. This is a legitimate licensing arrangement, similar in intent and economic effect as the licensing of physicians: to control a potentially coercive market phenomenon. Physicians control access to addictive drugs, and lawyers and adoption agencies control access to babies offered for adoption. This reduces the threat of kidnapped babies. By centralizing access to the flow of babies offered for adoption, the civil government can more successfully impose restrictions on the market for babies by guaranteeing that parents make the decision to supply this market, not kidnappers.

fants, but the economics of modern adoption is similar to the Old Testament practice of buying children from resident aliens. Adoption is a very good practice. Children are bought out of slavery inside covenant-breaking households.

Rushdoony refers to kidnapping as "stealing freedom."[36] He comments: "The purpose of man's existence is that man should exercise dominion over the earth in terms of God's calling. This duty involves the restoration of a broken order by means of restitution. To kidnap a man and enslave him is to rob him of his freedom. A believer is not to be a slave (I Cor. 7:23; Gal. 5:1). Some men are slaves by nature; slavery was voluntary, and a dissatisfied slave could leave, and he could not be compelled to return, and other men were forbidden to deliver him to his master (Deut. 23:15, 16).... The purpose of freedom is that man exercise dominion and subdue the earth under God. A man who abuses this freedom to steal[37] can be sold into slavery in order to work out his restitution (Ex. 22:3); if he cannot use his freedom for its true purpose, godly dominion, reconstruction, and restoration, he must then work towards restitution in his bondage."[38]

Conclusion

Kidnapping is a crime against God, man, and the social order. It steals men's freedom. It asserts the autonomy of the kidnapper over the victim. It substitutes the kidnapper's profit for the calling God gives to each man. It attacks God through His image, man. The kidnapper is therefore subject to the death penalty, at the discretion of his victim.

The potential imposition of the death penalty produces unequal risks for different economic classes. The rich are more likely to be victims in a non-slave society, where the quest for a ransom payment is the primary motivation for the kidnapper. *Equality*

---

36. Rushdoony, *The Institutes of Biblical Law* (Nutley, New Jersey: Craig Press, 1973), p. 484.

37. Rushdoony obviously does not mean "freedom to steal"; he means a person who "abuses his freedom by stealing," or "in order to steal." The use of the infinitive, "to steal," could lead to confusion.

38. *Ibid.*, p. 485.

before the law is the fundamental principle of biblical law enforcement; *inequality of economic results* is therefore inescapable. By imposing a single penalty, death, the law increases the percentage of rich kidnap victims.

The legislated abolition of slavery reduces the market demand for stolen men, thereby reducing the profit accruing to kidnappers, and increasing the safety from kidnapping for the average citizen. To be effective, however, the majority of potential slave-owners must agree with the abolition, or else be fearful of violating the law. A profit-seeking black market in slaves would thwart the economic effects of this law, namely, reduced demand for slaves. The high penalty imposed on both kidnapper and buyer, if coupled with the moral education of potential buyers of slaves (the final users), reduces the size and therefore the efficiency of the slave market. (Remember Adam Smith's observation: the division of labor is limited by the extent of the market.)[39]

Finally, the death penalty overcomes the short-run, present-oriented time perspective of the potential kidnappers. The magnitude of the punishment calls attention to the magnitude of the crime. A death penalty forces the criminal to contemplate the possible results of his actions.

As with all other crimes except murder, the victim has the final authority to specify the appropriate penalty, up to the biblically specified limit of the law. Rushdoony does not consider the concept of victim's rights in his *Institutes*. He writes that "the death penalty is mandatory for kidnapping. No discretion is allowed the court. To rob a man of his freedom requires death."[40] I would agree with this statement if it were qualified as follows: "The death penalty is mandatory for kidnapping. No discretion is allowed the court, once the victim has specified the death of the kidnapper as his preferred penalty." To deny the victim the legal right to specify the appropriate sanction is to deny the concept of victim's rights.

---

39. Smith, *The Wealth of Nations* (1776), ch. 3.
40. Rushdoony, *Institutes*, p. 486.

4

THE COSTS OF PRIVATE CONFLICT

And if men strive together, and one smite another with a stone, or with his fist, and he die not, but keepeth his bed: If he rise again, and walk abroad upon his staff, then shall he that smote him be quit: only he shall pay for the loss of his time, and shall cause him to be thoroughly healed (Ex. 21:18-19).

The theocentric principle here is that man is God's image, and that for anyone to strike another person unlawfully or autonomously is an attempt to commit violence against God. It is man as God's representative that places him under the covenantal protection of civil government. The State is required by God to protect men from the physical violence of other men.

One of the primary earthly goals of any godly society is the elimination of conflict among its citizens. The establishment of a reign of peace is one of the most prominent promises in the Old Testament's prophetic messages. Peace is therefore a sign of God's blessing and also a means of attaining other blessings, such as economic growth. Men who strive together in private battle testify to their own lack of self-discipline, and a godly legal order must provide sanctions against such disturbances of public order.

The Bible reminds men that they are responsible before God and society for their private actions. Specific costs are imposed by biblical law on the victor in any physical conflict. The eventual loser is to be protected and so is his family, whose rights he cannot waive simply by stepping into the arena. The loser is to be compensated for his loss of time while in bed and also for his medical expenses. In short, the victor must make *restitution* to the loser.

The mere possession of superior strength or combat skills is not to be an advantage in the resolution of personal disputes.

We see a similar perspective in the Hittite laws: "If anyone batters a man so that he falls ill, he shall take care of him. He shall give a man in his stead who can look after his house until he recovers. When he recovers, he shall give him 6 shekels of silver, and he shall also pay the physician's fee. If anyone breaks a free man's hand or foot, he shall give him 20 shekels of silver and pledge his estate as security. If anyone breaks the hand or foot of a male or a female slave, he shall give 10 shekels of silver and pledge his estate as security."[1] Men must pay the costs of restoring the injured party to physical wholeness.

Winners and Losers

These economic restraints on victors remind men of the costs of injuring others. There are economic costs borne by the physical confrontation's loser. There are also costs borne by society at large. A man in a sickbed can no longer exercise his calling before God. He cannot labor efficiently, and the products of his labor are not brought to the marketplace. If he is employed by another person, the employer's operation is disrupted. By forcing the physical victor to pay for both the medical costs and the alternative costs (forfeited productivity on the part of the loser), biblical law helps to reduce conflict. The physical victor becomes an economic loser. The law also insures society against having to bear the medical costs involved. The immediate family, charitable institutions, or publicly financed medical facilities do not bear the costs.

The Mishnah, which was the legal code for Judaism until the late nineteenth century, establishes five different types of compensation. First, compensation for the injury itself, meaning damages for permanent injury that results from the occurrence. Second, compensation for the injured person's pain and suffering. Third, compensation for the injured person's medical expenses. Fourth,

---

1. "The Hittite Laws," paragraphs 10-12, in *Ancient Near Eastern Texts Relating to the Old Testament,* edited by James B. Pritchard (3rd ed.; Princeton, New Jersey: Princeton University Press, 1969), p. 189. Paragraphs 13-16 continue the restitution theme: monetary penalties for biting off noses and ears of free men or slaves.

compensation for the injured person's loss of earnings (time). Fifth, compensation for the embarrassment or indignity suffered by the victim.[2] Not all five will be found in each case, of course.[3]

The judicially significant point is that the person who wins the conflict physically becomes the loser economically. The one who is still walking around after the fight must finance the physical recovery of the one who is in bed. The focus of judicial concern is on the victim who suffers the greatest physical injury. Biblical law and Jewish law impose economic penalties on the injury-inflicting victors of such private conflicts. As Maimonides put it, "The Sages have penalized strong-armed fools by ruling that the injured person should be held trustworthy. . . ."[4]

Games of Bloodshed

The murderous "games" of ancient Rome, where gladiators slew each other in front of cheering crowds, violated biblical law. The same is true of "sports" like boxing, where the inflicting of injuries is basic to victory. The lure of bloody games is decidedly pagan. Augustine, in his *Confessions*, speaks of a former student of his, Alypius. The young man had been deeply fond of the Circensian games of Carthage. Augustine had persuaded him of their evil, and the young man stopped attending. Later on, however, in Rome, Alypius met some fellow students who dragged him in a friendly way to the Roman amphitheater on the day of the

---

2. *Baba Kamma* 8:1, *The Mishnah*, edited by Herbert Danby (New York: Oxford University Press, [1933] 1987), p. 342.

3. Emanuel B. Quint, *Jewish Jurisprudence: Its Sources and Modern Applications*, 2 vols. (New York: Harwood Academic Publishers, 1980), I, p. 126. Maimonides wrote: "If one wounds another, he must pay compensation to him for five effects of the injury, namely, damages, pain, medical treatment, enforced idleness, and humiliation. These five effects are all payable from the injurer's best property, as is the law for all who do wrongful damage." Moses Maimonides, *The Book of Torts*, vol. 11 of *The Code of Maimonides*, 14 vols. (New Haven, Connecticut: Yale University Press, [1180] 1954), "Laws Concerning Wounding and Damaging," Chapter One, Section One, p. 160. Maimonides made one strange exception: if a person deliberately frightens someone, but does not touch him, he bears no legal liability, only moral liability. Even if he shouts in a person's ear and deafens him, there is no legal liability. Only if he touches the person is there legal liability: *ibid.*, Chapter Two, Section Seven, pp. 165-66.

4. *Torts*, Chapter Five, Section Four, p. 177.

bloody games. He swore to himself that he would not even look, but he did, briefly, and was trapped. "As he saw that blood, he drank in savageness at the same time. He did not turn away, but fixed his sight on it, and drank in madness without knowing it. He took delight in that evil struggle, and he became drunk on blood and pleasure. He was no longer the man who entered there, but only one of the crowd that he had joined, and a true comrade of those who brought him there. What more shall I say? He looked, he shouted, he took fire, he bore away with himself a madness that should arouse him to return, not only with those who had drawn him there, but even before them, and dragging others along as well."[5] Only later was his faith in Christ able to break his addiction to the games.

In the city of Trier (Treves) in what is today Germany, alien hordes burned the town in the early fifth century, murdering people and leaving their bodies in piles. Salvian (the Presbyter) records what took place immediately thereafter: "A few nobles who survived destruction demanded circuses from the emperors as the greatest relief for the destroyed city."[6] They wanted the immediate reconstruction of the arena, not the town's walls, so powerful was the hold of the bloody games on the minds of Roman citizens.

Chaos Festivals

Roger Caillois, in his book, *Man and the Sacred* (1959), argues that the chaos festivals of the ancient and primitive worlds served as outlets for hostilities. These festivals are unfamiliar to most modern citizens, or in the case of the familiar ones, such as Mardi Gras in New Orleans, Carnival in the Caribbean, or New Year's Eve parties in many nations, they are not recognized for what they are. He writes: "It is a time of excess. Reserves accumulated over the course of several years are squandered. The holiest laws

---

5. *The Confessions of St. Augustine*, trans. by John K. Ryan (Garden City, New York: Image Books, 1960), Book 6, ch. 8.

6. Salvian, *The Governance of God*, in *The Writings of Salvian, the Presbyter*, Jeremiah F. O'Sullivan, trans. (New York: Cima Publishing Co., 1947), Bk. VI, Sect. 15, p. 178. Salvian was a contemporary of St. Augustine, in the fifth century. This was probably written around A.D. 440.

are violated, those that seem at the very basis of social life. Yesterday's crime is now prescribed, and in place of customary rules, new taboos and disciplines are established, the purpose of which is not to avoid or soothe intense emotions, but rather to excite and bring them to climax. Movement increases, and the participants become intoxicated. Civil or administrative authorities see their powers temporarily diminish or disappear. This is not so much to the advantage of the regular sacerdotal caste as to the gain of secret confraternities or representatives of the other world, masked actors personifying the Gods or the dead. This fervor is also the time for sacrifices, even the time for the sacred, a time outside of time that recreates, purifies, and rejuvenates society. . . . All excesses are permitted, for society expects to be regenerated as a result of excesses, waste, orgies, and violence."[7]

It was these festivals, he argues, that in some way drained off the violent emotions inherent in men. (On the contrary, such festivals stimulated violent emotions.)[8] The festivals, he argues, were therefore basic to the preservation of social peace. Without these ritual celebrations of lawlessness, he argues, there will be an increase of actual wars. In other words, men innately require the tension and release of violence. Prohibit the socially circumscribed ritual chaos of Mardi Gras, Carnival, and New Year, and we therefore supposedly risk the outbreak of war. Because modern man has suppressed such ritual chaos, he concludes, we have seen the increase of wars and their intensity and devastation.[9]

In contrast to Caillois' analysis stands the Bible. Leaders in a godly social order should strive to eliminate such chaos festivals and "circumscribed violence." The laws requiring restitution for anyone injured in a brawl are related to the general prohibition

---

7. Roger Caillois, *Man and the Sacred* (Glencoe, Illinois: The Free Press, 1959), p. 164.

8. It is interesting to note that modern political liberals criticize graphic violence on television because it may produce violent behavior, especially in children. In contrast, they argue that graphic sex in magazines, books, and moving pictures is harmless, and in no way can be shown to produce deviant sexual behavior. In other words, liberals are opposed to violence and favor open sex. Conservatives have a tendency to reverse these two preferences and argue the opposite positions.

9. *Ibid.*, ch. 4.

against individual violence. Lawlessness is to be suppressed. Man is not told to give vent to his feelings of violence; he is told to overcome them through self-discipline under God. Wars and violence come from the lusts of men (Jas. 4:1). These bloody lusts are to be overcome, not ritually sanctioned. The celebration of communion is God's sanctioned bloody ritual which gives men symbolic blood, but the Bible forbids the drinking of actual blood (Lev. 3:17; Deut.12:16, 23; Acts 15:20).

Biblical Law Confronts the "Honorable Duel"

The Bible informs us that the civil government is to protect human life. Each man is made in God's image, and men, acting as private citizens, do not have the right to attempt to attack God indirectly by attacking His image in other men. Men are not sovereign over their own lives or over the lives of others; God is (Rev. 1:18). God delegates the right of execution to the civil government, not to individual men acting outside a lawful institution in the pursuit of lawful objectives.

The private duel is just such a threat to human life and safety. Fighting is a threat to social peace. It is disorderly, willful, vengeful, and hypothetically autonomous. It poses a threat to innocent bystanders (Ex. 21:22-25). It can destroy property. When a death or serious injury is involved, a duel can lead in some societies — especially those that place family status above civil law — to an escalation of inter-family feuding and blood vengeance.

The premise of the duel or the brawl is the assertion of the existence of *zones of judicial irresponsibility*. Men set aside for themselves a kind of arena in which the laws of civil society should not prevail. There may or may not be rules governing the private battlefield, but these rules are supposedly special, removing men from the jurisdiction of civil law. The protection of life and limb which is basic to the civil law is supposedly suspended by mutual consent. "Common" laws supposedly have no force over "uncommon" men during the period of the duel. Somehow, the law of God does not apply to private warriors who defend their own honor and seek to impose a mutually agreed-upon form of punishment on their rivals.

The Costs of Private Conflict

But the laws of God *do* apply. "The Bible does not permit the use of force to resolve disputes, except where force is lawfully exercised by God's ordained officer, the civil magistrate. To put it another way, the Bible requires men to submit to arbitration, and categorically prohibits them from taking their own personal vengeance (Rom. 12:17-13:7)."[10]

An obvious implication of the biblical law against dueling is the prohibition of gladiatorial contests, which would include boxing. A boxer who kills another man in the ring should be executed. Another implication is the necessity of rejecting the notion of a "fair fight." There is no such thing as a fair fight. Flight is almost always preferable to private fighting, but where fighting is unavoidable, it should be an all-out confrontation. Should a person "fight fair" when his wife is attacked? Should women under attack from a man "fight fairly"? The answer ought to be clear.[11] Thus, the code of the duel is doubly perverse: first, it imputes cowardice to a man who would seek to keep the peace by walking away from a challenge to his honor; second, it restricts a man's lawful self-defense to a set of agreed-upon "rules of the game." Fighting is not a game; it is either an evil assertion of personal autonomy or else a necessary defense of life, limb, and perhaps property.

Duel to the Death: Murder

One implication of Exodus 21:18-19 is that a death resulting from a duel or a brawl is to be regarded as murder.[12] This is a concept of personal responsibility that is foreign to societies that allow private violence. In such societies, the quest for personal power and prestige overrides the quest for public peace. The

---

10. James B. Jordan, *The Law of the Covenant: An Exposition of Exodus 21-23* (Tyler, Texas: Institute for Christian Economics, 1984), p. 110.

11. *Ibid.*, p. 112.

12. Robert L. Dabney, *Lectures in Systematic Theology* (Grand Rapids, Michigan: Zondervan, [1878] 1972), pp. 404-6. Dabney was by far the most insightful Presbyterian theologian in the nineteenth-century South. He had served for several months, before becoming too ill to continue, as Gen. Thomas "Stonewall" Jackson's chaplain, as well as his Chief of Staff. He later wrote a biography of Jackson, so he cannot be considered a man hostile to military virtues. Cf. Thomas Cary Johnson, *The Life and Letters of Robert Lewis Dabney* (Richmond, Virginia: Presbyterian Committee of Publication, 1903), ch. 13.

autonomy of man is affirmed by the ritual practices of the duel and brawl. Wyatt-Brown writes of the antebellum (pre-1861) American South: "Ordinarily, honor under the dueling test called for public recognition of a man's claim to power, whatever social level he or his immediate circle of friends might belong to. A street fight could and often did accomplish the same thing for the victor. Murder, or at least manslaughter, inspired the same public approval in some instances. Just as lesser folk spoke ungrammatically, so too they fought ungrammatically, but their actions were expressions of the same desire for prestige."[13]

Under biblical law, injured bystanders are protected from deliberate violence on the part of other people on an "eye for eye" basis.[14] An injured loser who walks again is entitled to full compensation. But in the case where the loser dies, the judges are required to impose a capital sentence on a surviving fighter. When the loser cannot "walk abroad," the victor must not be "quit." At best, he would have to pay an enormous fine to the family of the dead man, but even this would seem to be too lenient, since

---

13. Bertram Wyatt-Brown, *Southern Honor: Ethics and Behavior in the Old South* (New York: Oxford University Press, 1982), p. 353.

14. A somewhat different problem is raised if a person defends himself from another person who has initiated violence. What if, in defending himself, a person injures a bystander? Clearly, it was not the bystander's fault. The person responsible for inflicting the injury should pay damages. Should it be the person who initiated the violence or the defender who inadvertently harmed the bystander? For example, what if a man attacks another man, and the second person pulls out a gun and fires at the attacker, hitting a bystander by mistake? A humanistic theory of strict liability would produce a judgment against the defender, for his defense was misguided, or excessive, or ineffective. But what if the attacker had grabbed the defender's "shooting hand," causing him to fire wildly? The injury to the bystander would seem to be the fault of the attacker. On the other hand, if the original attacker was using only his fists, and the defender had pulled out a gun and started shooting — a seemingly excessive response — would this make the original attacker a defender when he attempted to grab the weapon? Judgment is complicated, for life is complicated.

The Bible places restraints on violence. The goal of the God-fearing man should be to reduce private physical violence. Thus, if the attacker uses fists, and the defender has a weapon, the attacker should be warned to stop. The victim does have the right to identify the attacker and press charges. The civil government should inflict the penalty. But if the attacker still challenges the person with the weapon, then the person has the right to stop the attacker from inflicting violence on him.

the only instance of a substitution of payment for the death sentence involves criminal negligence — the failure to contain a dangerous beast which subsequently kills a man — but not willful violence (Ex. 21:29-30). The autonomous shedding of man's blood, even to "defend one's good name," is still murder. There is the perverse lure of such "conflicts of honor."

It is clear that if a biblically honorable man refuses to fight because the civil law supports his position by threatening him with death should he successfully kill his opponent, he can avoid the fight in the name of personal self-confidence. He says, in effect, "I know I can probably kill you; therefore, I choose not to enter this fight because I will surely be executed after I kill you." Thus, he can avoid being regarded as a coward. This breaks the central social hold that the *code duello* has always possessed: the honorable man's fear of being labeled a coward. But in order to deflect this powerful hold, the State must be willing to enforce the death penalty on victors.

Courts and Vigilantes

Legal predictability is crucial to the preservation of an orderly society. The breakdown of predictable justice in any era can lead to a revival of blood vengeance. Those who are convinced that the court system is unable to dispense justice and defend the innocent are tempted to "take the law into their own hands." The rise of vigilante groups that take over the administration of physical sanctions always comes at the expense of legal predictability. This is a sign of the breakdown in the legal order, and it is accompanied by a loss of legitimacy by "establishment" institutions.[15]

---

15. This appears to be beginning in large cities in the United States. Citizen's patrols became common in certain Jewish districts in the New York City area in the late 1960's. A parallel group of inner-city youths sprang up in the late 1970's, the Guardian Angels, initially composed mostly of Puerto Ricans. This group has spread across the United States. By 1988, its leaders claimed 60 chapters and 6,000 members. Citizen's patrols have now spread to black neighborhoods and middle class neighborhoods, especially in response to the advent of "crack" houses: the modern equivalent of the opium dens of the nineteenth century. In some cases, local police departments do cooperate with these citizen's patrols, and to this extent they are not pure vigilante organizations. See "Neighbors Join to Rout the Criminals in the Streets," *Insight* (Nov. 28, 1988), pp. 8-21.

Eventually, vigilante movements are either stamped out by the existing social order or else they become the foundation of a new social order: the warlord society. The various vigilante movements of the United States in the nineteenth century arose when the civil authorities would not or could not enforce the law.[16] Vigilantes were common in the American West after the Civil War prior to the establishment of local and regional judicial order. The most famous vigilante group in U.S. history is the Ku Klux Klan. The original Ku Klux Klan of the American South, 1865-71, was a defensive movement.[17] The organization was self-consciously occult in its regalia. Members wore white sheets with holes cut out for eyes, so that they would resemble the folklore version of ghosts, thereby adding to the terror of superstitious former slaves. The Klan was highly liturgical, its rituals filled with diabolic symbols, hidden signs, and other elements of secret societies, and it predictably degenerated into violence and lawlessness within a few years. It was officially disbanded in 1869, and when local "dens" persisted, it was stamped out by the U.S. military. An imitation of the old Klan rose again to national political prominence in the 1920's,[18] only to fade nationally in the 1930's and in the South in the 1940's. Today,

---

16. Richard Maxwell Brown, "The History of Vigilantism in America," in H. Jon Rosenbaum and Peter C. Sederberg (eds.), *Vigilante Politics* (Philadelphia: University of Pennsylvania Press, 1976); see also Brown, *Strain of Violence: Historical Studies of American Violence and Vigilantism* (New York: Oxford University Press, 1975).

17. The early twentieth-century trilogy of novels by Thomas Dixon eulogized this early Klan. *Birth of a Nation*, the epic D. W. Griffith silent film of 1915, was based on Dixon's second novel in this trilogy, *The Clansman* (1905). This moving picture was the first modern "spectacular," and was shown to large audiences across the United States. It had the support of President Woodrow Wilson (an old college classmate of Dixon's) and the Chief Justice of the U.S. Supreme Court, a former Klansman. See David M. Chalmers, *Hooded Americanism: The First Century of the Ku Klux Klan, 1865-1965* (Garden City, New York: Doubleday, 1965), pp. 26-27. The film, unfortunately, led to a revival of the Klan: *ibid.*, ch. 4. (The 17-year-old star of Griffith's movie, Lillian Gish, also starred in *The Whales of August* in 1987, making hers the longest film career in history.)

18. It was the victory of an anti-Klan candidate for governor in the Republican Party's primary in the state of Oregon which led the Klan to jump to the Democratic Party. They elected the Democratic candidate, plus enough members of the legislature to pass a law mandating that all children between the ages of eight and sixteen attend a government-operated school. Chalmers, *Hooded Americanism*, p. 3. This law

numerous local Klan-type groups exist, but they have little influence.[19] But the Klan's former power testifies to the fact that when civil courts fail to dispense justice and therefore lose their legitimacy in the eyes of large numbers of citizens, societies will eventually see the rise of private dispensers of "people's justice."

Without a sense of legitimacy, the authority of public courts is threatened. The courts need legitimacy in order to gain the long-term voluntary cooperation of the public, meaning self-government under law, without which law enforcement becomes both sporadic and tyrannical. No legal system can afford the economic resources that would be necessary to gain full compliance to an alien law-order in a society whose members are unwilling to govern themselves voluntarily in terms of that law-order.[20] If the courts do not receive assent from the public as legitimate institutions, they can maintain the peace only by imposing sentences whose severity goes beyond people's sense of justice, which again calls into doubt both legitimacy and legal predictability.

Judicial Pluralism and Social Disintegration

A civil government that refuses to defend a law-order that is seen as legitimate by the public is inviting the revival of the duel, the feud, and blood vengeance. If the public cannot agree on standards of decency, then the courts will be tempted to become autonomous. Widespread and deep differences concerning religion lead to equally strong disagreements over morality and law. Religious pluralism leads to moral and judicial pluralism, meaning unpredictable courts. Religious pluralism is an outgrowth of polytheism. Polytheism inescapably leads to what we might call "polylegalism." Too many law courts decide in terms of conflicting moralities. Only the strong hand of centralized and bureaucratic

---

was overturned by the U.S. Supreme Court in 1925 in a landmark case, *Pierce v. Society of Sisters*, which has remained the key Court decision in the fight for Christian schools.

19. As one southerner described the Klan: "It is made up mainly of gasoline station attendants and FBI informers. The members can easily spot the informers: they are the only ones who pay their monthly dues."

20. Gary North, *Moses and Pharaoh: Dominion Religion vs. Power Religion* (Tyler, Texas: Institute for Christian Economics, 1985), pp. 291-94.

civil government can enforce a single standard of law on a religiously divided public, which is why religious and judicial pluralism ultimately leads to tyranny: the grab for power. Long-term judicial pluralism is a myth: one group or another ultimately must decide what is right and what is wrong, what should be prohibited by civil law and what shouldn't.[21]

The myth of judicial pluralism has hidden from the people (including Christians) the reality of the inescapable *intolerance* of all civil government. There can no more be religious neutrality on earth than in heaven, and as time moves toward that final court decision, the impossibility of pluralism is becoming more obvious. Either God or Satan will execute final judgment; either God's law or man's law will be imposed on eternity. The covenant representatives of each kingdom will, on earth and in history, progressively present their respective supernatural sovereign's case to the world. There is no way to reconcile these competing claims. Marxism cannot be reconciled with Christianity, and neither system can be reconciled with Islam. The liberal humanist's hope in treaties, arms control, and endless tax-supported economic deals with Communist nations is as doomed to failure as the conservative humanist's faith in the peace-promoting reign of neutral natural law.[22] Elijah's challenge is inescapable: "How long halt ye between two opinions? If the LORD be God, follow him: but if Baal, then follow him." Then as now, the people delay making a decision: "And the people answered him not a word" (I Ki. 18:21).

They did not remain silent forever. The fire came from heaven and consumed the sacrifice on God's altar. The people saw, understood, and acted: they brought the 850 priests of Baal to Elijah, who killed them (I Ki. 18:40). The nation for the moment sided with God's prophet. The "priests of Baal" of any era can delay judgment for a while, but eventually *judgment comes in history*. Nevertheless, without a change in heart, the people eventually return

---

21. Gary North, *Political Polytheism: The Myth of Pluralism* (Tyler, Texas: Institute for Christian Economics, 1989).

22. Gary North, *Healer of the Nations: Biblical Blueprints for International Relations* (Ft. Worth, Texas: Dominion Press, 1987), ch. 3.

to their old ways. The Revolution consumes its own children. The prophet is again put on the run (I Ki. 19).

The humanist courts of our day appeal to religious pluralism, yet they are creating judicial tyranny.[23] The anti-feud, anti-clan,[24] anti-duel ethic of once-Christian Western bourgeois cultures — societies in which social peace has fostered economic growth — is being undermined by judges who are creating lawlessness in the name of a purified humanist legal system. Judicial pluralism must be replaced, but not from the top down, and not from the vigilante's noose outward. The satanic myth of legal pluralism must be replaced by the power of the Holy Spirit in the hearts of men. The Holy Spirit is the enforcer in New Testament times.

Conclusion

Social order requires a degree of social peace. When biblical law began to influence the civil governments of the West, an increase of social peace and social order took place. This, in turn, led to greater economic growth and technological development.[25]

Christian culture is orderly. The Christian West steadily abolished or redirected the chaos festivals of the pagan world, until the growth of humanism-paganism began to reverse this process.[26] Legal systems became predictable, as the "eye for eye" principle

---

23. Carrol D. Kilgore, *Judicial Tyranny* (Nashville, Tennessee: Nelson, 1977).

24. Weber wrote: "When Christianity became the religion of these peoples who had been so profoundly shaken in all their traditions, it finally destroyed whatever religious significance these clan ties retained; perhaps, indeed, it was precisely the weakness or absence of such magical and taboo barriers which made the conversion possible. The often very significant role played by the parish community in the administrative organization of medieval cities is only one of the many symptoms pointing to this quality of the Christian religion which, in dissolving clan ties, importantly shaped the medieval city." He contrasts this anti-clan perspective with that of Islam. Max Weber, *Economy and Society: An Outline of Interpretive Sociology*, edited by Guenther Roth and Claus Wittich (New York: Bedminster Press, [1924] 1968), p. 1244.

25. Gary North, *The Sinai Strategy: Economics and the Ten Commandments* (Tyler, Texas: Institute for Christian Economics, 1986), pp. 223-26.

26. Peter Gay aptly titled the first volume of his study of the Enlightenment, *The Rise of Modern Paganism* (New York: Knopf, 1966). The two-volume study is titled, *The Enlightenment: An Interpretation* (New York: Knopf, 1966, 1969).

spread alongside the gospel of salvation. The unpredictable violence of State power was thereby reduced. In private relationships, men were not allowed to vent their wrath on each other in acts of violence. Those who violated this law became economically liable for their actions.

The duel or brawl is by nature a direct challenge to the authority and legitimacy of the civil government. It transfers to individuals operating outside the State — the God-ordained monopoly of violence — a degree of legal immunity from civil judgment. It transfers sovereignty in the administration of violence from the State to the individual. It is not surprising, therefore, that one program of legal reform recommended by some contemporary libertarian anarchists is the legalization of dueling. The duel is seen as a private act between consenting adults and therefore sacrosanct. (Sacrosanct: from *sacro* = sacred rite, and *sanctum* = holy and inviolable. Also related to *sanction* = legal and sovereign authority, or a judgment by a legal and sovereign authority.)

5
LEGITIMATE VIOLENCE

If men strive, and hurt a woman with child, so that her fruit depart from her, and yet no mischief follow: he shall be surely punished, according as the woman's husband will lay upon him; and he shall pay as the judges determine. And if any mischief follow, then thou shalt give life for life, eye for eye, tooth for tooth, hand for hand, foot for foot, burning for burning, wound for wound, stripe for stripe (Ex. 21:22-25).

The theocentric principle here is that man is made in God's image and therefore must be protected by civil law. The husband of the victimized woman represents God the Judge to the convicted criminal. The State is required to impose sanctions specified by the husband. The violent person who has imposed on the woman and the child the risk of injury or death must compensate the family. The judges do retain some degree of authority in specifying the appropriate sanction. The criminal must pay "as the judges determine." In the absence of actual physical harm, there is no rigorous or direct way to assess the value of this risk of injury or death, so the State does not allow the husband to be unreasonable in imposing sanctions.

Where physical damage can be determined objectively, the criminal must pay on an "eye for eye" basis. This is the judicial principle known as the *lex talionis*. The punishment must fit the magnitude of the violation; the violation is assessed in terms of the damages inflicted.

Controversy Over Abortion

Exodus 21:22-25 has recently become one of the most controversial passages in the Old Testament. Prior to the 1960's, when the abortion issue again began to be debated publicly in the United States after half a century of relative silence,[1] only the second half of this passage was controversial in Christian circles: the judicial requirement of "an eye for an eye." The abortion aspect of the argument was not controversial, for the practice of abortion was illegal and publicly invisible. A physician who performed an abortion could be sent to jail.[2] It was clearly understood by Christians that anyone who caused a premature birth in which the baby died or was injured had committed a criminal act, despite the fact that the person did not plan to cause the infant's injury or death. The abortion described in the text is the result of a man's battle with another man, an illegitimate form of private vengeance for which each man is made fully responsible should injury ensue, either to each other (Ex. 21:18-19) or to innocent bystanders. If this sort of "accidental" abortion is treated as a criminal act, how much more a deliberate abortion by a physician or other murderer! Only when pagan intellectuals in the general culture came out in favor of abortion on demand did pro-abortionists within the church begin to deny the relevancy of the introductory section of the passage.

This anti-abortion attitude among Christians began to change with the escalation of the humanists' pro-abortion rhetoric in the early 1960's. Christian intellectuals have always taken their ideo-

---

1. Marvin Olasky, *The Press and Abortion, 1838-1988* (Hillsdale, New Jersey: Lawrence Erlbaum Associates, 1988), ch. 6. This book shows that in the late nineteenth century, the battle over abortion, as revealed in the press, was widespread.

2. Julius Hammer, the millionaire physician father of (later) billionaire Armand Hammer, in 1920 was sent to Sing-Sing prison in Ossining, New York, for performing an abortion in 1919. The woman had died from the operation. Hammer was convicted of manslaughter. (If all women died after an abortion, there would be fewer abortions performed.) Predictably, several physicians protested the law, but to no avail. Armand Hammer, *Hammer* (New York: Putnam's, 1987), pp. 74-82. Contrary to Hammer's recollections, the press was hostile to Julius Hammer. See Joseph Finder, *Red Carpet* (New York: Holt, Rinehart & Winston, 1983), p. 18. (This book was reprinted in paperback by the American Bureau of Economic Research, Ft. Worth, Texas, in 1987). Julius Hammer had been a member of the Socialist Labor Party, a precursor of the American Communist Party. He became a millionaire by trading in pharmaceuticals with the USSR. He actually served as commercial attaché for the USSR in the United States. *Ibid.*, pp. 12-16.

logical cues from the humanist intellectuals who have established the prevailing "climate of opinion," from the early church's acceptance of the categories of pagan Greek philosophy to the modern church's acceptance of tax-funded, "religiously neutral" education. As the humanists' opinions regarding the legitimacy of abortion began to change in the early 1960's,[3] so did the opinions of the Christian intellectual community. Speaking for the dispensationalist world of social thought, dispensationalist author Tommy Ice forthrightly admitted in a 1988 debate: "Premillennialists have always been involved in the present world. And basically, they have picked up on the ethical positions of their contemporaries."[4] (He defended this practice, it should be noted.) The shift in Christian opinion regarding the illegitimacy of abortion took place throughout the 1960's and early 1970's.

The moral schizophrenia of contemporary pietism can be seen when anti-abortion picketers confront killer physicians at their offices with some variation of "Smile! God loves you" or "God hates abortion but loves abortionists." On the contrary, God hates abortionists, and He demands that the civil government execute them. Where are Christian protesters who pray the imprecatory psalms, such as Psalm 83? Where are they calling publicly on God to bring judgment against abortionists and their political allies?[5] Only when Christian anti-abortionists freely and enthusiastically admit that the Bible demands the public execution for all convicted abortionists, and also for the women who pay for them, will they at last be proclaiming the Bible's judicial requirements.

The fact that they draw back from proclaiming this testifies to the appalling lack of biblical thinking that prevails in contemporary Christianity. *The vast majority of Christians hate God's revealed law far more than they hate either abortion or abortionists.* They would

---

3. Olasky, *The Press and Abortion*, chaps. 10, 11.

4. Cited in Gary DeMar, *The Debate Over Christian Reconstruction* (Ft. Worth, Texas: Dominion Press, 1988), p. 185. The debate was Dave Hunt and Tommy Ice vs. Gary North and Gary DeMar. A pair of audio cassette tapes or a videotape of this April 14, 1988 debate are available from the Institute for Christian Economics.

5. Gary North, *When Justice Is Aborted: Biblical Standards for Non-Violent Resistance* (Ft. Worth, Texas: Dominion Press, 1989), pp. 88-94.

far rather live in a political world that is controlled by humanists who have legalized abortion than in a society governed by Christians in terms of biblical law. So, God has answered the desire of their hearts. He has done to modern Christians what He did to the Israelites in the wilderness: "And he gave them their request; but sent leanness into their soul" (Ps. 106:15).

The Legalized Slaughter of the Innocents

I do not intend to deal in detail with the question of abortion in this context.[6] There is no doubt that these verses apply to abortion.[7] The legal issue is clear: *victim's rights*. In all cases of public evil that the Bible prohibits, there must be judicial representatives of God: the victims are the primary representatives, and the various covenant officials are secondary representatives. When the victims cannot defend their interests, then the covenantal officers become the legal representatives of the victims.[8] The potential victims in this case are the unborn infants whose lives are sacrificed on the altar of convenience. Because they are incapable of speaking on their own behalf, God empowers their fathers to speak for them, or in cases where a father remains silent, God empowers the civil government to speak for them: first to prohibit abortion, and second to impose the death penalty on all those who are involved with abortion, either as murderers (mothers) or as their paid accomplices (physicians, nurses, office receptionists, and so forth).

---

6. J. J. Finkelstein points out that some variation of this law — the jostled woman who aborts her infant — is found in many of the ancient law sources. Finkelstein, *The Ox That Gored* (Philadelphia: American Philosophical Society, 1981), p. 19n. It is treated at length in Hammurabi's laws (209-14), Hittite laws (17-18), and Middle Assyrian laws (21): *Ancient Near Eastern Texts Relating to the Old Testament*, edited by James B. Pritchard (3rd ed.; Princeton, New Jersey: Princeton University Press, 1969), Part II, Legal Texts. Finkelstein argues that the text is probably a literary device rather than legal, since the likelihood of an abortion occurring in this way is minimal. What he does not consider is that as a case law, it was intended to be a minimal application example: if, in this biologically unlikely situation, the one causing harm is fully liable, how much more the liability of an actual abortionist.

7. R. J. Rushdoony, *The Myth of Over-Population* (Fairfax, Virginia: Thoburn Press, [1969] 1975), Appendix 3.

8. North, *When Justice Is Aborted*, ch. 2.

False Prophets

All this is conveniently ignored by Christian abortionists and their academically respectable false prophets.[9] Examples of pro-abortionists, especially physicians, in evangelical churches can be found in a book put out in 1969 by the Christian Medical Society, *Birth Control and the Christian: A Protestant Symposium on the Control of Human Reproduction*, edited by Walter O. Spitzer and Carlyle L. Saylor.[10] Bruce K. Waltke, then a Dallas Theological Seminary professor, and later a professor at Westminster Theological Seminary in Philadelphia, explicitly stated in that book that Exodus 21:22 teaches that "the fetus is not reckoned as a soul."[11] (He subsequently reversed his pro-abortion stance.) Dr. M. O. Vincent, psychiatrist, reported that the symposium moved him to conclude that "the foetus has great and developing value, but is less than a human being. It will be sacrificed only for weighty reasons."[12] Predictably, he refused to spell out in detail what these weighty reasons are. Dr. William B. Kiesewetter, before leading the reader to his conclusion that a Christian physician friend was doing the right thing when he "terminated the pregnancy" (never seen as terminating the baby) of a missionary's wife, warns us against "Rigid, authoritarian evangelicals [who] so often extract from the Word of God precepts which they then congeal into a legalism by which everyone is admonished to live."[13] (His main problem is not with rigid, authoritarian evangelicals. His main problem is with the rigid, authoritarian God who commanded Moses to write Exodus 21:22-25. This is the main problem faced by all false prophets who blithely deny the continuing judicial authority of God's Bible-revealed law, and who then proceed to recommend the violation of God's law whenever convenient.)

In short, it is not necessarily immoral to take money for performing an abortion, provided that you are licensed by the medical profession to do so. These self-deluded physicians would

---

9. *Ibid.*, Appendix A.
10. Wheaton, Illinois: Tyndale House, 1969.
11. *Ibid.*, p. 11.
12. *Ibid.*, p. 213.
13. *Ibid.*, p. 561.

bring a non-physician to court for practicing an abortion – an infringement on their state-licensed monopoly – but not a licensed colleague. Such is the state of twentieth-century medical ethics, including the ethics of self-professed Christians.

A book by D. Gareth Jones, Professor of Anatomy at the University of New Zealand, *Brave New People: Ethical Issues at the Commencement of Life* (1984), created a national Christian protest in the United States against its neo-evangelical, "liberal whenever remotely possible" publisher, Inter-Varsity Press. The book promotes a view of the "foetus" that would allow abortion in uncertain, undefined cases. Franky Schaeffer, the son of Francis Schaeffer (*Whatever Happened to the Human Race?*), mounted a protest in 1984 which led to the resignation of the editor of IVP and the scrapping of the book. Eerdmans republished it the next year. It is still published by IVP in Britain.[14]

A Question of "Barbaric" Sanctions

Christian scholars generally choose to ignore Exodus 21:22-25, and then they spend their time defending mass murder in the name of biblical ethics and "compassion" – compassion for murderous women and their well-paid, state-licensed accomplices. Meanwhile, these critics of biblical law are busy challenging any defenders of the law with criticisms along these lines: "You would reimpose the barbaric principle of poking out a man's eye or cutting off his hand. This is nothing but vengeance, a return to savagery. What possible good would it do the victim to see the assailant suffer physical damage identical to his own? Why not impose some sort of economic restitution to the victim? To inflict permanent injury on the assailant is to reduce his productivity and therefore the wealth of the community. By returning to Old Testament law, you are returning to the tribal laws of a primitive people."[15] (This line of criticism incorrectly assumes that the *lex*

---

14. For a critique of this book, see Gary North, *Moses and Pharaoh: Dominion Religion vs. Power Religion* (Tyler, Texas: Institute for Christian Economics, 1985), pp. 350-58.

15. Henry Schaeffer wrote a book called *The Social Legislation of the Primitive Semites* (New Haven, Connecticut: Yale University Press, 1915). The title is revealing. He did not comment on the "eye for eye" passages.

talionis principle was not in fact designed by God to encourage economic restitution to the victim from the criminal. Chapter 12 will demonstrate that *lex talionis* promotes economic restitution.)

Nevertheless, the question remains: *Which is truly "barbaric," mass murder through legalized abortion or the required judicial sanctions revealed in biblical law?* The Christian antinomians of our day — that is to say, virtually all Christians — have voted for the barbaric character of biblical law. They are faced with a choice: Minimal sanctions against abortion or the civil enforcement of biblical law? Their answer is automatic. They shout to their elected civil magistrates, "Give us Barabbas!" Better to suffer politically the silent screams of murdered babies, they conclude, than to suffer the theocratic embarrassment of calling for the public execution of convicted abortionists.[16] The babies who are targeted for destruction have only a confused, inconsistent, waffling, squabbling, rag-tag army of Christians to speak for them authoritatively in God's name inside the corridors of political and judicial power. Their defenders are agreed: "Abortion is the lesser of two evils, if the alternative is theocracy."[17]

In stark contrast is the tiny handful of Christians[18] who confidently believe in the whole Bible, including Exodus 21:22-25, and

---

16. We must not miss the point: the inevitable issue here is *theocracy*. When a Christian calls for the execution of the convicted abortionist, he is necessarily calling for the enforcement of God's revealed law by the civil magistrate. This fear of being labeled a theocrat is why James Dobson chooses to weaken his response to a pro-abortion physician by not dealing forthrightly with Exodus 21:22-25: "Do you agree that if a man beats his slave to death, he is to be considered guilty only if the individual dies instantly? If the slave lives a few days, the owner is considered not guilty (Exodus 21:20-21)[?] Do you believe that we should stone to death rebellious children (Deuteronomy 21:18-21)? Do you really believe we can draw subtle meaning about complex issues from Mosaic law, when even the obvious interpretation makes no sense to us today? We can hardly select what we will and will not apply now. If we accept the verses you cited, we are obligated to deal with every last jot and tittle." Dobson, "Dialogue on Abortion," in James Dobson and Gary Bergel, *The Decision of Life* (Arcadia, California: Focus on the Family, 1986), p. 14.

17. Christian anti-abortionists will attempt to find a third choice. It may be natural law. It may be emotion. It may be the will of the people. It may be to some less familiar version of common-ground philosophy, meaning baptized humanism. What it will not be is an appeal to the whole Bible as the sole authoritative will of God.

18. Christian Reconstructionists or theonomists.

who have therefore confidently voted against abortion as the true barbarism and for biblical law as the sole long-term foundation of Christian civilization. But most Christians have self-consciously suppressed any temptation to think about this dilemma, one way or the other. The thin picket lines in front of abortion clinics testify to the thoughtlessness of Christians in our day. (So do the thin shelves of the Christian bookstores.)[19]

Restitution and Vengeance

The "eye for an eye" principle is known by the Latin phrase, *lex talionis*, or "law of retaliation." The English word, "retaliate," is derived from the same Roman root as "talionis." Today, "retaliate" means to inflict injury, but earlier English usage conveyed a broader meaning: *to pay back or return in kind*, including good will.[20] According to one source, the *lex talionis* was a Roman law that specified that anyone who brought an accusation against another citizen but could not prove his case in the courts would suffer the same penalty that he had sought to inflict on the defendant.[21] (This was a perverted version of the biblical principle of the law governing deliberate perjury, found in Deuteronomy 19:16-21, which concludes with a restatement of the "eye for eye" requirement in verse 21. The law reads: "Then shall ye do unto him [the false witness], as he had thought to have done unto his brother: so shalt thou put the evil away from among you" [v. 19].[22] Only

---

19. James Jordan's book, *The Law of the Covenant: An Exposition of Exodus 21-23* (Tyler, Texas: Institute for Christian Economics, 1984), was removed from the shelves of a local Christian bookstore in Tyler when the store's owner discovered that Jordan had called for the execution of the aborting physician and the mother. The owner dared not take the heat for selling a book which announced: "Until the anti-abortion movement in America is willing to return to God's law and advocate the death penalty for abortion, God will not bless the movement. God does not bless those who despise His law, just because pictures of salted infants make them sick" (p. 115).

20. See the *Oxford English Dictionary*: "retaliate."

21. *Cyclopaedia of Biblical, Theological, and Ecclesiastical Literature*, edited by John McClintock and James Strong (New York: Harper & Bros., 1894), vol. X, p. 165: "Talionis, Lex."

22. The same rule applied in Hammurabi's Code: "If a seignior came forward with false testimony in a case, and has not proved the word which he spoke, if that case was a case involving life, that seignior shall be put to death. If he came forward

if the innocent person could prove perjury on the part of his accuser could he demand that the civil government impose on the latter the penalty that would have been imposed on him.)[23]

Not every Bible commentator has seen the "eye for eye" sanction as primitive. Shalom Paul writes: "Rather than being a primitive residuum, it restricts retaliation to the person of the offender, while at the same time limiting it to the exact measure of the injury – thereby according equal justice to all."[24] W. F. Albright, the archeologist who specialized in Hebrew and Palestinian studies, wrote: "This principle may seem and is often said to be extraordinarily primitive. But it is actually not in the least primitive. Whereas the beginnings of *lex talionis* are found before Israel, the principle was now extended by analogy until it dominated all punishment of injuries or homicides. In ordinary Ancient Oriental jurisprudence, men who belonged to the higher social categories or who were wealthy simply paid fines, otherwise escaping punishment. . . . So the *lex talionis* (is) . . . the principle of equal justice for all!"[25] Albright understood some of the implications of the passage for the principle of equal justice for all, meaning equality before the law. Nevertheless, the myth of "primitive" legislation still clings in people's minds.[26] It seems to some Christians to be a needlessly bloody law. In a reaction against the rigor of this judicial principle, liberal scholar Hans Jochen Boecker goes so far as to argue that Old Testament law was not actually governed by *lex talionis*,[27] that it only appears in

---

with (false) testimony concerning grain or money, he shall bear the penalty of that case." CH, paragraphs 3-4: *Ancient Near Eastern Texts*, p. 166.

23. A moral judicial system would impose on the accuser or his insurance company all court costs, plus the costs incurred by the defendant in defending himself.

24. Shalom Paul, *Studies in the Book of the Covenant in the Light of Cuneiform and Biblical Law* (Leiden: E. J. Brill, 1970), p. 40.

25. W. F. Albright, *History, Archaeology, and Christian Humanism* (New York, 1964), p. 74; cited in *ibid.*, p. 77.

26. Hammurabi's "code" has similar rules: "If a seignior has destroyed the eye of a member of the aristocracy, they shall destroy his eye. If he has broken a(nother) seignior's bone, they shall break his bone." CH, paragraphs 196-97. If an aristocrat has destroyed the eye of a commoner, however, the *lex talionis* did not apply: he paid one mina of silver (CH 198). *Ancient Near Eastern Texts*, p. 175.

27. Hans Jochen Boecker, *Law and the Administration of Justice in the Old Testament*

three instances, and that it is a holdover of early nomadic law.[28]

"Vengeance Is Mine"

Vengeance in the Bible is God's original responsibility. "To me belongeth vengeance, and recompence; their foot shall slide in due time: for the day of their calamity is at hand, and the things that shall come upon them make haste" (Deut. 32:35). "If I whet my glittering sword, and mine hand take hold on judgment; I will render vengeance to mine enemies, and will reward them that hate me. I will make mine arrows drunk with blood, and my sword shall devour flesh . . ." (Deut. 32:41-42a). All nations are required to rejoice because of God's willingness and ability to avenge His people: "Rejoice, O ye nations, with his people: for he will avenge the blood of his servants, and will render vengeance to his adversaries, and will be merciful unto his land, and to his people" (Deut. 32:43). These passages, and many others in the Old Testament, are the foundation of Paul's summary statement: "Vengeance is mine; I will repay, saith the Lord" (Rom. 12:19b). "For we know him that hath said, Vengeance belongeth unto me, I will recompense, saith the Lord. And again, The Lord shall judge his people" (Heb. 10:30).

God makes it clear that He sometimes intervenes personally in history and brings bloody vengeance on His enemies. The State, under limited and Bible-defined circumstances, possesses an analogous authority. It is therefore highly inaccurate to say that the authority to impose vengeance in history is exclusively God's prerogative. God has delegated to the civil government its limited and derived sovereignty to impose physical vengeance. The State is allowed, by the testimony of witnesses, to impose the death penalty and other physical punishments. *Perfect justice must wait until the day of judgment; so must perfect vengeance.*[29] But men do not have to wait until the end of time in order to see preliminary justice done, and therefore preliminary vengeance imposed.

---

and Ancient East, translated by Jeremy Moiser (Minneapolis, Minnesota: Augsburg, [1976] 1980), pp. 171-72.

28. *Ibid.*, pp. 174-75.

29. North, *Moses and Pharaoh*, ch. 19: "Imperfect Justice."

Vengeance is a form of *restitution*. "Vengeance is mine; I will *repay*." This repayment is in the form of punishment and even permanent judgment. God *pays back* what is owed to the sinner. It is *repayment in kind*, an original meaning of "retaliate." Capital crimes require the public execution of the guilty person. In the case of crimes less repugnant to God than capital crimes, economic restitution is often paid by the criminal to the victim. But restitution is ultimately owed to God.[30] The victim, as God's image bearer, deserves his restitution, just as God deserves His. When repayment in kind is not made, a sense of injustice prevails. The victim, or the family members who survive the victim, understand that a convicted criminal who is not forced to make restitution has evaded justice. Such an escape is seen as being unfair.

Fair Warning

God reminds His people that His ultimate justice cannot be evaded. This testimony of a final judgment is provided by the sanctions imposed by the authorities. Historical sanctions are designed by God to fit the crime in order to persuade men that *the universe is ultimately fair, for both time and eternity are governed by the decree of God*. God's people should not despair because some men escape the earnest (down payment) of the final justice that is coming. The 73rd Psalm is a reminder of the seeming injustice of life, and how the wicked are finally rewarded according to their deeds. "For I was envious at the foolish, when I saw the prosperity of the wicked" (Ps. 73:3). David was beaten down by events (v. 2), yet he saw all the good things that come to the wicked in life (vv. 4-5, 12). He flayed himself with such thoughts, "Until I went into the sanctuary of God; then understood I their end. Surely thou didst set them in slippery places: thou castedst them down into destruction. How are they brought into desolation, as in a moment! They are utterly consumed with terrors" (vv. 17-19). David finally admits: "So foolish was I, and ignorant: I was as a beast before thee" (v. 22).

The relationship between covenantal faithfulness and external

---

30. R. J. Rushdoony, *The Institutes of Biblical Law* (Nutley, New Jersey: Craig Press, 1973), pp. 525-30.

prosperity is clearly taught in the Bible (Deut. 28:1-14). So is the relationship between covenant-breaking and calamity (Deut. 28:15-68). This system of sanctions applies to the whole world, not just in Old Testament Israel. Deny this, and you have also denied the possibility of an explicitly and exclusively Christian social theory. Christians who deny the continuing relevance of Deuteronomy 28's sanctions in post-Calvary, pre-Second Coming history should be warned by David's admission that he had been foolish to doubt these relationships. The concept of *slippery places* is not often discussed, but it is very important. God sets people high *in order to make them slide*, visibly, before the world. God said to Pharaoh: "For now I will stretch out my hand, that I may smite thee and thy people with pestilence; and thou shalt be cut off from the earth. And in very deed for this cause have I raised thee up, for to show in thee my power; and that my name may be declared throughout all the earth" (Ex. 9:15-16). The temporary prosperity of the wicked must not be viewed as evidence that would call into question the long-term relationship between covenant-breaking and destruction.

Conclusion

Vengeance is legitimate, but not as a private act. It is always to be covenantal, governed by God's institutional monopoly, civil government. James Fitzjames Stephen said it best: "The criminal law stands to the passion of revenge in much the same relation as marriage to the sexual appetite."[31] The private vendetta is always illegitimate; public vengeance is sometimes legitimate. There are many examples of private vengeance not sanctioned by God: gangster wars, clan feuds, the murder of those who testify against a criminal or syndicate, and murders for breaking the code of silence of a secret society. It is a crime against God Himself to take any oath that testifies to the right of any private organization or voluntary society to inflict physical violence, especially death, for breaking the oath or any other violation of the "code," even if

---

31. James Fitzjames Stephen, *A History of the Criminal Law in England* (London: Macmillan, 1863), II, p. 80. Cited by Ernest van den Haag, *Punishing Criminals: Concerning a Very Old and Painful Question* (New York: Basic Books, 1975), p. 12.

Legitimate Violence 111

this oath's invoked penalties are supposedly only "symbolic" rather than literal. I refer here to Masonic oaths,[32] but also to any other similar oath. For example, the oath of an Entered Apprentice of the Masonic order ends with these words: ". . . binding myself under no less penalty than that of having my throat cut from ear to ear, my tongue torn out by its roots and buried in the rough sands of the sea at low-water mark where the tide ebbs and flows twice in twenty-four hours, should I ever knowingly or willingly violate this my solemn oath and obligation as an Entered Apprentice Mason."[33] Such an oath affirms the legitimacy of private institutional vengeance — vengeance applied by institutions that have not been assigned the State's limited sovereignty to serve as God's agency of vengeance.[34] This sort of physical vengeance is prohibited by biblical law, but the Bible does not condemn all earthly vengeance. The State is an agency of God's vengeance. So is the church, but the church may not lawfully impose physical vengeance, while the State can. Therefore, no church can legiti-

---

32. That the Freemasons adopt a covenantal view of the self-maledictory oath is admitted in *The Encyclopedia of Freemasonry*, a standard Masonic publication. The author of the section on "Oath" discusses the objections raised in the nineteenth century by the Roman Catholic Church and the Scottish seceders to Masonic oaths. He refers to the "sacred sanction" of an oath, and insists on the legitimacy of "the invocation of the Deity to witness" the oath. He cites Dr. Harris' *Masonic Discourses*: "What the ignorant call 'the oath,' is simply an obligation, covenant, and promise, exacted previously to the divulging of the specialties of the Order, and our means of recognizing each other; . . ." Explaining away the accusation that these secret oaths are taken in religious ceremonies, the author says: "Oaths, in all countries and at all times, have been accompanied by peculiar rites, intended to increase the solemnity and reverence of the act. . . . In all solemn covenants the oath was accompanied by a sacrifice; . . ." He admits that a Masonic oath may have sanctions attached, even a capital penalty. All oaths do, he insists. This is "an attestation of God to the truth of a declaration, as a witness and avenger; and hence every oath includes in itself, and as its very essence, the covenant of God's wrath, the heaviest of all penalties, as the necessary consequence of its violation." Albert G. Mackey, *The Encyclopedia of Freemasonry and Its Kindred Sciences*, 2 vols. (rev. ed.; New York: Masonic History Co., 1925), II, pp. 522-23.

33. *King Solomon and His Followers* (New York: Allen Pub. Co., 1943); cited in E. M. Storms, *Should a Christian Be a Mason?* (Fletcher, North Carolina: New Puritan Library, 1980), p. 63.

34. Gary North, *The Sinai Strategy: Economics and the Ten Commandments* (Tyler, Texas: Institute for Christian Economics, 1986), pp. 55-58.

mately invoke oaths or oath signs similar in form to secret society blood oaths. A church that does this has marked itself as a cult.

6
THE RANSOM FOR AN EYE

If men strive, and hurt a woman with child, so that her fruit depart from her, and yet no mischief follow: he shall be surely punished, according as the woman's husband will lay upon him; and he shall pay as the judges determine. And if any mischief follow, then thou shalt give life for life, eye for eye, tooth for tooth, hand for hand, foot for foot, burning for burning, wound for wound, stripe for stripe (Ex. 21:22-25).

The question must be raised: Is the concern of humanists for the "brutality" shown by the Bible's "eye for eye" principle misguided? Shouldn't their concern be focused on the brutality of the criminal against the innocent victim? Is the *lex talionis* principle not a deterrent to crime, especially repeated crimes by a criminal class? Shouldn't our concern be with the victims of violent crime rather than with the criminals who commit them?

We read of Adoni-bezek in the first chapter of Judges. Adoni-bezek (Lord of Bezek) was a Canaanitic king. The Israelites fought him and defeated him. "But Adoni-bezek fled; and they pursued after him, and caught him, and cut off his thumbs and his great toes. And Adoni-bezek said, Threescore and ten kings, having their thumbs and their great toes cut off, gathered their meat under my table: as I have done, so God hath requited me. And they brought him to Jerusalem, and there he died" (Jud. 1:6-7). This Canaanitic king's confession reveals that he recognized the justice of the punishment imposed on him by his conquerors.[1] He had cut off the toes and thumbs of kings; now he

---

1. The Hammurabi Code specifies mutilations on an "eye for eye" basis, para-

had suffered the same punishment. He had removed their anatomical "tools of dominion"; now he had his removed.[2]

Problems of Interpretation

This incident raises some difficult exegetical questions. Was the "eye for eye" principle literally applied in ancient Israel after the defeat of Canaan? Did Israel's courts really poke out people's teeth and eyes? If not, why not? Or is it merely that there are no clear-cut biblical records of such physical penalties being imposed by Israelite judges on Israelite citizens?

The incident also raises some difficult historical questions. In the Christian West, judges have consistently refused to impose "eye for eye" physical penalties. In non-Christian societies, permanent physical vengeance is quite common, e.g., Islam's *Shari'a* law. Why not in the West? What is it about inflicting permanent physical mutilation — in contrast to whippings or other relatively impermanent forms of physical violence — that so repels Westerners?

The West's Future-Orientation

The West's impulse toward dominion in history is one possible answer. The West has been future-oriented, as a direct result of its Christian eschatological heritage: *a faith in linear history*, with a God-created beginning, a God-sustaining providence, and a God-governed final judgment.[3] This vision of linear time made possible the development of modern science.[4] The future-orientation of the West, especially from the seventeenth century onward,

---

graphs 196-201. *Ancient Near Eastern Texts Relating to the Old Testament*, edited by James B. Pritchard (3rd ed.; Princeton, New Jersey: Princeton University Press, 1969), p. 175.

2. Without a thumb, a person cannot grasp a tool or weapon. Without a big toe, he cannot balance himself easily. See James B. Jordan, *Judges: God's War Against Humanism* (Tyler, Texas: Geneva Ministries, 1985), pp. 4-5.

3. Karl Löwith, *Meaning in History* (University of Chicago Press, 1949), ch. 11: "The Biblical View of History."

4. Stanley Jaki, *The Road of Science and the Ways to God* (University of Chicago Press, 1978), chaps. 1, 2; *Science and Creation: From eternal cycles to an oscillating universe* (Edinburgh and London: Scottish Academic Press, [1974] 1980); "The History of Science and the Idea of an Oscillating Universe," in Wolfgang Yourgrau and Allen D. Beck (eds.), *Cosmology, History, and Theology* (New York: Plenum Press, 1977).

and especially in Protestant societies, led to faith in long-term progress, including long-term economic growth.[5] Western people have understood the importance to the community of full production from all members. There is (or was) the psychological and social phenomenon called "the Protestant Ethic."[6] Begging, for example, has not been favored in Protestant nations. Idleness has been frowned upon. Therefore, the realization that physical punishment can permanently reduce the productivity of any citizen repels the Westerner. The Western judge asks: What happens to the criminal after he has "paid his debt"? Why should the criminal, his family, his future employers, and consumers be deprived of his full future productivity? Why should any man be hampered in working out his own salvation with fear and trembling (Phil. 2:12)? Wouldn't permanent physical mutilation tend to impair his future employment, thereby luring him back into a life of crime? What if he should experience a moral transformation in the future? Western justice seems to recognize such problems, and so it has rejected physical mutilation as a legal sanction.

Figuratively Speaking?

Are we to interpret the "eye for eye" passage figuratively? Jesus said in the Sermon on the Mount, "If thy right eye offend thee, pluck it out, and cast it from thee. . . . And if thy right hand offend thee, cut it off, and cast it from thee" (Matt. 5:29a, 30a). We recognize that He spoke figuratively. He meant that the lusts of the flesh are so dangerous spiritually that even the loss of eye or hand is to be preferred. Therefore, avoid moral contamination; avoid lust (5:28). But the issue in Exodus 21:24-25 is that there has been physical injury inflicted on another person. The eye which the victim has lost is a literal eye. To interpret the "eye for eye" passage figuratively because Jesus interpreted "eye" figuratively in a very different context is not legitimate.

---

5. Gary North, "Medieval Economics in Puritan New England, 1630-1660," *Journal of Christian Reconstruction*, V (Winter 1978-79), pp. 157-60.

6. Max Weber, *The Protestant Ethic and the Spirit of Capitalism* (New York: Scribner's, [1904-5] 1958). See also Gary North, "The 'Protestant Ethic' Hypothesis," *Journal of Christian Reconstruction*, III (Summer 1976); Daniel T. Rodgers, *The Work Ethic in Industrial America, 1850-1920* (University of Chicago Press, 1978).

There is no doubt that the "thumb for thumb" penalty was literally applied to Adoni-bezek. He recognized the justice of the penalty. Permanent physical mutilation is legitimate when applied to one who has committed a crime that has produced the same mutilation in another person. Yet the resistance of Western judges to impose this physical penalty on their own nation's citizens indicates that they have sought other ways to deal with criminals and victims in crimes involving permanent physical mutilation. Question: In cases other than manslaughter — the death of an innocent third party as a result of unwarranted violence — as in the abortion of Exodus 21:22-23, *may some other penalty legitimately be imposed*, one which meets God's standards of justice, as well as men's sense of justice?

Option: Economic Restitution

Say that an ox has been known to gore people in the past. It gets loose again and kills someone. The owner in this instance is held legally liable; in fact, he is to be put to death (Ex. 21:29). However, Exodus 21:30 provides an exception to the requirement that a crime that results in a person's death be punished by the execution of the person responsible. "If there be laid on him a sum of money, then he shall give for the ransom of his life whatsoever is laid upon him." The death penalty is set aside at the discretion of the judges and the victim's heirs. *The man pays a ransom for his life*. The text does not specifically say that the ransom is paid to the victim's next of kin, but this is the familiar pattern in the Old Testament. The payment would become part of the dead person's estate, as if he were still alive and had been merely injured by the beast. The ransom is a restitution payment. There is no evidence that the ransom would go anywhere else except to the victim's heirs.

The question can be raised: If the death of the owner of the ox does not benefit the victim's heirs, while the ransom does benefit them, does the *lex talionis* allow a comparable solution to the problem of the physically mutilated person? Instead of physically mutilating the criminal, may the judges legitimately impose a restitution payment?

Jewish Commentaries

Traditional Jewish explanations of the *lex talionis* principle point to a payment in lieu of physical mutilation. Nachmanides wrote in the thirteenth century concerning "eye 'tachath' (for) eye":

> It is known in the tradition of our rabbis that this means monetary compensation. Such a usage [of the term *tachath* to indicate] monetary compensation is found in the verse: *And he that smiteth a beast mortally shall pay for it; life 'tacheth' life* [Lev. 24:18], [in which case *tacheth* surely indicates monetary compensation]. Rabbi Abraham ibn Ezra commented that Scripture uses such a term to indicate that he really is deserving of such a punishment, [that his eye be taken from him], if he does not give his ransom. For Scripture has forbidden us to take *ransom for the life of a murderer, that is guilty of death* [Num. 35:31], but we may take ransom from a wicked person who cut off any of the limbs of another person. Therefore we are never to cut off that limb from him, but rather he is to pay monetary compensation, and if he has no money to pay, it lies as a debt on him until he acquires the means to pay, and then he is redeemed.[7]

Nachmanides' citation of Abraham ibn Ezra indicates that he was disturbed by the literal wording of the "eye for eye" stipulation. By refusing to call for a literal application of the verse in the case of a poor criminal, and also by their refusal to call for indentured servitude as a way to repay the debt, these two Jewish medieval commentators softened the threat of the punishment.

There are difficulties with this interpretation. It is ingenious, but it has no explicit biblical precedent, and it may therefore be incorrect, even though it appears to conform to the implicit meaning of "eye for eye." It involves speculation that relies heavily on the precedent of economic restitution in the case of the ox that gores someone to death (Ex. 21:30) – a separate case law that may not apply to the *lex talionis* law of Exodus 21:24-25. But this view became common in the interpretation of Jewish law. Rabbi Samson Raphael Hirsch commented on Exodus 21:25 in the early nineteenth century: ". . . the taking of this legal canon literally,

---

7. Rabbi Moses ben Nachman [Ramban], *Commentary on the Torah: Exodus* (New York: Shiloh, [1267?] 1973), p. 368.

in the sense of an eye for an eye, would be morally impossible for any idea of equity; . . ." Further, "the whole spirit of the text is what the traditional Halacha [Jewish law] teaches, viz., that here it is only speaking of monetary compensation for the injury inflicted. . . ."[8]

Restitution and Equity

In principle, the interpretation of the *lex talionis* as allowing economic restitution in place of physical mutilation raises some fundamental questions. First, is the requirement of vengeance compromised by the imposition of a restitution payment? Is there some fundamental aspect of justice, or men's sense of justice, that should allow a man to "buy his way out" of an injury that he has inflicted on another person? If so, what is this long-neglected aspect of justice?[9]

Second, does this law so interpreted lead to class antagonism? What if the criminal is poor? He cannot pay what a rich man can afford to pay. Is it fair to allow a rich man to forfeit only money, when the poor man must forfeit his eye or tooth or else become an indentured servant to pay off the debt? Will violent rich people become more careless than violent poor people with regard to injuring others? Are the rich being taught to care less for the law of God than the poor do? If the rich can buy their way out, is society thereby allowing the development of resentment among the poor, who feel that the law is working against them? Is society implicitly subsidizing rich criminals?

The most important questions are these: Has the "eye for eye" principle been abandoned when economic restitution is substituted for physical punishment? Will God honor a society that abandons this literal principle?

But what if the economic interpretation of *lex talionis* is denied? Would the requirement that all criminals pay the full physical

---

8. Samson Raphael Hirsch, *The Pentateuch Translated and Explained*, translated by Isaac Levy, 5 vols., *Exodus* (3rd ed.; London: Honig & Sons, 1967), p. 315.

9. I argue that three principles of justice lead us to such a view of *lex talionis*: victim's rights, the criminal's right to seek mercy through making a substitute payment, and the limitation of the judges' authority.

price rather than economic restitution really be beneficial to their victims? The victim may need additional capital to compensate for his loss of productivity as a result of the injury. What benefit is it to him that the criminal becomes equally hampered physically?

Furthermore, there are important social consequences of denying the economic interpretation. What benefit is it to society that two people now will suffer from some physical impairment rather than only one? Is the dominion covenant better fulfilled when two men lose an eye or an arm rather than only one man? After he makes economic restitution to the victim, the criminal can work hard and perhaps regain his lost wealth, but he can never regain a lost eye. Society may benefit more in the long run because of the productivity that the convicted man retains. If he repents and becomes a law-abiding member of the community, his greater productivity increases the wealth of all those consumers whom he will serve as a producer.

These questions deserve biblical answers. We can begin to discover answers by examining in detail how the substitution of economic restitution for physical mutilation might work.

Establishing a Fair Payment

Let us begin with the case of a victim who has lost his eye. A partially blinded person could insist on a particular restitution payment from the convicted criminal. He could say to the judges, "Tell that man that he can keep his eye, but only if he pays me 100 ounces of gold." The judges would then present this option to the criminal: *your gold or your eye.*

If the criminal values his body more highly than he values the economic restitution demanded by the victim, he can pay the money. This is the principle of *victim's rights* in action. On the other hand, if he values the payment higher, or if he simply cannot afford to pay, then he can forfeit his eye. This is the principle of *maximum specified sanctions* in action. The criminal could also make payment by selling himself into indentured servitude, with the buyer paying the victim. But perhaps the convicted man would prefer to lose the use of part of his body rather than becoming a bondservant. He could reject the demand of the victim for economic restitution and insist instead on his legal right under biblical law: to suffer the same physical mutilation that he had imposed on the victim.

The Right to Punishment

Each of the parties in this judicial dispute has biblically specified legal rights. The victim has the right to insist on the biblically specified maximum physical sanction: eye for eye. He also has the right to offer the criminal an alternative, one which appears to be less severe than the biblically specified physical sanction. If the alternative offered to the criminal is not regarded by him as less severe, then he has the legal right to insist on the imposition of the biblically specified maximum sanction. He therefore possesses the *right to be punished by the specified biblical sanction*. His punishment is limited by the extent of the injury which he imposed on his victim. The punishment fits the crime.

It is basic to the preservation of liberty that the State not be allowed to deny to either the victim or the criminal his right of punishment. While this principle of the right to punishment is at least vaguely understood by most people with respect to the victim, it is not well understood with respect to the criminal. The right to be punished is a crucial legal right, one which Paul insisted on at his trial: "For if I be an offender, or have committed any thing worthy of death, I refuse not to die: but if there be none of these things whereof these accuse me, no man may deliver me unto them. I appeal unto Caesar" (Acts 25:11).

If the State can autonomously substitute other criteria for deserved punishment, such as personal or social rehabilitation, then society loses its right to be governed by predictable laws with predictable judicial sanctions. The messianic State then replaces the judicially limited State. Neither the victim nor the criminal can be assured of receiving justice, for justice is defined by the State rather than by God in the Bible. If punishment is not seen as *deserved* by the criminal, and therefore his *fundamental right*, then he is delivered into the "merciful" hands of elitist captors who are not bound by written law or social custom. No one has described this threat more eloquently than C. S. Lewis: "To be taken without consent from my home and friends; to lose my liberty; to undergo all those assaults on my personality which modern psychoytherapy knows how to deliver; to be re-made after some pattern of 'normality' hatched in a Viennese laboratory to which I never professed allegiance; to know that this process will never end until either my captors have succeeded or I grown wise enough to cheat them with apparent success — who cares whether this is called Punishment or not? That it includes most of the elements for which any punishment is feared — shame, exile, bondage, and years eaten by the locust — is obvious. Only enormous ill-desert could justify it; but ill-desert is the very conception which the Humanitarian theory has thrown overboard."[10]

The State represents God in history in His capacity as cosmic Judge (Rom. 13:1-7). When a civil government's leaders say that the State represents any other agent or principle, the State has begun its march toward either tyranny or impotence. Either it will bring judgment on men and other states in the name of its deity, its official source of law,[11] or else some other State will bring judgment on it and those governed by it in the name of a foreign deity. Only a rare nation like Switzerland can defend its borders for centuries, and then only by renouncing all thought of conquest in the name of defense and international neutrality.[12]

The mark of this transformation of the State is when the State insists on imposing the punishment in terms of the supposed "needs of society," meaning ultimately the needs of the State's officers. When the State collects fines for use by the State rather than to pay victims, when it imposes prison sentences paid for by the taxes of law-abiding citizens, and when it insists that every

---

10. C. S. Lewis, "The Humanitarian Theory of Punishment," in Lewis, *God in the Dock: Essays on Theology and Ethics*, edited by Walter Hooper (Grand Rapids, Michigan: Eerdmans, 1972), pp. 290-91.

11. R. J. Rushdoony, *The Institutes of Biblical Law* (Nutley, New Jersey: Craig Press, 1973), p. 4.

12. It had better have high mountains, civil defense, an armed population, and services such as private banking and a geographical "King's X" facilities for overthrown rulers. See John McPhee, *La Place de la Concorde Suisse* (New York: Farrar, Strauss, Giroux, 1984).

convicted criminal "pay his debt to society," then the messianic State has arrived. God has specified that the victim is His representative in criminal cases, not the State, unless the victim is legally unable to represent himself, in which case the State acts as his trustee. Only if the State is the victim can it lawfully demand restitution. When the State presents itself as the universal victim of all crime to which is owed universal restitution by criminals and taxpayers alike, it has asserted its own divinity.

Benefits of Alternative Sanctions

The proposed economic solution to the dilemma of the *lex talionis* offers at least three very real benefits. The first benefit is judicial: *the victim has the right to specify the appropriate punishment.* This punishment is limited only by the maximum penalty specified by biblical law, *eye for eye*. The biblical principle of victim's rights is upheld by the judges. If the victim believes that the criminal's act was malicious, and if he wishes to inflict the same damage on the criminal which he himself suffered, this is his legal option.

To take this retributive approach, however, he necessarily forfeits all the economic advantages he might have received from a restitution payment from the criminal. He can exercise his legitimate desire for vengeance — his desire to reduce the criminal to a physical condition comparable to his own — but this desire for vengeance has a price attached to it. He is made no better off financially because of his enemy's suffering. In fact, he could be made slightly worse off: he, as a member of the economic community, loses his portion of the other man's lost future productivity, assuming the man cannot overcome the effects of his lost eye or limb. *Vengeance in the Bible's judicial system has a price tag attached to it*. This inevitably reduces the quantity of physical vengeance insisted on by victims, for biblical civil justice recognizes the judicial legitimacy of a fundamental economic law: "The higher the price of any economic good, the less the quantity demanded."

The second benefit of this interpretation of *lex talionis* is also judicial: *the criminal who is about to lose his eye or tooth is permitted to make a counter-offer*. He has the right to be punished to the limit of the written law, but he also can suggest a less onerous punishment — less onerous for him, but possibly more beneficial to his victim. He can legally offer money or services in exchange for the continued preservation of his unmutilated body. The system puts him in the position of being able to pay in order to retain his limbs. *He places a price tag on his body.*

This price tag makes it costly for the victim to pursue an emotion which, had there been no crime, would be called envious: the desire to tear another person down, irrespective of the direct benefits to the person who is envious.[13] But because there has been a crime, envy is legitimate in this case. It must be understood that "getting even" with a convicted criminal is a legitimate goal for the victim of a crime. God eventually "gets even" with Satan and his followers who have sinned against Him; He pulls them down from their positions of power and influence. This process of pulling Satan down began with Jesus' ministry, an event which was manifested by the power of His disciples. "And the seventy returned again with joy, saying, Lord, even the devils are subject unto us through thy name. And he said unto them, I beheld Satan as lightning fall from heaven. Behold, I give unto you power to tread on serpents and scorpions, and over all the power of the enemy: and nothing shall by any means hurt you" (Luke 10:17-19). The victims of violent crime are in an analogous position with God: innocent people who deserve to be avenged. But grace still abounds in history, so the criminal is allowed to make a counter-offer to his victim, just as the sinner can make a counter-offer to God.[14]

The third benefit of this interpretation is social: *the integrity of the legal system is upheld in the eyes of all the nation.* Members of society

---

13. Of course, the desire to gain compensation would be regarded as jealousy, in the absence of a crime: the desire to gain at another person's expense. The crime, naturally, does make a difference: the right of the State to avenge the victim is crucial; pseudo-envy or pseudo-jealousy are just that: pseudo. These are legitimate emotions when a crime has been committed that has cost the victim the use of part of his body.

14. When sick or injured people learn that they are about to die, one common reaction is to make a deal with God: specific service for an extension of the gift of life. Contrary to secular humanists and theological liberals, this makes good sense. The dying individual is thereby admitting that God is in control of life and death. This is another reason why dying people deserve to be told that they are dying.

at large cannot complain that the judges are playing favorites. The judges are not "respecting persons." If a rich man loses money, while the victim has lost the use of his body, this result has been the decision of the victim, not the judges. What is essentially a private dispute, victim vs. criminal, rather than a conflict between classes, has been settled by the disputants. The victim has made his choice. Outsiders therefore have no valid moral complaint against the judicial system. This keeps the ideology of class conflict from spreading to the general population. This is a very important feature of the justice system in an era of class conflict, meaning an era of rhetoric by competing elites in the name of various classes.

Insurance for Criminals?

Should the victim be denied the option of specifying the form of vengeance? Does it thwart justice to set up a judicial system where a rich criminal can offer to "buy his way out"?[15] Worse, what if his rich insurance company can offer to buy his way out?

If criminals could escape the likelihood of physical violence by means of monetary restitution, they might start buying insurance contracts that would enable them to escape the economic penalty of inflicting physical violence. This could be regarded as licensing criminal behavior. No one is going to co-insure another man's eye with his own eye, but the public has already set up co-insurance for monetary claims. Thus, by allowing economic restitution for crimes of violence, criminal behavior might be made less costly to the criminals.

One answer to this objection is that insurance companies are unlikely to insure a person from claims made by victims if the man is a repeat violator. The risk of writing such contracts is too high. Private insurance contracts are designed to be sold to the general public, and to keep premiums sufficiently price competitive, sellers exclude people known to be high risks. Low-risk buyers do not want to pay for high-risk buyers. Furthermore, insur-

---

15. If the criminal could "buy his way out" by bribing the judges, then justice would be thwarted. But judges in a biblical system represent the victims, not the State. If they represent a victim who wishes to be "bought off," where is the injustice?

ance policies often specify that the coverage is for civil damages rather than criminal acts. This is true of most automobile insurance policies. Policies specify exactly what is to be covered — the famous insurance industry principle of "the large print giveth, but the fine print taketh away."

Policies actually designed by criminals to co-insure would be extremely unlikely. Violent criminals seldom think ahead. They do not work well with others. They are essentially anti-social people. A system of insurance company-subsidized crime could not last very long without government financial aid.

The Auction for Human Flesh

By allowing the substitution of an economic payment for actual physical disfigurement, the judges unquestionably do authorize an auction for human flesh. If a convicted criminal is allowed to pay the victim in order to avoid physical mutilation, he is participating in an auction. Such an implicit auction may sound crass, but so does poking out an innocent person's eye. So does all criminal behavior. Covenant-breaking men may not like to think of criminal behavior in such terms, but this is what the Bible teaches. Sin is the evil, not economic restitution.

We begin our economic analysis of this auction process with a consideration of the victim. Let us assume that he has lost his eye. He tells the judges that he wants to see the other man's eye poked out, just as his was. He offers the criminal no choice between mutilation and restitution. Because the victim initially offers no alternative sanction, the criminal is then allowed to make a single counter-offer, if he wants to. Assume that he makes this counter-offer: 100 ounces of gold instead of losing his eye.[16] Perhaps he is a skilled craftsman who needs both eyes. Perhaps

---

16. As we shall see, this counter-offer is allowed because the victim did not offer the criminal a choice between mutilation and economic restitution. If the victim specifies a choice between mutilation and a money payment, he is not entitled to accept less money, since this would indicate that he had not been honest when he specified the initial conditions. On the other hand, if the criminal should propose a non-monetary payment, the victim would be entitled to consider it, since this would constitute a different kind of offer from that specified by the victim. See subsection below, "Limiting One's Original Demands."

he fears disfigurement. In any case, he places a high premium on his eye. He bids 100 ounces of gold to retain it.

Once the victim receives an offer from the criminal, he may change his mind about his commitment to seeing the criminal disfigured. Perhaps he did not suspect that he could get this much money from the criminal. Perhaps his wife has seen the wisdom of taking the money. He may conclude that he would much prefer 100 ounces of gold to the joy he would receive in seeing (with his remaining eye) his enemy brought low. After all, seeing his enemy part with 100 ounces of gold is also seeing him brought low, and the event brings other benefits, such as all the pleasures or security the 100 ounces of gold can buy. So he accepts the counter-offer. The criminal keeps his eye.

In this case, the criminal is the high-money bidder. The victim values the gold more than he values the criminal's eye. The criminal places more value on his eye than the gold. Each man gets what he most prefers. The criminal has bought the right to determine what happens to his own body. He has bought the right to avoid mutilation.

Consider the victim's other possible choice. He is still outraged at what has befallen him. He wants the criminal to share the same physical limitation. He is unwilling to accept the financial counter-offer. Now, economically speaking, the criminal had just placed 100 ounces of gold into the victim's lap. He had been willing to pay. The victim is not impressed, or not sufficiently impressed. He figuratively hands the 100 ounces of gold back to the criminal. "Keep your filthy money, you butcher! Keep your only remaining eye on your money." The victim has now matched the money bid of the criminal. He has forfeited the 100 ounces of gold that he might have received. He places a higher value on his legal ability to blind the other man's eye than he does on 100 ounces of gold. So the victim gets what he values most, the joy of seeing the other man lose his eye. But he pays 100 ounces of gold for this pleasure. The pleasure is biblically legitimate, but it is expensive.

The criminal's 100 ounces of gold did not constitute a high enough bid. The victim might have agreed for more than the 100 ounces, but the criminal had not been willing to pay this much. The criminal keeps what he wants: the 100+ ounces of gold that the victim might have accepted in payment, but which the criminal refused to offer. The criminal would rather have this larger quantity of gold than keep his eye. There is what the economists call "reservation demand" for this money; the criminal pays with his eye for his continued possession of the money.

None of this suggests that the criminal can buy justice. Justice is what the court provides when it tries the case and imposes the victim's preferred sanction, up to the limit of the law. The criminal is buying a specific sanction that he prefers by offering the victim an alternative which the criminal hopes the victim will prefer. It is an auction for flesh, not an auction for justice.

The Private Slave Market

To give the criminal access to capital sufficient to make the offer, the State must allow another auction for flesh: a slave market. Deny this, and the criminal is thwarted in gaining what he wants, and so is his victim. The most valuable asset a criminal may possess is his own ability to work. If he is denied the legal right to capitalize this asset, he may not be able to offer a sufficiently high bid to the victim to avoid mutilation.

The modern democratic theorist professes horror at such a thought. Why? *Because the modern State's disciples want the State to have a monopoly on the slave market.* The State imposes prison as the alternative to both restitution and slavery — an alternative which benefits neither the victim nor the potentially productive criminal.

At this point, we return once again to the basic theme of the Book of Exodus: *the choice between slavery to man and service to God.* It is therefore the question of *representation*: Who is represented by the State, God or autonomous man? When autonomous man is represented by the State, then tyranny or impotence is the result. Autonomous man seeks to enslave others, for he seeks to imitate God, just as Satan imitates God. The State becomes the primary agency of this enslavement process. It should not be surprising to learn that the call for the abolition of chattel slavery in the United States began in the 1820's in the Northeast, where the new state prison systems were also being implemented.[17]

Slavery may seem brutal. The *lex talionis* also may seem brutal. Judicially unregulated violence is more brutal. Injustice in the face of crime is more brutal yet. The high penalty imposed on the convicted criminal is intended to impress the criminal, potential criminals, and all ethical rebels of *the majesty of God's law*, and the high price God will impose eternally on those who break it. This no doubt repels the sense of justice of covenant-breakers, but God is not concerned about the ethical sensibilities of covenant-breakers. He is concerned primarily about His own majesty, which is reflected in His law, including the penalties imposed on those who transgress its provisions.

Technological Progress and Restitution

With the advent of modern technology, it might be possible for the victim to secure a replacement eye. He might demand an operation, with the criminal's eye being transplanted as a replacement. Or an exchange might be set up: the criminal's eye goes to an eye bank in exchange for an eye that might be more compatible biologically with the victim's system. Alternatively, the judges could allow the criminal to pay for an operation for the victim, and give the victim an additional payment equal to the value of the operation. The criminal would lose the money, but the victim would see again.

This sort of economic resolution to the problem of "eye for eye" standard is ideal: the victim gains what he had lost, and the criminal pays for it, plus restitution for the victim's pain, fear, and trouble. The technological advances brought by Western — and initially Christian[18] — civilization make possible the best solution for both parties, namely, the restoration of the injured man's sight, but at the expense of the criminal. The technological pro-

---

17. David J. Rothman, *The Discovery of the Asylum: Social Order and Disorder in the New Republic* (Boston: Little, Brown, 1971). This same era saw Horace Mann's call for the establishment of a "theologically neutral" tax-financed day school movement, meaning a call for social morality without Christian supernaturalism. When American society began to abandon the God of the Bible, it also began to abandon the institutional foundations of freedom.

18. See footnote #8, above.

gress that would be brought by a thoroughly Christian civilization would make possible a better set of options for both victim and criminal. The more faithful society's commitment to enforcing God's law, the more rapid the technological progress is going to be.

Limiting One's Original Demands

The threat of actual physical mutilation for the convicted violent criminal will always be present in a biblical legal order. The victim has lost his eye or tooth; the criminal deserves to lose his. But few criminals would sacrifice an eye if they could make restitution in some other way. They might sacrifice a tooth, but not an eye. The victim can legitimately demand the removal of the other man's eye, but there is not much doubt that he would prefer a large cash settlement to help him recover his lost productivity and forfeited economic opportunities. He might even be able to get a new eye through surgery. The rich man is allowed to "buy his way out," but only at the discretion (and direct economic benefit) of the victim. On the other hand, the victim can demand his "pound of flesh," but only by forfeiting the money that he might have been paid.

What if the victim is really vindictive? What if he demands 1,000 ounces of gold for the other person's tooth? In all likelihood, the criminal would prefer to forfeit the tooth. *Under this kind of judicial system, the victim must estimate carefully in advance just what the convicted person might be willing and able to pay.* There must be no "fall-back position" after the victim submits his pair of demands to the judges: physical mutilation or a specified financial restitution payment.

Under a biblical system of economic substitution, the victim would be required by the court to specify the minimum amount of money he would be willing to accept in exchange for not having mutilation imposed on the criminal. The victim would not be allowed to present a false estimate about how much restitution he would be willing to accept. This would be false witness, or perjury. He could not come back a second time, after the criminal had refused to pay the 1,000 ounces of gold, and say, "All right,

I'll accept 500 ounces of gold instead of his tooth." By lowering his new demand, he would be admitting that his initial offer had been higher than his minimal demand. In short, the injured victim must know in advance that by making an excessive initial financial demand, he might "price himself out of the market"; he therefore has to be reasonable if he is really after money. He might wind up with nothing except the pain and disfigurement of the criminal as his reward. He must ask for less money in order to increase his likelihood of collecting anything.

The judges would present the victim's specified choices to the criminal, and the criminal would have the option of refusing to pay the 1,000 ounces. The judges would then have the physical penalty imposed.

The man condemned by the victim to permanent physical mutilation would have the option of making a counter-proposal if the victim had offered no option to mutilation. The victim could then consider it. Again, the criminal would be allowed only one offer; if the victim still says no, and the criminal then makes a higher offer, he can be presumed to have given false witness when he made the first offer. By limiting the victim to presenting the criminal with only one set of options, and by giving the criminal the opportunity to make a single counter-offer only when no alternative option has been offered by the victim, the judges can obtain honest offers from the beginning.

The court would allow only one form of second-chance bids. If the criminal is unwilling to pay the victim the money payment demanded, but he is willing to pay in some other way than money, he would have the opportunity to present the alternative or group of alternatives for the victim to choose from. But if the victim turns this counter-offer down, the criminal will then have to undergo mutilation. He is governed by the equivalent rule that governs the victim: honest bidding. He offers his highest price or best bid. If it is rejected, he must suffer the physical consequences.

The Authority of the Judges

The integrity of society's covenantal civil judges is fundamental to the preservation of social order. The Bible warns rulers and judges to render honest judgment. They are forbidden to take bribes (although it is *not* forbidden for righteous people to offer bribes to corrupt judges).[19] Judges are to render honest judgment because the Bible requires it and because God requires it, not because it is made personally profitable for them to do so. When citizens distrust the judicial system, a fundamental weakness exists in the society. Bribes are a sign of such weakness and distrust.

The judges establish the initial penalty payment in the case of a notorious ox that has killed a person (Ex. 21:30). What about in the case of the crime of mutilation? Shouldn't the judges set the penalty? In the case of a non-injurious, accidental, premature birth caused by another man's violent behavior, the husband establishes the penalty, and the judges then impose it. "If men strive, and hurt a woman with child, so that her fruit depart from her, and yet no mischief follow: he shall be surely punished, according as the woman's husband will lay upon him; and he shall pay as the judges determine" (Ex. 21:22). This implies that the judges can overrule the husband if the penalty is thought by them to be excessive. The authority of the judges is supreme in this case.

If it is true that the Bible requires the judges to assess the penalty in the case of bodily mutilation, just as they do in the case of criminal manslaughter (the owner of the notorious ox), then they must make the decision: economic restitution or physical restitution. Both are legitimate forms of vengeance; both are true forms of restitution. If the judges are solely responsible for making this determination, then sovereignty is transferred to them and away from the victim and the criminal, who might prefer to come to a different, more mutually beneficial transaction. This raises the question of righteous judgment. Why should the victim and the criminal be excluded from the process of the setting of the penalty? After all, in the case of the non-injurious premature birth, the husband has the opportunity of setting a preliminary penalty. Why not in the case of mutilation?

---

19. Cf. Gary North, "In Defense of Biblical Bribery," in Rushdoony, *Institutes of Biblical Law*, Appendix 5; North, *Tools of Dominion: The Case Laws of Exodus* (Tyler, Texas: Institute for Christian Economics, 1989), pp. 793-800.

One solution to this dilemma would be to allow the judges to assess the original penalty, estimating what the defense of an eye is worth in the open market, and then make a preliminary announcement of the size of the payment. Then either of the two contending parties could make a counter-offer, which the judges would accept if both parties agree. In this way, the authority of the law would have a visible manifestation — rule by the judges — but the type of restitution could be modified at the discretion of the affected parties. It would be analogous to parents making an arranged marriage: either of the two children can legitimately protest and refuse the other, but initiating the marriage would be the right of the parents.

It is important that collusion between the judges and either the victim or the convicted criminal be prevented. To help prevent such collusion, dual rights are established: the right of the victim to demand different restitution from that set by the judges, and the right of the criminal to make a counter-offer to the victim when he receives notice of the judges' initial proposal.

There is another factor to consider. Economic value is both objective and subjective.[20] The judges are required by God to attempt to assess the cost to the victim, as well as the cost to the criminal, but they may make a mistake. There is no scientifically or theoretically valid way for judges to assess the comparative costs of injuries, since these costs are based on other people's subjective utilities. For example, if either the victim or the criminal is a right-handed skilled craftsman whose hand is his calling, and he has lost (or is faced with the threat of loss of) his right hand, the penalty is not easily fitted to the crime. Say that the victim has lost his right hand, and he is the craftsman. The criminal is a left-handed lawyer whose right hand is seemingly less crucial to him than the right hand of the victim. Is the loss of the criminal's right hand really a case of "hand for hand"? How can the judges determine what is a really comparable penalty? Hasn't the victim suffered far greater loss? Of course, the reverse could be true: a left-handed lawyer loses his right hand, and the

---

20. Gary North, *The Dominion Covenant: Genesis* (2nd ed.; Tyler, Texas: Institute for Christian Economics, 1987), ch. 4.

criminal is a right-handed craftsman. Is the *physically* identical penalty really comparable in terms of the costs to each person?

The System in Operation

Consider a hypothetical case. A criminal is convicted for having mutilated another man's hand. Let us consider three possible outcomes. *First*, the judges determine that the criminal should lose his hand. Why would they impose this penalty? Perhaps the criminal is a known brawler. He used a weapon to bash a victim's hand, making it permanently useless. The judges decide that the best thing for society would be for the criminal to have his hand bashed into uselessness or amputated, so that he could not easily repeat the offense.

The victim at this point might prefer economic restitution. The brawler also might be willing to pay to keep his hand. In such a case, the judges would be placing their perception of the public's need for future social peace above the economic needs of the victim.

The victim would have the option of asking for a different kind of punishment. The victim may want money, so he appeals the decision, and demands monetary compensation. The judges then go to the criminal. Is he willing to pay the victim the proposed monetary restitution? The criminal has three choices: pay the money, accept the judges' original penalty, or offer a third proposal to the victim. If the criminal turns down the request of the victim to be paid, and if the victim rejects the criminal's counter-offer, then the judges' original sentence would be carried out. He would lose the use of his hand.

Second, the judges impose a monetary penalty that is too low in the opinion of the victim. He demands more money. The criminal has a new set of choices: pay the higher penalty, make a counter-offer of something other than money, or lose his hand. He no longer has the option of paying the original penalty established by the judges. The victim has overruled the judges on the question of the appropriate monetary penalty.

Third, the judges impose a monetary penalty. The victim is outraged. He believes that the criminal should lose his hand, just as he lost his. The judges then go to the criminal. You must lose your hand, the victim says. Do you wish to offer the victim more money than we determined originally, or offer something other than money? The criminal makes his decision. If he decides to offer more money or another non-monetary option, he has only one opportunity to persuade the victim. If the victim refuses to accept the counter-offer, the criminal loses his hand.

By allowing the victim to demand different compensation — money or service rather than physical mutilation, or more money than the judges have imposed, or physical mutilation rather than money — the proposed restitution process allows subjective value to assert itself. The *victim* determines whether or not the judges have really offered him what his loss is worth to him personally. If he thinks he is being cheated, he can demand that his enemy pay more or suffer the same physical loss. The *criminal* also has the right to substitute the loss of an appendage, if the judges determine that he should lose the appendage, rather than pay what he believes is an excessive economic demand by the victim, if the demand is higher than the judges originally set.

The Bible does not anywhere indicate that the criminal has any legal, formal ability to overturn the final decision of the highest civil court of appeal. If the judges impose a particular penalty — mutilation, for example — and the victim is satisfied, then the criminal has no formal right of appeal. He cannot override the decision of the judges. But in fact he really does have the indirect ability to appeal — an appeal through the victim. He or his representatives can approach the victim with a counter-proposal. "Look, I would be willing to pay 100 ounces of gold if you would appeal the decision of the judges to have me mutilated." If this is satisfactory to the victim, he then appeals the decision, and the criminal agrees to the new terms of restitution. The judges are not allowed to overturn this mutually agreed-upon form of restitution.

If the court sets an economic penalty, and the victim agrees, the criminal still has a legal, formal ability to substitute his own mutilation for the economic restitution. He can demand the explicit physical sanction of the law: *lex talionis*. This means that the law upholds his right to demand the punishment specified by God. Bargaining is legitimate, but both the victim and the criminal can insist on the specified penalty. If the victim insists on physical multilation, the criminal has no choice. If the criminal insists on physical mutilition, the victim has no choice. Bargaining, however, is likely.

By establishing the three-way system of establishing penalties — judges, victim, and convicted criminal — the judicial system receives a means of making *objective* approximations of the inescapably *subjective* "eye for eye" standard — subjective to both victim and criminal. By permitting subjective estimations of loss by both the victim and the criminal, the judges find a way to offer compensation to the victim that he believes is comparable to the crime. The criminal, however, is allowed to counter-offer a different, economic form of restitution penalty if he believes that the cost of a physical penalty is too high.

Conclusion

My discussion of the possible outworkings of the "eye for eye" passage should not be understood as the last word on the subject. It is, however, a "first word." I want readers to understand that the biblical justice system is just, workable, and effective. The *lex talionis* should not be dismissed as some sort of peculiar juridical testament of a long-defunct primitive agricultural society. What the Bible spells out as judicially binding is vastly superior to anything offered by modern humanism in the name of civic justice.

The problems in dealing with the actual imposition of the *lex talionis* principle are great. The history of the people of God testifies to these difficulties. We have few if any examples of Christian societies that have attempted to impose the "eye for eye" principle literally. The basic principle is clear: *the punishment should fit the crime.* By allowing the victim to demand restitution in the form pleasing to him, and by allowing the criminal to counter-offer something more pleasing to him, the penalty comes close to matching the effects of the crime, as assessed by the victim.

Each party gets to make one offer. If the victim offers a choice between penalties, the criminal chooses which one he prefers, or can offer something completely different. If the victim specifies one and only one penalty, mutilation, the criminal is entitled to counter-offer. If the victim specifies only a money payment, but the criminal prefers mutilation on an "eye for eye" basis, then he has the right to choose mutilation.

The judges can establish the original restitution payment, whether physical or economic, but the two affected parties should have the final determination. This places limits on the State. The economic assets involved in this auction process are transferred (or retained) by the person who is more concerned with economic capital than with physical mutilation. In this way, biblical justice is furthered.

The modern Western world has not imposed deliberate, permanent physical mutilation on violent criminals. These criminals, when convicted, have been imprisoned. They have been compelled to pay fines to the State. In very few cases have they been compelled to make monetary restitution to the victims. The result has been escalating violence against private citizens, as well as the escalating power of the State.

Biblical law imposes penalties on violent criminals that tend to reduce the amount of violent crime. Biblical penalties encourage criminals to count the cost in advance. In the case of "crimes of passion," the convicted passionate criminals would be reminded of the benefits of self-control. That stump at the end of an arm is a better reminder than a string tied around a finger. So is the loss of several years' worth of savings, or several years as an indentured servant. What men sow, that shall they also reap (Gal. 6:7-8). A godly society's criminal justice system, organized around the *lex talionis* principle, provides criminals with a glimpse of (or preliminary down payment to) this cosmic principle of justice.

7

THE RANSOM FOR A LIFE

If an ox gore a man or a woman, that they die: then the ox shall be surely stoned, and his flesh shall not be eaten; but the owner of the ox shall be quit. But if the ox were wont to push [gore] with his horn in time past, and it hath been testified to his owner, and he hath not kept him in, but that he hath killed a man or a woman; the ox shall be stoned, and his owner also shall be put to death. If there be laid on him a sum of money, then he shall give for the ransom of his life whatsoever is laid upon him. Whether he have gored a son, or have gored a daughter, according to this judgment shall it be done unto him (Ex. 21:28-31).

The Bible tells us that we live in a universe which was created by God at the beginning of time and history, and that this world is sustained by Him, moment by moment. The doctrines of creation and providence are therefore linked. The universe which God created, He presently sustains. We live in a world of cosmic personalism.[1] God's answer to Job, beginning in Chapter 38 and continuing through Chapter 40, presents a summary of the total control of all events by God.

In such a world, men cannot escape full responsibility for their actions. God holds them responsible for everything they think, say, and do. "But I say unto you, That every idle word that men shall speak, they shall give account thereof in the day of judgment" (Matt. 12:36). "But I say unto you, That whosoever looketh on a woman to lust after her hath committed adultery

---

1. Gary North, *The Dominion Covenant: Genesis* (2nd ed.; Tyler, Texas: Institute for Christian Economics, 1987), ch. 1.

with her already in his heart" (Matt. 5:28). Everything people do is done within a personally sustained, God-ordained universe (Rom. 9). They succeed or fail in terms of God's decree. They run to God ethically, or they run away from God unethically; they cannot run away from Him metaphysically. God is everywhere; there is no escape: "Whither shall I go from thy spirit? Or whither shall I flee from thy presence? If I ascend up into heaven, thou art there: if I make my bed in hell, behold, thou art there" (Ps. 139:7-8). "Am I a God at hand, saith the LORD, and not a God afar off? Can any hide himself in secret places that I shall not see him? saith the LORD. Do not I fill heaven and earth? saith the LORD" (Jer. 23:23-24).

Human action is always personal, never impersonal. First, it is personal primarily with respect to God. God is the ultimate, inescapable fact of man's environment, not sticks and stones. Second, human action is secondarily personal with respect to oneself: one's goals, choices, and assets. Third, human action is personal with respect to other human actors, both as individuals and as covenantal groups. Fourth, human action is personal with respect to the environment, which God has created and presently sustains, and over which He has placed mankind. Man's responsibility extends *upward* to God, *inward* to himself, *outward* toward other men, and *downward* toward the environment. It is comprehensive responsibility. When we speak of "responsible men," we should have this four-part, comprehensive responsibility in mind, not just one or two aspects. A person may appear to be responsible in one or two areas of his life, but whether he likes it or not, or whether he is adequately instructed or not, he is covenantally responsible before God in all four ways, and he will be held totally accountable for his thoughts and actions on the day of judgment.

Though God holds each person fully responsible, no agency of human government has the power to do so. This is why we must affirm as Christians that with respect to the decisions of human governments regarding men's personal responsibility, there must always be *limited liability*. No agency of human government is omniscient; none possesses the ability of God to read the human heart or to assess damages perfectly. We must wait for perfect justice until the day of final judgment. To insist on perfect justice from human government is to divinize that agency. It will also lead to its bankruptcy and the destruction of justice.[2]

Responsibility: Upward and Downward

Man's responsibility outward and downward is seen in this section of Exodus. A man owes protection to his fellow man, which includes women, as the passage at the beginning of the chapter clearly points out. This passage also teaches that "dumb animals" under a man's personal administration are responsible, through him, for their actions. They are responsible upward to mankind through their master, as well as outward to other beasts through their master (Ex. 21:35). Human society enforces sanctions against lawless behavior, whether in the animals or their owners. Domesticated animals are responsible to mankind through their owners, and therefore society holds the owners responsible for those animals under their control. Animals that are not domesticated — neither trained nor tamed — are to be under physical restraint, at the owner's expense.

The shedding of man's blood is illegal, either by man or beast. "But flesh with the life thereof, which is the blood thereof, shall ye not eat. And surely your blood of your lives will I require; at the hand of every beast will I require it, and at the hand of man; at the hand of every man's brother will I require the life of man. Whoso sheddeth man's blood, by man shall his blood be shed: for in the image of God made he man" (Gen. 9:4-6). The ox that gores a man to death cannot escape the sanctions of biblical law. Neither can other man-killing animals. In the case of the ox, the animal is presumed to be domesticated, for if it were dangerous, the owner would be required to restrain it. The owner becomes legally liable because what was, in fact, a dangerous animal had been publicly treated by him as if it had been safe. *The owner deliberately or inadvertently misinformed the public about the risks.* He did not place restraints on it. The victim died because of the neglect

---

2. Gary North, *Moses and Pharaoh: Dominion Religion vs. Power Religion* (Tyler, Texas: Institute for Christian Economics, 1985), ch. 19: "Imperfect Justice."

of the owner. The owner should have placed restraints on the beast, or else he should have placed warnings for bystanders. Why shouldn't bystanders recognize that the animal is dangerous? Why are they considered judicially innocent? Don't people know that bulls charge people and gore them? They do know, which is why the Hebrew usage, as in English, indicates that "ox" in this case must refer to a castrated male bovine. The castrated beast is not normally aggressive. It is easier to bring under dominion through training. In this sense, a castrated male bovine is unnaturally subordinate.

As an aside, the question of unnatural subordination (lack of male dominion) can also be raised with respect to the prohibition against eunuchs worshipping in the congregation (Deut. 23:1). Presumably, this was because eunuchs could not produce a family, and to that extent they were cut off from the future. Rushdoony writes (unfortunately using the present tense): "Because eunuchs are without posterity, they have no interest in the future, and hence no citizenship."[3] This was true enough in ancient Israel, where land tenure, bloodlines, political participation (elders in the gates), and the national covenant were intermixed. The New Testament forever abolished this biological-geographical intermixture. Spiritual adoption[4] became forthrightly the foundation of heavenly citizenship (Phil. 3:20), and therefore the only basis of church membership. The baptism of the Ethiopian eunuch by Philip the deacon (Acts 8)[5] indicates that the Old Testament rule lost all meaning, once Jesus, the promised seed, had come and completed His work.

The goring ox is also judicially guilty. He is therefore treated as a responsible moral agent — not to the extent that a man is, of course, but responsible nonetheless. We train our domestic animals. We beat them and reward them. Modern scientists call this

---

3. R. J. Rushdoony, *The Institutes of Biblical Law* (Nutley, New Jersey: Craig Press, 1973), p. 100.

4. John 1:12; Romans 8:15; Galatians 4:5; Ephesians 1:5.

5. That a deacon performed this baptism, as well as many others in Samaria, creates a presently unsolved theological problem for all denominations that specify elders as the only ordained church officers with a lawful call to baptize.

training "behavior modification." In other words, we deal with them on the assumption that they can learn, remember, and discipline themselves. Anyone who has ever seen a dog that looks guilty, which slinks around as if it has done something it knows is wrong, can safely guess that the dog *has* done something wrong. It may take time to find out what, but the search must begin. The dog *knows*.

An Ethically Unclean Beast

The goring ox is to be treated as if it were an unclean beast. It has become an ethically unclean beast. Because of its ethical uncleanness, it is still subject to this punishment in New Testament times, despite the New Testament's abandonment of the category of physical and ritual uncleanness. James Jordan comments on the biblical meaning of unclean animals:

> All unclean animals *resemble the serpent* in three ways. They eat "dirt" (rotting carrion, manure, garbage). They move in contact with "dirt" (crawling on their bellies, fleshy pads of their feet in touch with the ground, no scales to keep their skin from contact with their watery environment). They revolt against human dominion, killing men or other beasts. Under the symbolism of the Old Covenant, such Satanic beasts represent the Satanic nations (Lev. 20:22-26), for animals are "images" of men. To eat Satanic animals, under the Old Covenant, was to "eat" the Satanic lifestyle, to "eat" death and rebellion.
>
> The ox is a clean animal. The heifer and the pre-pubescent bullock have sweet temperaments, and can be sacrificed for human sin, for their gentle, non-violent dispositions reflect the character of Jesus Christ. When the bullock enters puberty, however, his temperament changes for the worse. He becomes ornery, testy, and sometimes downright vicious. Many a man has lost his life to a goring bull. *The change from bullock to bull can be seen as analogous to the fall of man*, at least potentially. If the ox rises up and gores a man, he becomes unclean, fallen. . . .
>
> The *unnaturalness* of an animal's killing a man is only highlighted in the case of a clean, domesticated beast like the ox. Such an ox, by its actions, becomes unclean, so that its flesh may not be eaten. . . .
>
> The fact that the animal is stoned indicates that the purpose of the law is not simply to rid the earth of a dangerous beast. Stoning in the Bible is the normal means of capital punishment for men. Its application to the animal here shows that animals are to be held accountable to

some degree for their actions. It is also a visual sign of what happens when a clean covenant man rebels against authority and kills men. Stoning is usually understood to represent the judgment of God, since the Christ is "the rock" and the "stone" which threatens to fall upon men and destroy them (Matt. 21:44). In line with this, the community of believers is often likened to stones, used for building God's Spiritual Temple, and so forth. In stoning, each member of the community hurls a rock representing himself and his affirmation of God's judgment. The principle of stoning, then, affirms that the judgment is God's; the application of stoning affirms the community's assent and participation in that judgment.[6]

Covenantal Hierarchy and Guilty Animals

"But if the ox were wont to push [gore] with his horn in time past, and it hath been testified to his owner, and he hath not kept him in, but that he hath killed a man or a woman; the ox shall be stoned, and his owner also shall be put to death." The owner had been warned that the beast was dangerous. (We shall consider in the next section what constitutes valid evidence of habitual goring.) He had withheld this information from the victim. How? By refusing to place adequate restraints on the beast. The victim had every reason to believe that the ox was fully domesticated, meaning that it was *self-disciplined* under the general authority of its owner. Again, it is *self-government under God's law* which is the crucial form of government.

The Bible is unique in establishing the judicial requirement of self-government to beasts in general. At the very least, any beast is to be held accountable if it kills a human being. (Maimonides made one exception regarding a domesticated beast: it is not responsible if it kills a heathen, meaning a gentile.)[7] Since the days of Noah, they have had the fear of man placed in them by

---

6. James B. Jordan, *The Law of the Covenant: An Exposition of Exodus 21-23* (Tyler, Texas: Institute for Christian Economics, 1984), pp. 122-24.

7. "If an ox kills a person anywhere, whether an adult or a minor, a slave or a freeman, it incurs death by stoning whether it is innocuous or forewarned. However, if it kills a heathen, it is exempt in accordance with heathen law." Moses Maimonides, *The Book of Torts*, vol. 11 of *The Code of Maimonides*, 14 vols. (New Haven, Connecticut: Yale University Press, [1180] 1954), "Laws Concerning Damage by Chattels," Chapter Ten, Section One, p. 36.

God (Gen. 9:2). A beast must somehow suppress this fear — an internal warning from God — in order to kill a man. Beasts are responsible creatures; they are to be hunted down and killed for this form of rebellion. Some domesticated beasts are responsible outward to other beasts, upward to man, and, through their masters, upward to God.[8]

The Bible deals with the liability problem by making owners personally responsible for the actions of their animals. If their animals cause no problems, there will be no penalties. The more dangerous the animals, the more risky the ownership. Clearly, Exodus 21:30 is a case-law application of a general principle regarding the responsibilities of ownership. The principle can be extended to ownership of other animals besides oxen, and also to related instances of personal financial liability for damages in cases not involving animals.

The law makes it clear that the owner may not profit in any way from the evil act of the beast. He is not permitted to salvage anything of value. The beast is stoned — the same death penalty that a guilty human would receive — and the owner does not receive the carcass. Its flesh may not be eaten (v. 28). The beast is treated as if it were a human being. Its evil act brings death — not the normal killing of oxen, which allows owners to eat the flesh or sell it to those who will, but the death of the guilty. The guilty beast is no longer part of the dominion covenant. It can no longer serve the economic purposes of men, except as an example. It has to be cut off in the midst of time, just as a murderer is to be cut off in the midst of time.

Why Stoning?

J. J. Finkelstein discusses at considerable length the question of the stoning of the ox. While similar laws regarding the goring ox are found in many ancient Near Eastern law codes, the Hebrew law is unique: it specifically requires stoning of the ox that

---

8. The incomparable biblical example of upward responsibility of an animal toward man is Balaam's ass. "And the ass said unto Balaam, Am not I thine ass, upon which thou hast ridden ever since I was thine unto this day? Was I ever wont to do so unto thee? And he said, Nay" (Num. 22:30).

kills any human being, even a slave. Finkelstein concludes that this requirement testified to the ox's crime as being of a different order than the crime of its negligent owner. It points to *treason*, a rebellion against the cosmic order, a crime comparable to a Hebrew's enticing of a family member to worship foreign gods, which was also to be punished by stoning (Deut. 13:6-11). It is an offense against the whole community, and the whole community is therefore involved in the execution. "The real crime of the ox is that by killing a human being — whether out of viciousness or by an involuntary motion — it has objectively committed a *de facto* insurrection against the hierarchic order established by Creation: Man was designated by God 'to rule over the fish of the sea, the fowl of the skies, the cattle, the earth, and all creatures that roam over the earth' (Gen. 1:26, 28). Simply by its behavior — and it is vital here to stress that intention is immaterial; the guilt is objective — the ox has, albeit involuntarily, performed an act whose effect amounts to 'treason.' It has acted against man, its superior in the hierarchy of Creation, as man acts against God when violating the Sabbath or when practicing idolatry. It is precisely for this reason that the flesh of the ox may not be consumed."[9]

Finkelstein traces this biblical law forward into the Middle Ages. In medieval Europe, trials for animals were actually held by the civil government. Defense lawyers in secular courts were hired at public expense to defend accused beasts. Witnesses were called. Guilty animals were destroyed as a civic act. In some cases, they were publicly hanged.[10] Few people know about this side of European history, although specialized historians have known all along. Some of the great minds of Western philosophy, including Aquinas and Leibniz, attempted to explain this practice rationally.[11] Yet the specialized historians have generally remained silent, and few professional historians have ever heard of such

---

9. J. J. Finkelstein, *The Ox That Gored* (Philadelphia: American Philosophical Society, 1981), p. 28.

10. A painting of the hanging of a pig in Normandy in 1386 appears on the cover of the 1987 reprint of E. P. Evans' 1906 book, *The Criminal Prosecution and Capital Punishment of Animals* (London: Faber & Faber). The painting shows the pig dressed in a jacket.

11. Nicholas Humphrey, Foreword, *ibid.*, p. xviii.

goings-on, nor are they aware that in ancient Athens, the courts tried inanimate objects, such as statues that had fallen and killed someone. If convicted, the object was banished from the city.[12] Why the silence? Why don't these stories get into the textbooks? As Humphrey asks: "Why were we never told? Why were we taught so many dreary facts of history at school, *and not taught these?*"[13]

He answers his own question: modern historians can make little sense out of these facts. There seems to be no logical explanation for the way our ancestors treated guilty animals. What is a guilty animal, anyway — a legally convicted guilty animal? How can such events be explained? Finkelstein cites the theory of legal scholar Hans Kelsen that such a practice points to the "animism" of early medieval Europe, since to try an animal in court obviously points to a theory of the animal's possession of a soul.[14] Kelsen says that this reflects early Europe's older primitivism. Finkelstein then attacks Kelsen's naive approach to an understanding of this practice. In contrast to primitive societies, it is only in the West that such legal sanctions against offending animals have been enforced. "*Only* in Western society, or in societies based on the hierarchic classification of the phenomena of the universe that is biblical in its origins, do we see the curious practice of trying and executing animals as if they were human criminals."[15] Then he makes a profound observation: "What Kelsen has misunderstood here — and in this he is typical of most Western commentators — is the sense, widespread in primitive societies (as, indeed in civilized societies of non-Western derivation), that the extra-human universe is *autonomous* and that this autonomy or integrity is a quality inherent in every species of thing."[16] Because Western society long denied such autonomy to the crea-

---

12. W. W. Hyde, "The prosecution of animals and lifeless things in the middle ages and modern times," *University of Pennsylvania Law Review* (1916). Finkelstein is somewhat suspicious of these accounts.

13. Humphrey, "Foreword," p. xv.

14. Finkelstein, *Ox That Gored*, p. 48. He cites Kelsen, *General Theory of Law and State* (1961), pp. 3-4.

15. Finkelstein, *op. cit.*, p. 48.

16. *Ibid.*, p. 51.

tion, it has in the past adhered to the biblical requirement of destroying killer animals; in Europe, they were even given a formal trial.

Expiation

What none of the scholars discusses is the need for expiation, a need which is both psychological and covenantal. The animal's owner and the community at large, through its representatives, must publicly disassociate themselves from the killer beast. They must demonstrate publicly that they in no way sanction the beast's murderous act. There is an Old Testament precedent for the need for this sort of formal expiation: the requirement in ancient Israel that civic officials sacrifice a heifer when they could not solve a murder that had taken place in a nearby field (Deut. 21:1-9). "So shalt thou put away the guilt of innocent blood from among you, when thou shalt do that which is right in the sight of the LORD" (v. 9). In New Testament times we no longer need to sacrifice animals (Heb. 9, 10), but the need for formal procedures for the expiation of the crime of man-killing is still basic. To ignore this need is to unleash the furies of the human heart.

The medieval world understood this to some degree, however imperfectly; the modern humanistic West does not understand it at all, and seeks to deny it by abolishing any trace of such ritual practices. We cannot make sense of the so-called "primitive folk practices" of medieval and early modern Western history that dealt with this fundamental civic and personal need, and so we refuse even to discuss them in our history books. We execute murderers in private when we execute them at all. (In the State of Massachusetts in the early 1970's, the median jail term served by a murderer was under two and a half years.)[17] Humanist intellectuals in the non-Communist West seek to persuade the public that society is itself ritually guilty for maintaining the "barbarous" practice of capital punishment. Meanwhile, in the year of our Lord 1988, in the streets of southern California, motorists were shooting each other during traffic jams, and teenage

---

17. James Q. Wilson, *Thinking About Crime* (New York: Basic Books, 1974), p. 186.

gang members were executing at least one victim per day.[18] God is not mocked at zero cost to the mockers.

Personal Liability and Self-Discipline

The convicted owner of the habitually goring ox in Exodus 21:28 implicitly misinformed the ox's victim. He had known that the ox had been violent in the past, yet he did not take steps to restrain it. The beast was roaming around as if it had no prior record of violence. The victim did not recognize the danger involved in being near the beast.

The Bible does not reveal in these passages regarding goring oxen the evidence that constitutes judicially binding prior knowledge. What kind of information did the owner have to possess in order for the court to declare him guilty? The rabbinical specialists in Jewish law said that the animal had to have gored someone or other animals on three occasions before the owner became personally liable.[19] Maimonides spelled it out in even greater detail: any domesticated animal must first kill three heathen (gentiles), plus one Israelite; or kill three fatally ill Israelites, plus one in good health; or kill three people at one time, or kill three animals at one time.[20] This is an excessive number of prior infractions in order to activate capital sanctions. Subsequent victims need more protection than these Talmudic rules would provide. It is far more reasonable to conclude that a single prior conviction should suffice to identify the beast as dangerous.

We know that an ox that had gored another ox had to be sold by its owner to a third party (Ex. 21:35). Thus, to be the owner of an ox that had been convicted of goring, he would have had to go out and repurchase the offending ox, or else he is the person who bought the offending ox. In either case, he had taken active steps to buy a known offender. To have done this, and then to have refused to take active measures to restrain it, should make him legally vulnerable to the charge of negligence.

---

18. An estimated 80,000 gang members were in the county of Los Angeles.

19. Albeck, *Jewish Law*, col. 322.

20. Maimonides, *Torts*, "Laws Concerning Damage by Chattels," Chapter Ten, Section Three, p. 36.

Would other evidence rather than a prior conviction be a sufficient warning? What if neighbors had reported the beast to the authorities? If the authorities had issued a formal warning to the owner, would this serve as evidence of its status as a habitual offender? If we answer yes, then this raises the issue of "innocent until proven guilty." There had been no proven evidence against the beast. Perhaps neighbors were hostile to the ox's owner, and reported false information. On the other hand, perhaps they were telling the truth, and the owner was negligent in not taking steps to restrain the ox.

The Double Witness Principle vs. the Messianic State

The easiest way to resolve the issue is to rely on the biblical principle of the double witness (Deut. 17:6). If two different witnesses each reports a different infraction — neither of the infractions had a double witness — then the authorities must issue a warning to the owner. This formal warning can then serve as evidence in a future trial.

The differing criteria of evidence should be discussed in terms of the differing impact of the crime and differences in the resulting liability: the death of a human being vs. the death of someone else's ox. Maimonides fails to recognize that the formal criteria that govern evidence of liability in the case of an ox that kills another ox are less rigorous because the crime is less damaging. In a case of an ox that slays another ox, biblical law does not require that a formal warning be given by the authorities to the owner; prior general knowledge is sufficient to convict: "Or if it be known that the ox hath used to push [gore] in time past, and his owner hath not kept him in; he shall surely pay ox for ox; and the dead shall be his own" (Ex. 21:36). *Public knowledge rather than a formal complaint to the civil authorities is sufficient to convict the owner in this instance*. It can be safely assumed by the judge that if the public knew about the beast's habits, then the owner must have known. In contrast, the potential liability of the owner is far greater when an ox kills a human being. It is too dangerous to allow the judge to make his ruling in terms of the assumption of general knowledge. By requiring more rigorous standards of evidence, biblical law restrains the discretionary authority of the State's representative in the more serious cases of negligence. This restrains the State.

Here is the viewpoint of the modern humanistic State: the State as an agency that possesses the judicial authority and obligation to search men's hearts, and to render formal judgment in terms of its findings. This view of State power asserts that the State possesses an ability that only God possesses: the ability to know man's heart. The prophet Jeremiah asked rhetorically: "The heart is deceitful above all things, and desperately wicked: who can know it?" (Jer. 17:9). His answer was clear: "I the LORD search the heart, I try the reins, even to give every man according to his ways, and according to the fruit of his doings" (Jer. 17:10). The human judge can make causal connections based on public evidence, but he cannot search the defendant's heart. Any assertion to the contrary necessarily involves an attempt to divinize man, and in all likelihood, divinize man's major judicial representative, the State.

The Goring of a Slave or a Child

"If the ox shall push [gore] a manservant or a maidservant; he shall give unto their master thirty shekels of silver, and the ox shall be stoned" (Ex. 21:32). Normally, the death penalty could be imposed on the owner of the ox. In this case, however, the penalty was fixed by law: 30 shekels of silver.

The wording here is peculiar. To "push" means, in this instance, to kill. In verse 29, "push" did not mean to kill. "But if the ox were wont to push with his horn in time past, and it hath been testified to his owner, and he hath not kept him in. . . ." Had "to push" meant "to kill," the ox would have been executed upon conviction. An ox that killed someone was stoned to death (v. 28). Thus, "push" in verse 29 had to mean something other than killing. But with respect to servants, the word "push" or "gore" is used in the sense of "gore to death." This is why the ox is executed: a human being has died.

Why the comparatively small penalty?[21] Why is the death of

---

21. Thirty pieces of silver were a lot of money in terms of what they could buy, but not compared to what the victim's heirs could normally impose.

a servant dealt with less severely? Because the servant's owner has not suffered a loss comparable to the loss suffered by the heirs of a free man or woman. He has lost part of an investment in human capital — one which he would have had to part with after a set term of years. He has not suffered the loss of a relative. The primary issue is covenantal. The owner has not suffered a covenantal loss; he has suffered only an economic loss. He is not entitled to place penalties on the owner of the goring ox larger than the economic penalty specified by law.

If a male bondservant had brought a wife and children into the household of the owner, they would now go free, which serves them as a form of compensation. The master would have recouped his investment from the owner of the ox, thereby freeing the slave's heirs from further service. What if the deceased bondservant had married after becoming a bondservant? In this instance, the heirs probably would have had the option of either remaining as servants in the owner's household or going free. Whether they would go free or not would depend on the size of the penalty payment to the bondservant-owner, compared to what he had paid for the bondservant. If the death occurred shortly before the bondservant was to have gone free, then the penalty payment would have constituted an overpayment, and the extra money probably would have functioned as a release price for the wife and children of the bondservant. But if the penalty payment was approximately what the owner had spent to pay off the bondservant's debt — the original cause of his going into slavery — then the bondservant's family would have remained with the owner, as specified in Exodus 21:4.

An interesting connection can be seen between the death of Christ on the cross and the death of the gored servant. James B. Jordan has commented on this connection: "As we have seen, our Lord Jesus Christ was born into the world as a homeborn slave-son, for His incarnation was His ear's circumcision. On the cross, he was made sin for us, and thus came under condemnation of death. He became an abject slave, that we might be elevated into the status of adopted slave-sons. He was killed by the wild beasts, the lions of paganism, and the apostate unclean goring bulls of

Israel: 'Many bulls have surrounded Me; strong ones from Bashan have encircled me. They open wide their mouth at me, as a ravening and a roaring lion. . . . Save Me from the lion's mouth; and from the horns of the wild oxen Thou dost answer Me' (Ps. 22:12, 13, 21). Thus, the price given for Christ's death was the price of the gored slave, thirty pieces of silver (Matt. 26:15). At His resurrection, however, our Lord overcame the bulls and trampled on the silver for which He was sold: 'Rebuke the beasts of the reeds, the herd of bulls with the calves of the peoples, trampling under foot the pieces of silver; He has scattered the people who delight in war' (Ps. 68:30). Thus, Judas found no joy in his silver, and it was used to buy a burying field for dead strangers, pagans destroyed by the wrath of God (Matt. 27:2-10)."[22]

The Goring of a Child

"Whether he have gored a son, or have gored a daughter, according to this judgment shall it be done unto him" (Ex. 21:31). This is an important biblical principle: the imposition of a fine rather than the execution of the ox's owner or his child (a pagan practice of the ancient Near East). The Bible places this example under the general rule that allows the substitution of a fine for the death of the owner. This means that the evil practice of the ancient Near East, killing a man's child if he kills another man's child, is prohibited.[23] The Hammurabi Code specified: "If a builder constructed a house for a seignior, but did not make his work strong, with the result that the house which he built collapsed and so has caused the death of the owner of the house, that builder shall be put to death. If it has caused the death of a son of the owner of the house, they shall put the son of that builder to death."[24]

This sharp difference from Babylonian law would appear to

---

22. Jordan, *Law of the Covenant*, pp. 127-28.

23. Dale Patrick, *Old Testament Law* (Atlanta, Georgia: John Knox Press, 1985), p. 78.

24. Code Hammurabi, paragraphs 229-30. *Ancient Near Eastern Texts Relating to the Old Testament*, edited by James B. Pritchard (3rd ed.; Princeton, New Jersey: Princeton University Press, 1969), p. 176.

be an application of the principle of Deuteronomy 24:16: "The fathers shall not be put to death for the children, neither shall the children be put to death for the fathers: every man shall be put to death for his own sin."

Criminal Negligence

We know from the text that the ox's owner had been warned about the dangerous ox, yet he did nothing visibly to restrain it. Why would an owner neglect a warning from someone else regarding the threat of his ox to others? There are several possible reasons. First, he may not trust the judgment of the person bringing the warning. The beast may behave quite well in the owner's presence. Is he to trust the judgment of a stranger, and not trust his own personal experience? But once the warning is delivered, he is in jeopardy. If the beast injures someone, and the informant announces publicly that he had warned the owner, the owner becomes legally liable for the victim's suffering.[25]

The owner may be a procrastinator. He fully intended to place restraints on the ox, but he just never got around to it. This does not absolve him from full personal liability, but it does explain why he failed to take effective action.

Another reason for not restraining the ox is economics. It takes extra care and cost to keep an unruly beast under control. For example, over and over in colonial America, the town records reveal that owners of pigs, sheep, and cattle had disobeyed previous legislation requiring them to pen the beasts in or put rings in their noses. Apparently, the authorities were unable to gain compliance, for this complaint was continual and widespread throughout the seventeenth century.[26] The costs of supervising the animals or maintaining fences in good repair were just too high in the opinion of countless owners. Even putting a ring in the beasts'

---

25. Because a serious penalty could be imposed on the liable owner, the informant would have to have proof that he had, in fact, actually warned the owner of the beast's prior misconduct. Otherwise, the perjured testimony of one man could ruin the owner of a previously safe beast which then injured someone.

26. Carl Bridenbaugh, *Cities in the Wilderness: The First Century of Urban Life in America, 1625-1742* (New York: Capricorn, [1938] 1964), pp. 19, 167, 323.

noses, making it easier for others to put a rope through the ring and pull a beast home or to some other location, was simply too much trouble.[27] Boston imposed stiff fines on the owners of wandering animals, which helped to reduce the problem.[28]

In one case, the unwillingness or inability of a woman to control her wandering pig literally changed the political history of the United States. Litigation over the ownership of a wandering pig between Goodwoman ("Goodie") Sherman and the well-to-do Boston merchant, Robert Keayne, led in 1644 to a deadlock in the General Court (legislature) of Massachusetts between the deputies or direct representatives of the people (who favored Sherman) and magistrates (who favored Keayne). The result was the division of the two groups into separate legislative houses – the origin of bicameralism in America.[29] As Bridenbaugh notes, "The frequency with which the hog appears in town records is mute proof that despite many 'good and sufficient' measures the problem was never solved, and the bicameral legislature of Massachusetts remains a monument to its persistence."[30] Passing laws is not sufficient. Sanctions must be imposed that alter human behavior.

The Bible establishes the principle of cosmic personalism as the foundation of the universe.[31] There is no way that men can escape their responsibilities before God. Because biblical law recognizes this principle, it establishes the judicial principle of restitution to victims by the negligent. The general rule is: an eye for an eye, a life for a life.

---

27. In my research on my doctoral dissertation on colonial American Puritanism, I came across no case where an owner was executed for the act of his beast, nor do I recall locating an example where heavy restitution was paid to a victim.

28. Bridenbaugh, *Cities in the Wilderness*, p. 168.

29. On the "sow" incident, see Charles M. Andrews, *The Colonial Period of American History*, 4 vols., *The Settlements* (New Haven, Connecticut: Yale University Press, [1934] 1964), I, pp. 450-51. Cf. Gov. John Winthrop, *Winthrop's Journal: "History of New England,"* 1630-1649, edited by James Kendall Hosmer, 2 vols. (New York: Barnes & Noble, [1908] 1966), II, pp. 64-66, 120-21.

30. Bridenbaugh, *Cities in the Wilderness*, p. 19. I put a question mark in the margin of my book upon first reading it. I had not yet heard of the Keayne-Sherman conflict, and Bridenbaugh never explained what he meant. Scholars can sometimes be too cryptic.

31. North, *The Dominion Covenant: Genesis*, ch. 1.

Conclusion

The Bible affirms the principle of limited liability before men. The State is not God. It cannot know every aspect of historical causation. Neither can men. The State therefore cannot lawfully impose unlimited liability on those convicted of negligence, irrespective of their knowledge, decisions, and contractual arrangements.

In this unique instance, the case of a dangerous ox that kills a person, the guilty owner can legitimately escape death, though his beast cannot, because the victim's heirs are allowed to impose an economic restitution payment on the negligent individual.

8

THE PRINCIPLE OF LIMITED LIABILITY

If an ox gore a man or a woman, that they die: then the ox shall be surely stoned, and his flesh shall not be eaten; but the owner of the ox shall be quit. But if the ox were wont to push with his horn in time past, and it hath been testified to his owner, and he hath not kept him in, but that he hath killed a man or a woman; the ox shall be stoned, and his owner also shall be put to death. If there be laid on him a sum of money, then he shall give for the ransom of his life whatsoever is laid upon him. Whether he have gored a son, or have gored a daughter, according to this judgment shall it be done unto him (Ex. 21:28-31).

The Bible imposes liability on owners of animals known to be dangerous. Penalties are imposed that vary according to the nature of the infraction and the degree of prior knowledge by the owner. These penalties are intended to reduce uncertainty about potentially violent beasts. By extending the principle of legal liability, we can derive principles of liability for owners of inanimate objects.

Man is a limited creature. His knowledge is therefore limited. Because his knowledge is limited, God limits man's legal liability. Man is not to be judged by standards that could apply justly only to an omniscient being. If a State seeks to impose perfectionist standards of liability, the legal system will cease to function. It will begin to produce unjust decisions, and there will be an increase of uncertainty and also an increase of arbitrary decisions — precisely what biblical law is designed to prevent. Such judicial uncertainty would make economic decision-making prohibitively expensive. The economy would be threatened.

Consider the case of a potentially dangerous beast which broke its rope or knocked down a restraining fence in Old Testament Israel. The owner would be in the same position as a man who was using an axe which he thought was safe. The axe head flew off and killed someone. This was a case of accidental manslaughter. Immediately, the man would have fled to a city of refuge, in order to escape the dead man's avenger of blood. At that point, the avenger of blood would have demanded a trial, and the elders of the city would have held it. If judged guilty of premeditated murder, the guilty man would have been delivered up to the avenger. If judged innocent, he would have had to remain in the city until the death of the high priest (Num. 35:22-28).

A Broken Rope

Consider the dangerous beast in our day which breaks his restraining rope and kills someone. The victim's heirs sue the owner. They argue that the owner should have used a more sturdy rope. If convicted, the owner then has to prove that the rope's manufacturer was the true culprit. The court then investigates the rope manufacturer. Should he be held liable? To defend himself, he charges the hemp growers with selling a substandard product. Each stage in the case gets more technical and more expensive. The quest for perfect justice is suicidal. It increases the costs of litigation to such an extent that real victims cannot ever afford to attain restitution, for the case never ends. The courts become clogged with expensive cases that can never be resolved by anyone other than God. Only the lawyers profit. God's law does not exist in order to create employment for lawyers.

The State that attempts to impose standards of personal responsibility that imply omniscience and omnipotence will eventually make life impossible. Sometime before civilization grinds to a strangled halt, however, the bureaucrats will back down or else there will be a revolution which removes these messianic standards of personal and corporate responsibility from the law books. The price of perfect liability laws, like the price of perfect justice, or the price of a risk-free society, is death.[1] Such justice will be

---

1. It should be understood that the selection of "socially appropriate risk" is like any other selection process: it involves subjective valuation and "aggregation" through politics and market forces of the "socially appropriate" mixture of risk and productivity.

available only at the end of history. At that point, it will not only be available, it will be inescapable.

This passage therefore has implications for the concept so popular in modern economies, that of *limited liability*. The modern corporation is protected by limited liability laws. In case of its bankruptcy, creditors cannot collect anything from the owners of the corporation's shares of ownership. The corporation is liable only to the extent of its separate, corporate assets.

Legitimate Limitations

Certain kinds of economic transactions that limit the liability of either party, should one of them go bankrupt, are valid. For example, a bank that makes a loan to a church to construct a building cannot collect payment from individual members, should the church be unable to meet its financial obligations. It can repossess the building, of course, something that few banks relish doing. It is bad publicity, and a church building is a kind of white elephant in the real estate world: only churches buy them, and almost all of them are short of funds. This is why bankers prefer to avoid making loans to churches, other things being even remotely equal.[2]

The same sorts of limited liability arrangements ought to be legally valid for other kinds of associations, including profit-

---

See Mary Douglas and Aaron Wildavsky, *Risk and Culture: An Essay on the Selection of Technological and Environmental Dangers* (Berkeley: University of California Press, 1982).

2. A wise banker would recommend to the church's officers that church members refinance their homes or assume debt using other forms of collateral, and then *donate* the borrowed money to the church. This ties the loans to personal collateral that a banker can repossess without appearing to be heartless. It makes church members personally responsible for repayment. (Co-signed notes are also acceptable from the banker's point of view, but questionable biblically: e.g., prohibitions against "surety.") Members cannot escape their former financial promises by walking away from the church. It also keeps the church out of debt as an institution, which is godly testimony concerning the evil of debt (Rom. 13:8a). Since a loan is not taxable to the recipient as income (in U.S. tax laws), and since repayments on interest for home loans are tax-deductible, and since donations to a church are tax-deductible, the borrowers receive tax advantages through this arrangement. The interest payments would not constitute a tax advantage if the church borrowed the money, since income to churches is not normally taxable. This approach is illegal in the state of Texas, however; it is illegal to refinance your home in Texas, except to make home improvements — a very stupid law that is left over from the older "populist" mentality.

seeking corporations,[3] limited partnerships, or other private citizens who can get other economic actors to agree voluntarily to some sort of limited liability arrangement. For example, a "daredevil" who accepts a very dangerous job, such as putting out an oil well fire, is probably willing to release his employer from all legal damages in case he gets killed. He is paid more than a normal wage for his services in order to compensate him for the risk. A normally dangerous job, such as uranium mining or handling radioactive substances, may carry with it an economic obligation to release the employer from any responsibility for injury or death. The very existence of the danger keeps other workers from applying, thereby lowering the competition and keeping economic wages higher than would have been the case, had the job been safe. The laborer is compensated fairly. He gets more money for being willing to bear greater risk. Without the limited liability provision, the employer might not be willing to employ anyone. The dominion assignment might not be completed in this field until some new technological development reduces risk. Some tasks in life cannot be actuarially insured at a profit, but this does not mean that they should not be performed by people who are aware of the risks and who agree to "self-insure" themselves.[4]

---

3. Robert Hessen, *In Defense of the Corporation* (Stanford, California: Hoover Institution, 1979). I disagree with R. J. Rushdoony's condemnation of limited liability. See Rushdoony, *Politics of Guilt and Pity* (Fairfax, Virginia: Thoburn Press, [1970] 1978), Part III, ch. 8: "Limited Liability and Unlimited Money." What persuaded me that he is incorrect here was a careful consideration of the legal implications of the imposition of unlimited personal liability of church members for the decisions of pastors and church officers. Could the church function if every member were made potentially liable to the limits of his capital for the illegal activity of the church's officers?

4. After the fatal explosion of the launch vehicle of the Challenger space shuttle in January of 1986, it was revealed that the seven military-employed "astronauts" had been required by the government to forego all but minimal life insurance benefits as a condition of participating in the launch. The one civilian, a school teacher, had been given anonymously a one-trip life insurance policy for a million dollars, insured by Lloyd's of London. Months later, the heirs of four of the astronauts received payments totalling $7.7 million, or about $1.9 million per family. (Gold: $350/oz.) The federal government paid 40% of this, and the firm that constructed the rocket paid 60%. This was a political decision; the actual figures paid were kept secret by the government, and only became public fifteen months later when legal action was taken by seven news organizations. *New York Times* (March 8, 1988). It is not yet public knowledge what was paid to the heirs of the other three astronauts.

Other Cases

On the other hand, consider the case of citizens who once lived near an atomic bomb test site. They were assured by government officials (who were presumed to be knowledgeable and therefore were legally responsible) that there were no excessive risks involved in remaining where they were, when there is evidence that these officials knew or should have known about the risks. The citizens who sustain long-term radiation-related injuries as a result of the explosion have every reason to sue and collect from the federal government, even if those officials cannot be located today, or are dead. It is the policy of deliberate misinformation ("disinformation") concerning risks which is the issue. The civil government cannot escape these responsibilities. "I was just following orders," is no excuse for some bureaucrat's deliberately misinforming the civilian victims.

There are other cases that are more difficult to assess. A chemical firm buries toxic wastes. It uses means that are at the time of burial believed to be safe by private health experts or government health officials — people whose tasks are part of the quarantine function of the civil government (cf. Lev. 13, 14). The firm's managers have not deliberately misinformed anyone. Neither have public health officials. They acted with good intentions to the best of their ability, according to the best technical knowledge generally available at the time of the decision. They are like a man who ties up a dangerous beast with a rope generally believed to meet standards of strength, but which snaps unexpectedly, allowing the beast to escape and injure or kill someone.[5] Men are limited creatures; they cannot be held to be liable for every unforeseen act. This was also the conclusion of the rabbinical experts of Jewish law.[6]

"Ransom" Insurance

The Bible provides only one explicit example of a capital crime that can be punished either by execution or a fine: this one.

---

5. Gary North, *Tools of Dominion: The Case Laws of Exodus*, (Tyler, Texas: Institute for Christian Economics, 1990), ch. 16.

6. Writes Shalom Albeck: "The foreseeability test as the basis of liability for damage led the rabbis to conclude that even where negligent the tortfeasor would only be liable for damage that he could foresee." *Principles of Jewish Law*, col. 322.

Murder has to be punished by the death penalty (Num. 35:31). In this case, the ox is executed, so the general principle of "life for life" is maintained. Genesis 9:4-6 is not violated by Exodus 21:28-30. The owner, because he is not directly guilty of committing a capital crime, although fully responsible before the law for the actions of his beast, can escape execution. It is not stated that the judges make this decision: death or restitution. The victim's family probably makes this decision. Perhaps both judges and family do.[7] Restitution is owed to the relatives, as heirs of his estate; legally, the payment is made to the dead victim. The economic incentive of the family is clear: money is more useful than the death of the victim.

The restitution payment normally would be high. A man has to pay. There is no escape. If he cannot pay what is demanded, either through liability insurance, personal capital, or selling himself into slavery, then he dies. Restitution is mandatory.

The development of personal liability insurance is one way that Western society has dealt with the problem of the catastrophic judgment. The question then arises: Should *criminal negligence* be covered? The civil government must face the questions raised by economic analysis. If the criminal is criminally negligent, yet covered by liability insurance, can the insurance firm be forced by law to pay, even if its contract with the convicted person says that it must? Is a third-party payment to the victim in the name of the criminal an immoral contract and therefore illegal? Does it reduce the economic threat of personal bankruptcy to such an extent that criminal negligence is thereby subsidized? Is criminal negligence a legitimate event to insure against? Should such contracts be made illegal — not just unenforceable in a court of law, but illegal?

There is another problem. If the "deeper pocket" of the insurance company is available for the victim's family to reach into, will they demand "all the traffic will bear," irrespective of justice? If the owner were not insured, would the victim's family ever demand such a high restitution payment? In the absence of insurance, the victim's heirs would probably have to limit their de-

---

7. J. J. Finkelstein, *The Ox That Gored* (Philadelphia: American Philosophical Society, 1981), p. 29.

mands. Question: Should judgments be based on the merits of the case or the "depth of the pocket" of the insurance company?

Limiting the Insurer's Liability

To sell personal liability policies, insurance companies have to limit their liability. They do so by placing maximum monetary limits on all pay-outs. They also limit their liability by insuring people who have reputations for being reliable. High-risk buyers raise the premiums that low-risk buyers are forced to pay. There is an economic incentive for companies to seek out lower-risk buyers for any given type of policy. They can insure a special class of higher-risk people, but only by charging all members high premiums. Eventually, they run out of volume sales when they seek out more and more high-risk buyers. They eventually stop selling policies to the highest-risk people. Personal liability insurance, to be profitable, must be sold to a *particular class* of insurable people. The very concept of "insurable class" refers to a group of people to whom the actuarial laws of probability apply. Groups to which these laws do not apply cannot be safely and profitably insured by private firms selling voluntary policies. Thus, insurance companies attempt to sell to people who are members of a large, insurable class.[8] Insurance firms limit their risk by enlarging the number of policy buyers within a particular large class. They do not want to be bankrupted by one or two large settlements; to avoid bankruptcy, they must sell large numbers of policies. The larger the number of policy holders, the closer the "fit" between the actuarial laws − "laws of large numbers" − and the actual number of cases in which the company must pay victims of negligence.

Liability insurance therefore will cover occasional cases of criminal negligence, for any given policy holder may occasionally be criminally negligent. For example, personal liability coverage on automobile drivers covers those rare cases in which a driver may be criminally negligent.[9] But the firms will not insure people who have received numerous traffic tickets for speeding, and espe-

---

8. Ludwig von Mises, *Human Action: A Treatise on Economics* (3rd ed.; Chicago: Regnery, 1966), p. 109.

9. Some policies may exclude such coverage. It is in the self-interest of policy-buyers to read the fine print of their insurance contracts before they buy.

cially for drunk driving. It is true that high-risk drivers can purchase automobile and liability insurance, but only because state governments require the auto insurance industry to set up high-risk pools for otherwise uninsurable drivers do the companies sell policies to these people. *Today's civil governments are requiring private firms to insure people who are more likely to be regarded by the courts as criminally negligent.* These laws reduce political pressures from those classified as criminally negligent; they continue to be allowed to drive. The states also avoid having to set up taxpayer-financed insurance programs for the high-risk drivers — programs that might bring complaints from low-risk drivers who also vote. The legislators require all drivers to carry personal liability policies — "ransoms for lives" — but they also require insurance companies to sell high-risk drivers this coverage. If the law did not compel the purchase of auto insurance, or strongly encourage it by requiring visible evidence of a driver's ability to self-insure himself, the insurance firms would be trapped. They could not easily pass on to low-risk drivers the added costs of insuring high-risk people. Low-risk drivers are forced by the state to pay higher premiums for their policies than would have been the case had the high-risk drivers been refused coverage and thereby forced off the roads.

Thus, the concern about criminals' escaping justice because of private insurance contracts is misplaced. The greater problem is the civil government's demand that people who are more likely to be convicted of criminal negligence be covered by insurance, whether or not they are insurable by private firms on a voluntary basis. It is not that the State *allows* insurance companies to pay "ransoms for the lives" of criminally negligent people; it is rather that the State *compels* private firms to sell such coverage to people or firms that are more likely to be convicted of criminal negligence.

The State as Insurer

The State even enters as the "insurer of last resort" when no private firms will insure extremely high-risk people or industries. One example in the United States — which is common in Western industrial nations, though not in Japan[10] — is the government-

---

10. H. Peter Metzger, *The Atomic Power Establishment* (New York: Simon & Schuster, 1972), p. 218.

The Principle of Limited Liability

guaranteed coverage for accidents connected with the generation of electricity through nuclear power. Power companies are government-licensed public utilities that possess regional monopolies. The "Price-Anderson" legislation of the 1950's sets relatively low ceilings for financial liability by such firms — $560 million per accident[11] — and then the federal government collects the premium money. By limiting its liability, the federal government forces residents who live near nuclear power sites to co-insure against a disaster, since there is a maximum pay-out per accident. The larger the local population that could be affected, the more each resident co-insures, for the lower the per capita payments would be. Taxpayers also co-insure: in case of an accident, the tiny federal nuclear accident insurance fund could not pay off more than 2 percent of a single $560 million damage suit. Money taken from the federal government's general fund would have to make up the difference. Because of this federal legislation, public utilities have been able to expand the use of nuclear power generation. In this sense, today's nuclear power industry has not been the product of a free market economy; it has been the product of special-interest legislation in the form of liability maximums and compulsory State insurance coverage.

Anti-nuclear power advocates tend to be anti-free market, and usually blame the free market for the nuclear power industry. Nuclear power proponents usually are pro-free market, so they seldom talk about the statist nature of the subsidy. But when the chips are down, the pro-nuclear power people accept federal subsidies to *their* program as being economically and ideologically valid. Writes nuclear power advocate Petr Beckman: "Yes, the American taxpayer has paid $1 billion to research nuclear safety, and I consider that a good investment. . . ."[12] He also argues that the Price-Anderson insurance program makes money for the federal government because power companies pay premiums to Washington, along with money sent to private insurance pools. "You call that a subsidy?" he asks.[13] Of course it is a subsidy.

---

11. *Idem.*

12. Petr Beckman, *The Health Hazards of NOT Going Nuclear* (Boulder, Colorado: Golem Press 1976). p. 154.

13. *Ibid.*, p. 156.

The premium rates are far below market rates, even assuming private firms would insure against a nuclear power plant disaster, which is doubtful. The maximum liability is fixed by law far below what would be demanded in a court if some major nuclear accident took place in a populated area. This is why the Price-Anderson legislation was enacted in the first place: to subsidize the power industry by reducing its legal liability and its insurance rates. Furthermore, taxpayers are co-insuring: the fund which is to cover all power companies nationally was $8 million as of 1976; the liability was $560 million per accident. Taxpayers would have to make up the difference.

I do not want to give the impression that I am against the development of nuclear power. What I support is the development of a free market in power generation. The economic ideal would be a system of power generation that is marked by open entry and price competition. There would be no public utility monopoly over power generation. This may not yet be technically feasible, but it is the ideal against which all proposals should be evaluated. For example, if the technology of solar power generation were sufficiently advanced (and marketed), and if battery technology were improved, then the power-user could "unplug" from the local power company. He could store the power on sunny days and use it at night or on cloudy days. Another example: space-based solar power generation and microwave transmission back to earth.

With respect to nuclear power, the main economic problem is the disposal of nuclear waste. The problem with today's waste-disposal techniques is that radioactive waste material is compacted and stored in large containers. The problem is the concentration of nuclear waste. A much more fruitful approach would be to search for technologies of waste dispersal rather than waste storage. If the radioactive isotopes were attached to tiny granules of matter and then dispersed from the air over wide ranges of the world's oceans, there would be little additional threat to the already radioactive world environment. The political fallout would be far more dangerous than the physical kind. One additional requirement: power-generating companies should be required to pay all waste disposal costs.

The Free Market's Response

Liability insurance is another example of a free market, scientific development that protects the victims without bankrupting those who are personally responsible. The victims receive more money than the private, uninsured citizen or firm would otherwise have been able to pay. The lifetime income loss suffered by the family of the victim is compensated by the insurance company. The negligent person still could be executed, should the plaintiffs desire it, but it is far more likely that they would prefer to accept money from the insurance firm. The "ransom for a life" is higher; thus, the guilty person is more likely to survive. This extends the dominion covenant; the victim's family carries on, but the guilty man suffers no loss of capital, except possibly his ability to buy insurance subsequently.

Does the State have a biblically sanctioned right to compel people to buy liability insurance or else proof of sufficient capital to make restitution? In the case of drivers' liability insurance, where death and serious injury to innocent parties are common, and the drivers are using the State's highway system, the answer is yes. The State can establish rules and regulations for drivers who wish to qualify to use its highways. One of these regulations is liability insurance. Another requirement might be an annual auto safety inspection.[14] The automobile is like a large beast; if it becomes dangerous through neglect by its owner, innocent people can be killed. Insurance companies can be used as screening agents. They may be able write cheaper policies for those who drive inspected automobiles.

Other forms of liability insurance should not be mandatory, unless the situation is comparable to the "dangerous beast in a State-owned place" analogy, but civil government should recognize the legitimacy of the victim's heirs to call for the execution of the criminally negligent party. This would encourage people to buy sufficiently large personal liability insurance policies so that the victim's heirs would have a strong financial incentive to

---

14. This assumes that there is statistically valid evidence that state-mandated auto inspections do in fact reduce accidents and injuries. This evidence is frequently unclear. What *is* clear is that such legislation provides an initial increase in the net worth of those who are granted the licenses to perform these inspections, and that a continuation of such laws brings a stream of rents to those who possess these licenses.

allow the guilty man to live.

Conclusion

This law of criminal negligence is much broader than simply oxen and owners; it applies to all cases of death to innocent parties that are the result of negligence on the part of owners of notorious beasts or notorious machinery — capital that is known to be risky to innocent bystanders. Automobiles, trucks, certain kinds of occupations, nuclear power plants, coal mines, and similar examples of dangerous tools are covered by this general principle of personal liability. This law should not be understood as applying to workers who voluntarily work in dangerous callings and who have been warned in advance of the risks by their employers, nor should it be used as a justification for the creation of a messianic State that attempts to discover criminal negligence in every case of third-party injury, despite the lack of knowledge of risks by the owners or experts in the field.

Personal liability insurance is a development of the West that allows criminally negligent people a greater opportunity to escape the death penalty by means of high payments to the heirs of their victims. Purchasing such insurance is not to become mandatory, except in cases related to the use of State-financed capital (e.g., highways). Nevertheless, the risk is so high — execution — and the cost of premiums so low in comparison to the risk, that personal liability coverage is available to most people. Only the very poor, who would not normally own "oxen" (expensive capital equipment), or people convicted repeatedly of criminal negligence or actions that would lead to convictions for criminal negligence (e.g., drunk driving), or people who manage or own businesses that create high risks for innocent bystanders, would normally be excluded from the purchase of such insurance coverage. They would have to learn to handle their "oxen" with care.

9

THE PITFALLS OF NEGLIGENCE

And if a man shall open a pit, or if a man shall dig a pit, and not cover it, and an ox or an ass fall therein; the owner of the pit shall make it good, and give money unto the owner of them; and the dead beast shall be his (Ex. 21:33-34).

Here is another variation of the restitution principle. A man digs a pit for some reason, and fails to cover it. This is negligent behavior. He knows that unsuspecting people or animals could fall into the pit and be harmed. His failure to go to the expense of covering the pit is an example of what economists call "externalities." He imposes the risk of an injured beast on the owner of the beast. *By saving time and money in not covering the pit, he thereby transfers the economic burden of risk to someone else.* This is a form of theft. Someone who cannot benefit from the use of the pit is expected to pay a portion of its costs of operation, namely, the risk of injury to any animal that might fall into it. This is the meaning of economic "externalities": those who cannot benefit from an economic decision are forced to pay for part of the costs of operation.

Biblical civil law settles the question of property rights and the responsibilities of ownership. Because the Bible affirms the rights of private ownership – meaning *legal immunities* from interference by either the State or other private citizens in the use of one's property – it therefore imposes *responsibilities* on owners. The law regulating uncovered pits is not an infringement on private property rights. On the contrary, it is an *affirmation* of such rights. By linking personal economic responsibility to personal, private ownership, biblical civil law identifies the legal owner of the pit, namely, the person who is required to pay damages should another person's animal be killed by a fall into the unsafe pit. He receives some sort of advantage from the pit, and therefore he must bear the expense of making it safe for other people's animals. "Pit" is a classification used for centuries by the rabbis to assess responsibility and damages. The Mishnah specified that any pit ten handbreadths deep qualifies as deep enough to cause death, and therefore is actionable in cases of death. If less than this depth, the pit is actionable in case of injury to a beast, but not if the beast died.[1] Writes Jewish legal scholar Shalom Albeck: "This is the name given to another leading category of tort and covers cases where an obstacle is created by a person's negligence and left as a hazard by means of which another is injured. The prime example is that of a person who digs a pit, leaves it uncovered, and another person or an animal falls into it. Other major examples would be leaving stones or water unfenced and thus potentially hazardous. The common factor is the commission or omission of something which brings about a dangerous situation and the foreseeability of damage resulting. A person who fails to take adequate precautions to render harmless a hazard under his control is considered negligent, since he is presumed able to foresee that damage may result, and he is therefore liable for any such subsequent damage."[2]

Samson Raphael Hirsch, the brilliant mid-nineteenth-century Jewish Torah commentator, analyzed the economics of negligence under the general heading of property, and property under the more general classification of guardianship. "Man, in taking possession of the unreasoning world, becomes guardian of unreasoning property and is responsible for the forces inherent in it, just as he is responsible for the forces of his own body; for property is

---

1. *Baba Kamma* 5:5, *The Mishnah*, edited by Herbert Danby (New York: Oxford University Press, [1933] 1987), p. 338.

2. "Avot Nezikin: (2) Pit," *The Principles of Jewish Law*, edited by Menachem Elon (Jerusalem: Keter, 1975?), col. 326. This compilation of articles taken from the *Encyclopedia Judaica* was published as Publication No. 6 of the Institute for Research in Jewish Law of the Hebrew University of Jerusalem.

nothing but the artificially extended body, and body and property together are the realm and sphere of action of the soul — i.e., of the human personality, which rules them and becomes effective through them and in them. Thus is the person responsible for all the material things under his dominion and in his use; and even without the verdict of a court of law, even if no claim is put forward by another person, he must pay compensation for any harm done to another's property or body for which he is responsible."[3] The guardian is always responsible before God for the administration of everything under his legal authority.

Hirsch goes so far as to say that our willingness to indemnify a victim is not enough, morally speaking; we must take care not to allow damage in the first place. "Once you have done harm the only thing you are able to do is to pay compensation; you can never undo the harm and wipe out all its consequences."[4] A righteous person should become a blessing for those around him. "You, with all your belongings, should become a blessing; be on your guard that you and your belongings do not become a curse! Watch over all your belongings so that they do no harm to your neighbour!" And also what you throw away or pour away — see to it that it do no harm; you ought to bring good, so do not bring evil!"[5] Thus, our economic responsibility is an *active* responsibility. We must actively seek to avoid harming others. It is within this moral framework that the Bible discusses the uncovered pit.

Animals and Children

This case law deals specifically with animals. It does not mention people. Why not? Because the pit is almost certainly located on the land of the person who digs it. An animal that wanders onto the man's property has no understanding of private property rights. Presumably, no fence has restrained it from coming onto the property. If a fence is present, then the animal would have to knock it down to get onto the property. The damage to

---

3. Samson Raphael Hirsch, *Horeb: A Philosophy of Jewish Laws and Observances*, trans. I. Grunfeld (New York: Soncino, [1837] 1962), pp. 243-44, paragraph 360.

4. *Ibid.*, p. 247, paragraph 367.

5. *Ibid.*, p. 248, paragraph 367.

the fencing would then be the responsibility of the owner of the animal. He should have restrained his animal. *The fence in such an instance serves as the legal equivalent of a cover.* But unrestrained access to the area of the uncovered pit places the responsibility on the land-owner. An animal is not expected to honor the law against trespassing.

What holds true for an animal is also true for a young child. If the child is not restrained by a fence or a cover over the pit, then the owner is liable. Like an ox with a reputation for violence, so is the uncovered pit. The owner is responsible. The parents of a child who is killed by a fall into an uncovered pit are entitled to the same restitution as the heirs of a victim of an ox that was known to be dangerous.

A responsible adult who comes onto another person's property and falls into a pit has to have a legitimate reason for being there. If the uncovered pit is located on a path over which a visitor might normally pass, and the pit is not easily visible, then the owner becomes legally responsible. The visitor, in this instance, is like a dumb animal: he is not aware of special prohibitions against walking in the vicinity of the uncovered pit. But if the visitor has climbed over a fence and is wandering over the property in the dead of night, where he has no reason to be, then the owner is innocent. If the intruder ignores "No Trespassing" signs, he is also unprotected by the "covered pit" law. He is not to be treated in a literate culture as if he were a dumb animal. Albeck comments: "If the *bor* [pit] (i.e., the hazard) is adequately guarded or left in a place where persons or animals do not normally pass, such as one's private property, no negligence or presumed foreseeability can be ascribed and no liability would arise."[6]

The pit-digger is required to reimburse the owner of the dead beast. The latter can then buy a replacement for the dead animal. The pit-digger becomes the owner of the dead animal. In Israel, he could have sold it or eaten it, since it died of a known cause; it did not die "of itself," which would have made it forbidden meat for Israelites (Deut. 14:21). The pit-digger does not suffer a total loss.

---

6. Albeck, "Pit," *Principles of Jewish Law*, col. 326.

The Pitfalls of Negligence

In modern times, people build swimming pools on their property. These are certainly uncovered most of the swimming season. They are holes in the ground. Are these the modern equivalent of a pit? No. A pit is a hole in the ground which is not expected. It is not readily visible. A swimming pool has a cement deck around it. It may have a diving board. It is plainly visible in the back yard. It is anything but inconspicuous. Besides, if an animal falls into it, it will swim out. If a small child falls into it, liability could be imposed on the owner only under the "railed roof" statute (Deut. 22:8), not under the "uncovered pit" statute. The pool is a place of entertainment and recreation, just as flat-roof housetops were in the ancient world. It is not a pit which men stumble into unexpectedly. The so-called "attractive nuisance" problem — a dangerous object to which small children are attracted — falls under the railing statute.

Prohibiting Future Violations

A modern application of this law would assess subsequent personal liability to someone who would place an abandoned refrigerator with a lock-latch in the alley behind his home without first removing the door. A child might play hide and seek by climbing into the refrigerator and shutting the door. Such stories were familiar throughout the 1940's and 1950's. Courts did not always impose penalties on the owners, but by the 1960's, the products were deemed innately unsafe by the authorities. The sale of lock-latch refrigerators was banned in the 1960's in the United States. Doors that can be pushed open from the inside were made mandatory for producers of refrigerators.

Such laws are passed primarily because judges have refused to honor the principle of holding owners personally responsible for "uncovered pits." The Old Testament did not require the civil government to impose fines on people who dug pits and then failed to cover them. It did not create an army of "enforcers." Instead, it assigned individual responsibility to owners of dangerous property. The civil government let men's *fear of their legal liability* serve as their incentive to make their property safer.

There are definite economic effects of legislation that assesses economic penalties before an accident occurs. These effects are seldom considered by legislators or by the special-interest groups that lobby for such legislation. In the case of lock-latch refrigerators, the original product had definite advantages. When the door was closed, it audibly snapped shut. The new no-lock doors sometimes fail to close tightly, but users are not always alerted (because of the absence of the old snap) when this happens. These doors are less efficient than older doors in this respect. When they are still being used in the kitchen, they are more easily left open by children who find them more difficult to close than the older design, which snapped shut easily. As a result, food rots from time to time, and the costs are borne by the owner.

It seems certain that a few lives are saved each year by this legislation, but there never were hundreds of cases of smothered children in any year. It was a newspaper-worthy occasional event. Millions of refrigerator owners are today subjected to the statistical risk of occasionally leaving a door open and rotting a week's food. Predictably, this cost is more difficult to bear for lower-income families, since food costs occupy a higher proportion of their household budgets.

It may seem callous to compare the cost of spoiled food, no matter how much, with the lives of children, no matter how few. But there are inescapable costs with every desirable benefit. *Legislation creates benefits; therefore, in a cursed, scarcity-bound world, it necessarily imposes costs.* Who benefits? How much? Who pays? How much? These questions should always be asked before any piece of legislation is voted on.

When society adopts a utopian legal code which proclaims "better millions of extra dollars spent by consumers on a safer product design than one child dead from an accident," it places an impossibly expensive burden on society — the expense of seeking an impossible goal, *risk-free existence*.[7] Besides, legislators honor the "better millions of dollars than . . ." principle only when it is cost-effective to them as politicians, that is, only when adversely

---

7. Mary Douglas and Aaron Wildavsky, *Risk and Culture: An Essay on the Selection of Technological and Environmental Dangers* (Berkeley: University of California Press, 1982).

The Pitfalls of Negligence

affected voters will not be numerous enough, or sufficiently well organized, to threaten them at the next election.

For example, far more children are killed in one year in home fires than ever died in abandoned refrigerators. Many lives could be saved by legislating *and continually enforcing* the installation of smoke detectors in every home. Legislators could also require fire escape drills on parents twice a year, with penalties for violating the rule. Parents today refuse to accept the level of perpetual interference in their lives by the police that the enforcement of such a law would require. So legislators in this case ignore the principle of "better millions of dollars than. . . ." They honor it only when few lives are involved (e.g., asphyxiated children in refrigerators), and only a few companies need be monitored (e.g., appliance manufacturers).

First, legislators refuse to make owners legally liable for damages, as the Bible requires. Second, they pass laws (or allow the bureaucracy to define and then enforce earlier laws) whose costs to the general public are not immediately perceptible (e.g., rotten food produced by no-lock latches). In short, they pass pieces of legislation with minimal political and statistical impact (for good or evil) in terms of the utopian "better millions of dollars than . . ." principle, but fail to honor it in statistically relevant cases, because of the equally relevant (to them) political backlash they would receive from voters. The proclamation of the "better millions of dollars than. . . ." principle has been, is, and will continue to be the product of economic ignorance and political hypocrisy.

This is not to say that it is always wrong to require owners to pay more in order to save lives. But the Bible provides us with the proper guidelines, not some hypothetically universal utopian principle that would necessitate the creation of a messianic State. The general principle is simple: those who own a known dangerous object are legally responsible for making it safer for those who are either immature or otherwise unwarned about the very real danger.

Public Pits

There are areas of life that are almost always the responsibility of the civil government. Highways are one example. If people are to use the highways, they need protection, both as drivers and pedestrians. The civil government erects stop signs and stop lights; it places other road signs along the highways, so that drivers can drive more safely and make better high-speed decisions. Similarly, residential areas and school zones are restricted to slower traffic. This protects pedestrians and home owners who would otherwise face the continual threat of high-speed vehicles that are difficult to control in tight quarters.

The posting of a speed limit is essentially the same as a private citizen who posts a "no trespassing" sign, or a "beware of dog" sign on his property. The sign serves as a substitute for the "cover for the pit"; the sign, like the cover, is a device for *protecting the innocent*. Where children in cities are forced to cross busy streets, local governments hire crossing guards to control traffic and help younger children across the street. Sometimes, older students in a grammar school serve as unpaid crossing guards in a safety patrol. In some communities, fenced, overhead ramps are built across busy highways. The fence serves as a means of protection for 1) pedestrians who might fall off the overpass and 2) motorists who face risks from vandals who would drop heavy rocks onto the passing cars beneath. But fences are expensive, and they cannot be built in every residential area. Thus, the civil government establishes speed limits, and it posts signs that warn drivers of these limits.

A philosophy of nearly risk-free existence would impose speed limits of no more than a few miles per hour on all drivers, except perhaps on specially designed highways. But voters, who are both pedestrians and drivers, would not long tolerate such utopian restrictions. In most places in the United States, voters drive far more hours during the day than they walk. So they will not allow defenders of the rhetoric of risk-free living to have their way. They make judgments as individuals that legislators must respect in the aggregate: *speed limits that meet the needs of voters*, both as drivers and pedestrians, or the parents of pedestrians. Once the speed limit is posted, people make personal adjustments, both as drivers (by slowing down to approach the legal limit, but letting pedestrians

The Pitfalls of Negligence						175

look out more for themselves) and as pedestrians (by reducing their watchfulness about cars, so long as cars are moving at or near the posted limit). Voters compromise: slower speeds close to schools, but faster speeds on highways.

Drivers who violate these limits are increasing the statistical risks of walking in a neighborhood. Residents believe that they have been granted a degree of safety by the authorities — not perfect safety, since automobiles are still permitted in the area, but *calculable safety*. They use the streets and sidewalks in terms of this greater degree of safety. But pedestrians and other (slower) drivers are threatened by those who refuse to honor the posted speed limit. They have made decisions in terms of a given environment ("25 m.p.h."), and a law-breaker unilaterally alters this environment. He has, in effect, torn down the protective fencing. He has "uncovered the pit."

Fines and Restitution

What is the proper remedy? Most communities impose fines for excessive speeding, with the fines proportional to the violations: a higher fine for a higher speed. Can a fine be justified biblically? Yes. *The fine is imposed because a specific victim cannot be identified*. No one was injured by the speeding vehicle. Therefore, the civil government collects a *restitution payment* in the name of all the victims who had their lives and property *threatened* by the speeder's act.

A statistically measurable risk of injury was transferred by the speeder to those in the area of his speeding vehicle. This is another case of "externalities": people are being forced by the speeder to bear risks involuntarily. The fines should be used to establish *a trust fund for future victims of "hit and run" auto accidents*, where the guilty party cannot be located and/or convicted. The perpetrator of this "victimless crime" becomes a source of restitution payments for the subsequent victims of this same criminal act by an unconvicted agent. *Fines are therefore an acknowledgement by the authorities of the limits placed on their knowledge*. If law enforcement authorities were omniscient, all restitution payments in a biblical society would go from the known criminal to the known victim.

Fines should be imposed by local authorities for a specific purpose: to make restitution payments to victims who reside in the same general neighborhood. The civil government acts as a *trustee* for future victims in cases where the authorities cannot locate or convict the violator. *Fines are not to be regarded as a normal source of revenue for the civil government.* The civil government must enforce biblical law without prejudice. The bureaucrats' fond hope of collecting municipal operating revenues from fines creates prejudice. In a biblical commonwealth, taxes are supposed to finance civil government — *predictable* taxes that are collected from every responsible adult in a community. Citizens must know what law enforcement is really costing them. Setting up "speed traps" along the highway so that non-residents can be forced to finance the local government is a gross perversion of the function of the fine. This subsidizes local bureaucrats rather than assisting future victims.

Drunk Drivers

An individual who deliberately distorts his own perceptions is implicitly attacking God and his God-created environment.[8] He is saying by his actions that God has not been fair to him in placing him in such an environment. He then makes decisions under the influence of alcohol or drugs that can physically damage others because of his self-induced distorted perceptions. Drunk drivers are therefore to be prosecuted as criminally negligent, should their acts cause damage. They have "torn off the pit cover" with impunity. Their injury-inflicting acts are not to be considered as accidents, meaning low-probability events that cannot reasonably be predicted in advance in the life of any specific individual. Their injury-inflicting actions are rather the product of an act of moral rebellion: the implicit denial of their own personal responsibility for their actions.

---

8. Obviously an exception is the person who has accepted an anesthetic in order to reduce his pain. Thrashing around in agony during a medical operation clearly reduces the likelihood of a successful operation. But such people are always placed under medical observation and supervision. They are not legally responsible agents during their period of distorted perceptions.

The Pitfalls of Negligence

Drunk drivers impose increased statistical risks on their potential victims. The victim or the heirs must be given the legal option of imposing a heavy restitution payment, under the guidance of the judges. Where there is no victim, the drunk driver must pay the fine.

Repeated convictions for drunk driving indicate moral rebellion. Here is a person who has the equivalent of a notorious ox: the lawless "beast" is inside him. Worse: he is responsible in a way that a beast is not. He has moral insights concerning the consequences of his acts that a beast does not possess. The authorities can legitimately "tie him up" by revoking his right to operate a vehicle until he has demonstrated his continued sobriety for a fixed period of time. Like a notorious ox that must be fenced until it becomes self-disciplined, so is the drunk driver, or the repeat speeder, or the driver who drives under the influence of drugs. There may not be identifiable victims, but there are certainly *statistical victims* whose interests need protection.

The same principles of economic analysis that apply to speeding and drunk driving can be applied to other areas of life in which the State is the primary protector of life and limb. Fines to the civil government should be imposed on convicted violators only in cases where the civil government is acting as a trustee for future unknown victims.

Political Hypocrisy

The problem today is that society refuses to accept the morally and legally binding nature of Old Testament legal principles of criminal negligence. First, legislators do not consistently make "pit owners" legally liable for damages, as the Bible requires. The most flagrant example is the failure of state and local governments to impose stiff fines on all drunk drivers, and capital punishment on drunk drivers whose unsafe driving leads to someone else's death. Furthermore, politicians do not impose fines on themselves or city employees for failing to repair public streets with potholes which cause damages to people's cars or which cause accidents.

Second, politicians pass safety laws (or allow the bureaucracy to define and then enforce earlier laws) whose costs to the general public are not immediately perceptible. They may require automobile companies to install seat belts that buyers do not want to pay for, and which occupants subsequently refuse to use, but politicians are not about to pass a law that would impose fines on families for refusing to install smoke detectors in their own homes. The first piece of legislation would not gain the reprisal of voters; the second probably would. Third, because of the rise of State-financed health care, politicians can justify intrusions into the lives of citizens on this basis: "Because taxpayers must pay for injuries that are the result of carelessness, it is the responsibility of the State to force people to be more careful." A good example of a compulsory personal safety law is the law requiring motorcyclists to wear crash helmets. In a free market social order, if a cyclist sustains head injuries in a one-man crash, he hurts only himself. But because of the spread of socialized medicine, politicians can justify helmet laws politically. This line of reasoning can be used to pass almost any kind of safety legislation in the name of reducing potential accidents. Safety laws become in principle open-ended if their justification is the possible burden to taxpayers that an injury might produce. The socialization of health care can lead, step by step, to the socialization of all of life.

This is not to say that it is always wrong to require owners to pay more in order to save lives, but the Bible provides us with the proper guidelines, not some hypothetically universal utopian principle that would necessitate the creation of a messianic State. The general principle is simple: *those who own a known dangerous object are legally responsible for making it safer for those who are either immature or otherwise unwarned about the very real danger.*

Conclusion

Ownership is a social function. There is a link between the costs and benefits of lawful ownership. He who *benefits* from the use of private property must also bear the *costs* of ownership. He cannot legitimately pass on the costs to other people who have not voluntarily agreed to accept these costs. He is also responsible for the risks of physical damage that he imposes on them without their prior knowledge and consent.

The pit-digger must cover the pit or be responsible for the consequences. The owner of an unpenned notorious ox is equally

The Pitfalls of Negligence 179

responsible. Beasts are not expected to understand property rights; the owner must fence his property, or cover his pit, or pay restitution to the dead beast's owner. He cannot legitimately pass on the risks associated with uncovered pits to his neighbors.

The civil government has an analogous responsibility to protect those who use the property which belongs to, or is administered by, the State. Thus, speed limits, crossing guards, and school safety patrols are created. Patrol cars monitor traffic in neighborhoods. Fines are collected from speeders and other traffic violators. Why fines? Because there are limits on the knowledge of law enforcement authorities; thus, fines are used as a way to collect restitution payments from known violators, and to make payments to victims of unknown violators.

Responsibility is personal, and it involves every area of authority exercised by any individual. The civil government has the obligation of setting forth principles of judicial interpretation that will prevail in any civil court. The court will look at the circumstances surrounding the injured party, and determine who was responsible. If the property owner was attempting to pass on involuntarily to innocent third parties the risks of ownership, the court will find the owner guilty. All property owners know this in advance, and they can take steps to reduce their legal risks by reducing involuntary risks borne by innocent third parties.

The Bible does not warrant the establishment of a huge bureaucracy to define every area of possible risk, promulgate minute definitions of what constitutes unlawful uses of property, and describe in detail every penalty associated with a violation. The Bible certainly does not indicate that the civil government is warranted to step in and proclaim a potentially injurious action illegal, except in cases where the violator could not conceivably make restitution to all the potential victims (e.g., fire codes) or in cases of repeated violations (the "notorious ox" principle). The Bible simply reminds property owners of the consequences of creating hazards to life and limb for third parties who were not consulted in advance concerning their willingness to bear the risks. The property owner is assumed to be competent to make judgments for himself concerning the consequences of his actions, and then take the steps necessary to reduce his risks.

10

RESTITUTION, REPENTANCE, AND RESTORATION

If a man shall steal an ox, or a sheep, and kill it, or sell it; he shall restore five oxen for an ox, and four sheep for a sheep. . . . If the theft be certainly found in his hand alive, whether it be ox, or ass, or sheep; he shall restore double (Ex. 22:1, 4).

Men have failed to understand the fundamental goal of biblical law: *restoration* — restoration between God and rebellious man, and restitution between the criminal and his victim. Rushdoony writes: "Emphatically, in Biblical law the goal is *not punishment but restoration*, not the infliction of certain penalties on criminals but the restoration of godly order."[1] Biblical law alone cannot restore sinful man to God, but it does serve as our reminder of our need for a way to repay God fully. Biblical law reminds us that we are dead in our sins (Rom. 7:9-13). Biblical law points to the work of the kinsman-redeemer, Jesus Christ.

Just as sinners need to be restored to God, the criminal needs to be restored to his victim. His victim is the representative and symbol of God, for all sin and crime is ultimately an attempted attack on God, the primary Victim. This is why the criminal is required by God's law to make restitution to his victim. Double restitution restores the victim's economic position prior to the crime, plus it increases his holdings to compensate him for the trouble the crime caused him. He is as fully repaid as the court system can lawfully determine. At the same time, making eco-

---

1. R. J. Rushdoony, *The Institutes of Biblical Law* (Nutley, New Jersey: Craig Press, 1973), p. 515.

nomic restitution restores the criminal legally and psychologically. He knows that he has paid his debt, not just to society but to his victim. He is made clean, analogous to the cleansing the sinner experiences when he accepts Jesus Christ's payment of his sins at Calvary. He is given a fresh start.

The restoration of peace between criminal and victim is accomplished by the criminal's payment of double restitution to the victim. Once this payment is made, the victim has no additional legal claim against the criminal. The matter is legally settled. Any attempt by the victim to extract anything else from the criminal is illegitimate. This is the legal basis of the criminal's covenantal restoration to society. Restitution is good for the victim, good for the criminal, and good for society.

When biblical law is enforced, innocent members of society can feel more confident about their lives and property because the State is obeying God and punishing criminals in a way that preserves the dominion covenant. They can work hard, knowing that the State is working to reduce crime and help them keep the fruits of their labor. At the same time, the criminal now knows that his debt is paid, and that *the one of the burdens of guilt is removed*. He can then return to a lawful calling and begin to exercise dominion as a free man. This is what Rushdoony means when he speaks of restoration as a means of maintaining godly order.

The restoration of peace with the victim is not the same as restoration of peace with God. It is analogous to this restoration, but not the same. What we must say as Christians is that double restitution to the victim is *necessary* for the criminal's restoration of wholeness before God, but it is *not sufficient*. Not only is double restitution to the victim needed, so is repentance before God. This raises a difficult question for biblical social order: To what extent should the civil government be involved in encouraging or enforcing repentance before God?

The Problem with Enforcing Repentance

The Bible teaches the need for restitution, repentance, and restoration. Only the first can be legitimately required by civil law. The criminal must make outward restitution to his victim, no matter what his inner feelings are. The State should lawfully enforce this. But it cannot enforce repentance, for this would involve the God-prohibited claim of the State to be God. The State is not God; its officials cannot know what is in men's hearts. Nevertheless, when a criminal today is sentenced, a reporter will sometimes add these words: "He showed no signs of remorse." This indicates that even in modern "secular" times, we potential victims expect criminals to show signs of repentance. Second, the criminal is morally required by God to repent, and to declare himself completely at the mercy of God. The penalty for failing to do this is an eternity of punishment in God's fiery prison, from which there is no escape. No human government can lawfully enforce this required repentance, as we have seen. Third, in response to both external restitution to the victim and internal repentance before God, God restores the sinner to wholeness. This is the gift of God's grace.

It must be stressed that the State cannot legitimately require the internal act of repentance; officers cannot know the criminal's heart. Men cannot and must not try to enforce repentance; our laws cannot legitimately be written in terms of the internal state of a person's mind. The State also cannot legitimately require a public statement of theological faith from all residents in a society. The "stranger within the gates" may believe what he wants about God, man, and law. This does not mean that the State cannot legitimately require a statement of faith from those who seek *citizenship* and therefore the right potentially to serve as *judges* "within the gates." If a person is not covenantally under law, he should not be allowed to become a judge — voter, juror, civil magistrate — who places others under that law. The covenant is hierarchical; to rule we must also serve. To enforce a law-order, we must be under it.

This may sound strange to Christians who for some reason still believe in the humanist myth of morally and religiously neutral law,[2] but everyone in the United States is governed by a humanist version of this covenantal principle of hierarchy and

---

2. Gary DeMar, *Ruler of the Nations: Biblical Blueprints for Government* (Ft. Worth, Texas: Dominion Press, 1987), ch. 3: "Plural Law Systems, Plural Gods."

oath. In the United States, citizens are required to uphold and defend the Constitution. While they make no profession of allegiance unless they serve as civil magistrates of some kind, merely by being born in the U.S. or in a family of U.S. citizens, they legally become citizens. (Some Christians may not believe in infant baptism — the child's possession of non-voting church membership from the day of his physical birth — but all Americans affirm the analogous civil principle of a child's non-voting civil citizenship. The child is protected by covenant civil law.) Aliens are required to make no such profession of civil faith, implicitly or explicitly. They are required to obey the terms of laws that are based on the Constitution, but they are not required by law to swear that they will uphold and defend the Constitution. (This is the main reason why foreign citizens should be exempt from military conscription: soldiers, as covenanted officials of the national government, are required to uphold and defend the Constitution. They wear the marks of their civil office — uniforms — and carry "swords": weapons.)

The State can legitimately claim only the right to compel outward conformity to the law, including the law of economic restitution. *Outward conformity to the law* is sufficient to create the conditions of *external social order*. This is the function of civil government: *the preservation of external social order through the administration of justice*. At the same time, we must recognize that apart from widespread inward repentance, no social order can be preserved in the long run, for men will chafe at the requirements of God's law, including the law of restitution. Men will not honor God's law indefinitely, apart from widespread conversions. *Regeneration ultimately undergirds long-term social order*.[3] Nevertheless, it is not the State's function to seek to enforce inward regeneration. The State is not the Holy Spirit.

(I dearly hope that this analysis puts to rest the nonsense about the Christian Reconstruction movement's supposed attempt to force everyone to become a Christian. This lie has been spread by a handful of people who know it is a lie, and then by many

---

3. Gary North, *Dominion and Common Grace: The Biblical Basis of Progress* (Tyler, Texas: Institute for Christian Economics, 1987), ch. 6.

people who think it is the truth. The founders of Christian Reconstructionism, being Calvinists, have always maintained that *God forces people to become Christians through His irresistible regenerating grace*, for without this regenerating grace people cannot accept the message of the gospel. The natural man does not receive the things of the spirit of God, according to I Corinthians 2:14. We take this verse literally. *It is God's sovereign and exclusive power to force men to believe in the saving work of Jesus Christ; therefore, no human institution can lawfully compel such faith.* For anyone who is curious as to why Christian Reconstructionism came out of historic Calvinism, here is a good place to begin looking for the answers. It is precisely *because* the founders of the movement were Calvinists that Christian Reconstructionism has *never* taught that the civil government should force residents of an ideal Christian commonwealth to believe in any particular religion. Every State can, must, and always does establish standards for *citizenship-judgeship* that are based on some kind of religious belief, for all law is at bottom religious, but no Christian State can legitimately establish a profession of Christian faith as a standard for law-abiding residency.)

Restitution to God

In the case of a murder or an accidental death that looks as though it might have been murder, the victim cannot prosecute the covenant lawsuit. The Old Testament specified that the victim's nearest male relative, the *go'el*, meaning the one who held the dual office of kinsman-redeemer and blood avenger, should prosecute the case, either directly, by killing the suspect in the highway, or in the court of the city of refuge to which the suspect had fled, or outside the walls of the city if the suspect left the protection that the city offered (Num. 35:16-27). If there was no known suspect, then God became the *go'el* who would prosecute the closest city to the suspected place of the murder.

Jesus is the kinsman-redeemer in history, and He is therefore the blood avenger. He is God's lawful representative who brings God's covenant lawsuit against humanity, prosecuting the covenant lawsuit both in history and at the final judgment. As the holder of this crucial office, He also made the required restitution payment to God. We must begin with the assumption that God requires this restitution payment; if we do not assume this, then Christ's death at Calvary becomes a case of cosmic overkill.

The concept of biblical justice requires that civil judges act as representatives of God, the victim, and the community, in this order. We see this in the Old Testament's requirements in the case of an unsolved murder. The elders of the nearest city (not the priests) were required to sacrifice a heifer, wash their hands over its carcass, and announce: "Our hands have not shed this blood, neither have our eyes seen it. Be merciful, O LORD, unto thy people Israel, whom thou hast redeemed, and lay not innocent blood unto thy people of Israel's charge. And the blood shall be forgiven them" (Deut. 21:7-8).[4] The priests came near to bless the elders, but they themselves did not conduct the sacrifice (v. 5).

The judges served in this case as the lawful intermediaries between God and the city. They had been unable to locate the murderer, and the victim's blood cried out to God for vengeance (Gen. 4:10). This language of animate blood served in the Old Testament as a covenantal symbol of the relationship between God and the dead victim. Because there was no identifiable culprit, God became the legal spokesman for the victim. Why? Because the victim in his capacity as victim had served the murderer as a judicial intermediary for God. Killing a human being is attempted murder of God, for men are made in God's image. This is the basis of capital punishment for murder (Gen. 9:5). God therefore became the blood avenger (*go'el*) of the victim in cases of unsolved murderers, and He threatens the community that refuses to acknowledge that a major crime against Him has been committed.

Guilt was to this extent collective, not in the sense that the local community was responsible for the murder, but in the sense that God required ritual expiation for the murder, which had been an indirect attack on His own image. The elders had to acknowl-

---

4. The imagery of the civil magistrate's washing his hands over the sacrificial animal was the heart of Pontius Pilate's attempt to escape personal responsibility for the community-authorized murder of Jesus. Unlike the elders in Israel, however, he knew exactly who was responsible for the murder.

edge ritually that God is the ultimate attempted Victim of all crime, but especially murder, and that He is therefore owed restitution. *The restitution payment in the form of a bloody sacrifice was the legal basis of the restoration of peace between the local community and God.*

Who is the intended victim of all sin? God is. Men break the law of God to express their own autonomy as law-makers and law-interpreters. Thus, restitution is always owed primarily to God, which He collects in history and at the final judgment. But crimes are public acts. God has established intermediaries to enforce the law. To the extent that a crime is committed against anyone, the victim becomes God's legal representative, since the crime was ultimately an attack of God's holiness. The victim becomes the God-designated agent who prosecutes God's covenant lawsuit against the suspected criminal. He acts as God's agent primarily, and as his own agent secondarily, as the secondary victim.

What if the victim, as God's agent and as the secondary victim, refuses to prosecute? I see no warrant in most cases for the State then to prosecute. The court can lawfully serve as the agent of the victim in certain exceptional cases. Two examples would be victims who are orphaned minors or mental incompetents. Nevertheless, under normal circumstances, a decision not to prosecute by a victim who is legally competent to initiate a covenant lawsuit is a binding decision. He thereby loses his legal claim on any future restitution payments by the convicted criminal. If he is willing to suffer this loss, then the State must honor his or her decision. The individual, not the State, is the victim; the principle of victim's rights is binding on the State. Only if the criminal act in some way also injured the State or society could the State then prosecute, but only on its own behalf.

The witness also serves as a potential redeemer for the criminal. His public testimony allows God's representatives to bring judgment in history before God brings it in eternity. This was Paul's argument for telling the Corinthian church to prosecute the incestuous member: "To deliver such an one unto Satan for the destruction of the flesh, that the spirit may be saved in the day of the Lord Jesus" (I Cor. 5:5). While men are alive in history, they can be brought into the covenant. Judgment in history is one way of bringing them in. God told Ezekiel something very similar regarding the role of a prophet:

> Son of man, I have made thee a watchman unto the house of Israel: therefore hear the word at my mouth, and give them warning from me. When I say unto the wicked, Thou shalt surely die; and thou givest him not warning, nor speakest to warn the wicked from his wicked way, to save his life; the same wicked man shall die in his iniquity; but his blood will I require at thine hand. Yet if thou warn the wicked, and he turn not from his wickedness, nor from his wicked way, he shall die in his iniquity; but thou hast delivered thy soul (Ezek. 3:17-19).

The Old Testament prophet served as an agent of God's ecclesiastical and final courts. The witness in ancient Israel served as an agent of God's civil court. The covenant-keeper today has the office of prophet, for he possesses God's word. He can lawfully bring an ecclesiastical covenant lawsuit against God's enemies within the church and a warning of eternal judgment to those outside. He is also a prince, for he can be a witness in civil trials. He can bring a civil covenant lawsuit against civil law-breakers. He is the defender of God's interests. If he refuses to serve in these offices, then he becomes God's victim. The blood of the guilty will be on his hands, God warned Ezekiel, as well as the blood of the innocent.

Concern for the Victim

Concern for the victim rather than with rehabilitation of the criminal often marked what today are dismissed as "primitive" societies.[5] English common law has also tended to focus on retribution, not the rehabilitation of the criminal. It seeks to punish men in specific ways for specific evil acts. There is a tight relationship between the nature of the crime and the kind of punishment administered by the civil authorities. Justice is concerned with measures, which is why the goddess of justice is pictured as a blindfolded woman holding scales. Punishment is *measured out* in

---

5. Stephen Schafer, *Compensation and Restitution to Victims of Crime* (2nd ed.; Montclair, New Jersey: Patterson Smith, 1970).

terms of the severity of the crime.

In contrast, modern humanistic theories of jurisprudence, in the name of humanitarianism, to a great extent have promoted a messianic view of the State. Prof. Lon Fuller has summarized the contrasting views, and the heart of the controversy is the assertion of the ability of the State to *recreate* man: "The familiar penal or retributive theory looks to the act and seeks to make the miscreant pay for his misdeed; the rehabilitative theory on the other hand, sees the purpose of the law as recreating the person, or improving the criminal himself so that any impulses toward misconduct will be eliminated or brought under internal control. Despite the humane appeal of the rehabilitative theory, the actual processes of criminal trials remain under the domination of the view that we must try the act, not the man; any departure from this conception, it is feared, would sacrifice justice to a policy of paternalistic intervention in the life of the individual."[6] This fear is well-deserved: continual interventions into the lives of men by a self-professed omniscient paternalistic State are precisely where a legal theory of "trying the man rather than his acts" do lead. A jury can make the criminal "pay for his crime" by paying the victim; members of the jury can make reasonable estimates of the economic effects of the convicted criminal's acts. On the other hand, jurors cannot read the convicted criminal's mind. All they can do is draw conclusions regarding his intentions based on the cross examination of public testimony and evidence that was obtained legally. When men try to read other men's minds, the result is tyranny.

Restitution by the criminal to the victim is one way of restoring wholeness to the victim. It also reduces the likelihood of private attempts at vengeance.[7] It is a way of dealing with guilt. In this sense, it is also a means of restoring wholeness to the criminal.

---

6. Lon Fuller (1969), cited by Richard E. Laster, "Criminal Restitution: A Survey of Its Past History and an Analysis of Its Present Usefulness," *University of Richmond Law Review*, V (1970), p. 97. Laster's study concludes that the role of the victim in criminal law has steadily diminished (p. 97).

7. Laster, *ibid.*, p. 75.

Israel's History

Israel's history can legitimately be classified in terms of a series of incidents by which this three-fold relationship — restitution, repentance, and restoration — was illustrated in a covenantal, communal, and national way. Israel's deliverance from Babylon is a good example of this restorative process. It is also illustrated in the instance of David's adultery and murder of Uriah the Hittite. David repented (II Sam. 12:13); the child died (12:18), and so did three of his adult sons — Amnon, Absalom, and Adonijah — thereby making four-fold restitution on a "four lives for one" basis. Fourfold restitution was the required payment for the slaughter of a lamb (Ex. 22:1). Nathan the prophet had used the analogy of the slaughtered ewe lamb in his confrontation with David (II Sam. 12:4). David recognized that the culprit was worthy of death (v. 5). David therefore could not escape making the four-fold restitution payment to God's sense of justice (adultery and murder are both capital crimes in the Bible); and David and Bathsheba were covenantally restored in their marriage, which God testified to publicly by the birth of Solomon (12:24), who became the lawful heir of David's throne.

We must understand capital punishment as a restitution payment to God. The death penalty is not a means of revenge alone or deterrence alone. The death penalty is God's required restitution payment which is imposed on Adam and his heirs, and was imposed also on the second Adam, Jesus Christ. For any civil crime too great to be compensated for by a monetary restitution payment to the human victim, God requires the civil magistrate to impose the death penalty, God's restitution payment. Homicide, for example, could not be paid for in Israel by anything less than the life of the murderer — life for life (Num. 35:31), a law which is without parallel in the laws of the ancient Near East.[8] It was only later rabbinic Judaism that abandoned the principle that all murderers are subject to the death penalty, in order to reduce the penalty for Jews who kill resident aliens or gentiles.[9]

---

8. Shalom Paul, *Studies in the Book of the Covenant in the Light of Cuneiform and Biblical Law* (Leiden: E. J. Brill, 1970), p. 61.

9. Maimonides wrote: "If an Israelite kills a resident alien, he does not suffer

Christian Theology

Restitution, repentance, and restoration are equally fundamental concepts in Christian theology. Without Christ's restitution payment to God for the sins of mankind, there could have been no history from the day Adam fell. Without repentance, the individual cannot claim to be free from the requirement to make the restitution payment to God. Eternal judgment is God's lawful vengeance on all those who have not made restitution, meaning all those who have not placed themselves at the mercy of God by claiming to be under Christ's general repayment. The righteousness of God is demonstrated by His eternal punishment of those who have not made full restitution. The punishment fits the crime of ethical rebellion against a sovereign, holy God.

Restitution in Recent American Jurisprudence

Various forms of restitution have been adopted by civil governments for centuries.[10] Experiments by state and local governments in the United States since the mid-1970's also indicated that such a system can provide significant benefits to victims. The state of Minnesota began its experiment in October of 1973. Based on one year's data, researchers made a study of opinions and results. Restitution was a condition of probation of the criminals in one-fourth of all probation cases. "Restitution was used in a straightforward manner by most courts. Full cash restitution was ordered to be paid by the offender to the victim in more than nine out of ten cases. Adjustments in the amount of restitution because of limited ability of the offender were rare. In-kind, or service, restitution to the victim or community was ordered in only a few cases. . . ."[11]

---

capital punishment at the hands of the court, because Scripture says, *And if a man come presumptuously upon his neighbor* (Exod. 21:12). Needless to say, one is not put to death if he kills a heathen." Moses Maimonides, *The Book of Torts*, vol. 11, *The Code of Maimonides*, 14 vols. (New Haven, Connecticut: Yale University Press, [1180] 1954), Chapter Two, Section Eleven, p. 201.

10. J. A. Gylys and F. Reidy, "The Case for Compensating Victims of Crime," *Atlanta Economic Review*, XXV (May/June 1975).

11. *Summary Report: The Assessment of Restitution in the Minnesota Probation Services*, prepared for the Governor's Commission on Crime Prevention and Control (Jan. 31, 1976), p. 1.

The program was limited primarily to non-violent criminal offenders who were considered able to pay, which generally meant white middle-class criminal offenders.[12] This limits the empirical reliability of the conclusions concerning the overall effectiveness of the program. Also, the amount of restitution was limited to the amount of the economic loss by the victims, not two-fold restitution, as required by the Bible. The original state-level trial program was dropped in 1976, but the principle has been instituted at the local level. Judges in every jurisdiction now impose restitution as a penal sanction.

The *Summary Report* states that "Most judges and probation officers favored the use of restitution. Similarly most judges and probation officers expressed the belief that restitution had a rehabilitative effect." Furthermore, "most victims believed that restitution by the offender to the victim is the proper method of victim compensation. Victims who were dissatisfied tended to be those who felt that they had not been involved in the process of ordering or aiding in the completion of restitution." And perhaps most revealing of all, "Most offenders thought that restitution as ordered was fair."[13] Only ten of the offenders (14.4%) would have preferred a fine or a jail sentence.[14] It is understandable why we have seen a renewed interest in restitution as a form of punishment.[15]

Conclusion

Social order requires that there be legal means of the restoration of peace between criminal and victim. If the crime is so horrendous that no economic restitution payment from the crimi-

---

12. *Idem.*
13. *Idem.*
14. *Ibid.*, p. 26.
15. Joe Hudson and Burt Galloway (eds.), *Considering the Victim: Readings in Restitution and Victim Compensation* (Springfield, Illinois: Charles C. Thomas, 1975); O. Hobart Mowrer, "Loss and Recovery of Community," in George M. Gazda (ed.), *Innovations to Group Psychotherapy* (Springfield, Illinois: Charles C. Thomas, 1975). Such interest has never been entirely absent: Irving E. Cohen, "The Integration of Restitution in the Probation Services," *Journal of Criminal Law, Criminology and Police Science*, XXXIV (1944), pp. 315-26.

nal is sufficient to compensate the victim, then God requires capital punishment, the maximum restitution payment which God collects personally because He was the ultimate target of the criminal. Most crimes in the Bible are not capital crimes, however. The focus of biblical law is on economic restitution as the means of the restoration of social peace.

The victims' interests are primary: God's and the actual human victim. Because God brings judgments in history against towns and nations that refuse to enforce His civil law-order, the community needs representatives to uphold God's law: witnesses and judges. They represent the claims of God, the victim, and the community against the criminal. In civil courts, they prosecute God's covenant lawsuit in the name of God, the victim, and the community. God warns that if the victim's rights are not upheld, He will execute judgment against the criminal and his ally, the community. The community must choose, just as Adam did, either to prosecute God and the victim by siding with the criminal, actively or passively, or to prosecute the criminal in the name of God and the victim. To do the former is to leave the blood of the innocents on the community.

11

PROTECTING THE VICTIMS

If a man shall steal an ox, or a sheep, and kill it, or sell it; he shall restore five oxen for an ox, and four sheep for a sheep. . . . If the theft be certainly found in his hand alive, whether it be ox, or ass, or sheep; he shall restore double (Ex. 22:1, 4).

We think of the criminal's victims as being people who have lost their animals or money. But there are other victims: the animals themselves. This is analogous to the crime of kidnapping. The restitution system that the Bible establishes for oxen and sheep reflects this special concern by God for helpless animals. What makes sheep and oxen special is their status in the Old Testament as symbolically helpless animals. So, biblical law protects both the animals and their owners. Let us consider each in turn.

A. Symbolically Helpless Animals

Why the requirement of five-fold restitution for a slaughtered or sold ox? Oxen require training, meaning a capital investment by the owner, in order to make them effective servants of man in the tasks of dominion, but so do other animals, such as horses and donkeys, yet only two-fold restitution is required for them. Also, a thief who is found with a living ox in his possession pays only double restitution. What makes a slaughtered or sold ox different? Answer: *the ox is symbolic of the employed servant.* It is my contention that this symbolism has more to do with its five-fold restitution penalty than the value of its training does.

The law forbids the muzzling of oxen when they are working

in the field (Deut. 25:4). Paul cited this verse on two occasions: first, to make the point that God cares for His people, and that our spiritual labors will not be in vain (I Cor. 9:9); second, to point out that the laborer is worthy of his reward, and that elders in the church are worthy of double honor (I Tim. 5:17-18). It pays to train an ox, just as it pays to train human workers in their jobs. Unquestionably, a trained ox is worth more to the owner than an untrained steer, just as a trained worker is worth more than an unskilled worker, and just as an elder is deserving of double honor (payment). Furthermore, the ox is a dominion beast, but the steer is only a source of food and leather. The ox is productive until the day it is killed by man or beast; the steer is simply fattened for the slaughter.

Sheep are undoubtedly quite different from oxen. They are stupid animals. Shepherds care for them, sheep dogs monitor their movements, but wise men do not invest a lot of time and energy in trying to train them for service. They are not active work animals like oxen, which pull plows; they are far more passive. A sheep is in fact the *classic passive animal* — an animal whose main purpose in life is to get *sheared*. They are helpless. For this reason, they are symbolic in the Bible of the poor.[1]

How do we make sense of the four-fold restitution payment for a stolen sheep which is subsequently killed or sold by the thief? Why is this loss (as indicated by the size of the restitution payment) so great to the owner, compared to the double restitution payment he receives if the stolen sheep is restored to him by the thief? Economic analysis of a sheep's output does not throw much light on this problem, except in a negative sense: there is no strictly economic reason. A beast of burden such as a donkey has to be trained, and was unquestionably a valuable asset in the Old Testament economy. So was a horse. Yet neither slaughtered horses nor slaughtered donkeys are singled out in the law as entitling their owners to four-fold or five-fold restitution. What is so special about a sheep? Is its wool production that much more valuable than the economic output of a horse or donkey? Clearly,

---

1. James B. Jordan, *The Law of the Covenant: An Exposition of Exodus 21-23* (Tyler, Texas: Institute for Christian Economics, 1984), pp. 267-69.

the answer is in the negative. We are forced to conclude that the distinguishing characteristic between a slaughtered stolen donkey and a slaughtered stolen sheep has nothing to do with the comparative economic value of each beast's output. Instead, it has a great deal to do with the sheep's *symbolic subordinate relationship to the owner*.

Of Sheep and Men

In the Bible, animals *image* man.[2] Sheep are specifically compared to men throughout the Bible, with God as the Shepherd and men as helpless dependents. The Twenty-Third Psalm makes use of the imagery of the shepherd and sheep. David, a shepherd, compares himself to a sheep, for God is described as his shepherd (Ps. 23:1). Christ called Himself the "good shepherd" who gives His life for His sheep (John 10:11). He said to His disciples on the night of His capture by the authorities, citing Zechariah 13:7, "All ye shall be offended because of me this night: for it is written, I will smite the shepherd, and the sheep of the flock shall be scattered abroad" (Matt. 26:31). He referred to the Jews as "the lost sheep of the house of Israel" (Matt. 10:6), echoing Jeremiah, "Israel is a scattered sheep" (Jer. 50:17a) and Ezekiel, "And they were scattered, because there is no shepherd: and they became meat to all the beasts of the field, when they were scattered" (Ezk. 34:5). Christ spoke of children as sheep, and offered the analogy of the man who loses one sheep out of a hundred. The man searches diligently to locate that one lost sheep and rejoices if he finds it. "Even so it is not the will of your Father which is in heaven, that one of these little ones should perish" (Matt. 18:14).

It is thus the *helplessness* of sheep rather than their value as beasts of burden or dominion that makes four-fold restitution mandatory.[3] Shepherds regard sheep as their special responsibil-

---

2. Animals in men's image: *ibid.*, p. 122. He cites Prov. 6:6; 26:11; 30:15, 19, 24-31; Dan. 5:21; Ex. 13:2, 13. When I use the noun "image" as a verb, I am reminded of one cynic's remark: "There is no noun in the English language that cannot be verbed."

3. Maimonides ignored all this when he insisted that if a thief "butchers or sells on the owner's premises (an animal stolen there), he need not pay fourfold or fivefold. But if he lifts the object up, he is liable for theft even before he removes it from the

ity. The position of sheep is therefore unique. *Sheep are representative of the utter helplessness of men.* An attack on the sheep under a man's control strikes at his position as a covenantally responsible steward. David risked his life to save a lamb (or perhaps lambs) captured by a bear and a lion, and he slew them both (I Sam. 17:34-36), taking the lamb, apparently unharmed, out of the mouth of the lion: "I caught him by his beard" (v. 35). As God had delivered him out of the paw of both lion and bear, David told Saul, so would He deliver him out of the hand of Goliath (v. 37). Again, David was comparing himself (and Israel) with the lamb, and comparing God with the shepherd. Thus, the recovery of a specific lost or stolen sheep is important to a faithful shepherd or owner, not just a replacement animal.

David and Bathsheba

Perhaps the best example of sheep as a symbol for defenseless humans is found in Nathan's confrontation with King David concerning his adultery with Bathsheba, wife of Uriah the Hittite. Nathan proposed a legal case for David to judge. A rich man steals a female lamb from a poor neighbor, and then kills it. "And David's anger was greatly kindled against the man; and he said to Nathan, As the LORD liveth, the man that hath done this thing shall surely die: And he shall restore the lamb fourfold, because he did this thing, and because he had no pity" (II Sam. 12:5-6). Then Nathan replied to him, "Thou art the man." Uriah had been the neighbor; Bathsheba is the ewe lamb who, biblically speaking, has been killed, the death penalty being applicable in cases of adultery (Lev. 20:10).

David recognized that the four-fold restitution was applicable in the case of stolen and slaughtered sheep. But in fact, Nathan was not talking about a lamb; he was talking about a human being. He used the symbol of the slaughtered sheep for the foolish woman who consented to the capital crime of adultery. The woman

---

owner's premises. Thus, if one steals a lamb from a fold and it dies on the owner's premises while he is pulling it away, he is exempt. But if he picks it up, or takes it off the owner's premises and it then dies, he is liable." Maimonides, *Torts*, "Laws Concerning Theft," Chapter Two, Section Sixteen, p. 67.

had been entitled to protection, especially by the king. Instead, she had been placed in jeopardy of her life by the king. The king had proven himself to be an evil shepherd.

What was the penalty extracted by God? First, the infant born of the illicit union would die, Nathan promised (II Sam. 12:14). On the seventh day, the day before its circumcision, the child died (v. 18). The next section of Second Samuel records the rape of Tamar by David's son Amnon. Absalom, her brother, commanded his servants to kill Amnon, which they did (II Sam. 13:29). Absalom revolted against David and was later slain by Joab (II Sam. 18:14). Finally, Adonijah attempted to steal the throne, but Solomon was anointed (I Ki. 1), and Adonijah tried again to secure the throne by asking Solomon to allow him to marry David's bed-warmer. Solomon recognized this attempt to gain the throne through marriage, and had him executed (I Ki. 2:24-25). Thus, four of David's sons died, fulfilling the required four-for-one punishment for his adultery and his murder of Uriah.[4]

Shepherds and Sheep

By striking at a man's lawful position of personal stewardship, the sheep-stealer takes an extra risk. It is far less risky to steal gold or silver and then sell it than to steal and sell a sheep; he will pay only two-fold restitution if he is captured for stealing and then selling gold. The sheep-stealer strikes at the very heart of a man's dominion assignment, in which a man has invested love and care on helpless, dependent beasts. *The shepherd's calling (vocation) is the archetypal calling: it points analogically to the cosmic personalism and providential goodness of God.* It is therefore specially defended by biblical law.

We see the archetypal nature of the shepherd's calling in the

---

4. The Jewish scholar Brichto recognizes the connection between Exodus 22:1 and the death of four of David's sons. His comment on the fourth of the four-fold penalty that God imposed on David is pertinent: "The execution of Adonijah, occurring after David's death has, in this context, escaped general notice: even of scholars, who have been conditioned not to count as significant (for biblical man) what happens to a man's son(s) after his demise." Herbert Chanan Brichto, "Kin, Cult, Land and Afterlife – A Biblical Complex," *Hebrew Union College Annual*, XLIV (1973), p. 42.

office of church elder. We call ministers of the gospel "pastors," a word derived from the same root as "pastoral." They are shepherds. Christ three times told Peter that his task would be to feed Christ's sheep (John 21:15-17). Peter later instructed elders of the church to "Feed the flock of God which is among you, taking the oversight thereof" (I Pet. 5:2a). The shepherd's role as caretaker and protector is analogous to God's care and protection of the world and Christ's care and protection of His church (John 10).

It is significant that the Israelites had been shepherds of cattle and sheep when they came into Egypt. The Egyptians despised shepherds. Because of this, Joseph instructed his brothers to ask Pharaoh for a separate land, Goshen, where the Israelites would not come into contact with the Egyptians (Gen. 46:33-34). God's law, delivered so soon after their escape from a land in which their calling was despised, dealt with that calling and its risks and responsibilities.

The Egyptians had despised shepherds, whose task is to care for flocks. These same Egyptians had placed the Israelites in bondage. The Egyptians were repulsed by an occupation that is based on a covenantal model of God's responsibility for the care and protection of His people. They were also repulsed by the concept of a society based on the idea of a ruler's covenantal responsibility for the care and protection of men. This hostility is understandable: Egypt was a bureaucratic, tyrannical State.[5] The Israelites' experience in Egypt was designed by God to teach them that men are not allowed to do to cattle and sheep something that they are unquestionably not to do to other men: treat them unmercifully and carelessly or steal them and illegally slaughter them. Thus, God imposed His four-fold restitution on the Egyptians: He destroyed them.

Sheep, being stupid, are inescapably dependent. They have to trust their master if they are to survive. The shepherd is not to betray this personal trust until it is time to kill the sheep for food or, in Old Testament times, for sacrifice. Christ pointed to the intimate relationship between the shepherd and his sheep:

---

5. Gary North, *Moses and Pharaoh: Dominion Religion vs. Power Religion* (Tyler, Texas: Institute for Christian Economics, 1985), ch. 2: "Imperial Bureaucracy."

"And when he putteth forth his own sheep, he goeth before them, and the sheep follow him: for they know his voice. And a stranger will they not follow, but will flee from him: for they know not the voice of strangers" (John 10:4-5). When removed from the care of their shepherd, forcibly or otherwise, the sheep become lost.

Symbolism or Training?

At this point, I must resort to a somewhat speculative hypothesis in order to make sense out of the four-fold restitution payment for a missing or dead sheep and the five-fold restitution payment for a missing or dead ox. I am arguing that the high penalties are imposed because of the symbolic nature of sheep and oxen, although I cannot absolutely prove it.[6] But to make sense of Exodus 22:1, we have to go beyond considerations of strictly financial profit and loss. Economics as such does not provide a clear-cut answer to a fundamental question: *Why doesn't God's law impose five-fold or four-fold restitution payments for the slaughter or sale of stolen horses or donkeys or other beasts of burden (dominion)?* They require the capital investment of training, just as an ox does. The value of this training is forfeited when the thief cannot return the actual stolen beast to the owner. We might presume that the principle of the four-fold and five-fold restitution payment does, by implication, apply to these other beasts, if they have received training or other capital investments that set them apart from untrained beasts of the same species. Nevertheless, the Bible never says this explicitly. It specifically singles out sheep and oxen. Why?

I see two possible reasons. First, unlike horses, donkeys, and other domesticated animals that might be trainable, sheep and oxen were commonly *slaughtered and eaten*, as they are today. Thus, they need special protection from thieves. A thief who slaughters an ox or sheep is subject to more stringent penalties. The higher penalty tends to restrain him in his blood-letting. This is a more strictly economic argument, one based on the economic effects of

---

6. Jordan, *Law of the Covenant*, Appendix G. I discussed my thesis in the present chapter with Jordan prior to the publication of his book, and he expanded on the idea.

the law. Second, both sheep and oxen are *symbolic in the Bible of mankind*: oxen for men of power or office, and sheep for dependent, spiritually helpless people. Oxen are normally peaceful, dominion beasts that are used for plowing the fields, never for war. Sheep are passive creatures that require special care on the part of shepherds. Thus, as archetypes of man in his relationship to God — *creatures in need of care* — oxen and sheep receive special consideration by the law.

Why a five-fold restitution payment for oxen? Why not fourfold? Probably because oxen are beasts of burden and therefore living tools of dominion. They are dependent,[7] though not so dependent as sheep, but they are also symbolic of God's dominion covenant. The number five is associated with the covenant in the Bible. Also, Israel marched in military formations based on the number five.[8] The number five is associated with dominion. By killing a stolen ox, the thief is symbolically sacrificing another person's economic future for the sake of his own present enjoyment. This is what Satan attempted to do to Adam, and only the grace of God in Christ prevented Satan's successful slaughtering of humanity.

This law of restitution singles out oxen and sheep as being special creatures. Other passages in the Bible do the same. What the stringent restitution penalties of Exodus 22:1 point to is a general principle: *how you treat oxen and sheep is indicative of how you treat other men.* The ox is worthy of his hire; how much more a man! The sheep is helpless, and is deserving of protection; how much more a man! A society whose legal order protects oxen and sheep from thieves who would slaughter them is a society whose legal order is likely also to protect men from oppression, kidnapping, and murder. A biblical social order offers special protection to oxen, sheep, and men.[9]

---

7. I believe that the male ox in this case law is castrated and not a bull. Castration reduces its threat to men, yet the animal's strength can still be harnessed for man's purposes. It is more dependent on man than a bull would be.

8. James B. Jordan, *The Sociology of the Church* (Tyler, Texas: Geneva Ministries, 1986), pp. 215-16.

9. David Daube's comments on the four-fold and five-fold restitution requirements acknowledge none of this. Instead, he returns to his favorite theme, like a dog

B. Owners

The penalty paid to the victim by the criminal *compensates him for his trouble*, while it simultaneously serves as a *deterrent to future criminal behavior*. Biblical restitution achieves both goals — compensation of the victim and deterrence of criminal behavior — by means of a single judicial penalty: restitution. In contrast, modern humanistic jurisprudence has until quite recently ignored the needs of the victim by ignoring restitution.

This two-fold purpose of criminal law was ignored by modern American jurisprudence until the 1960's, when the subject of restitution to victims at last became a topic of discussion among legislators and law enforcement authorities.[10] The Department of Corrections of Minneapolis, Minnesota, began a "restitution and release" experimental program in 1974, the Minnesota Restitution Center, in which criminals involved in crimes against other people's property compensate the victims. Only 28 men were admitted to the experiment during its first year. Violent criminals were not accepted.[11] By 1978, 24 of the 50 states in the United States had adopted some form of compensation to victims of violent crimes.

This policy had begun in the mid-1960's in Great Britain. In the United States, the first state to introduce such a program was California, in 1965. Such costs as legal fees, money lost as a result of the injured person's absence from work, and medical expenses

---

returns to its vomit: the "later addition" thesis. He contrasts the two-fold restitution requirement with the four-fold and five-fold requirements. The higher penalties are evidence of an earlier law. ". . . the older rule makes a rather primitive distinction between theft of an ox and theft of a sheep: for one ox you have to give five, but for one sheep only four. No such distinction occurs in the later rule. Whatever kind of animal you steal, you have to restore two for one." Daube, *Studies in Biblical Law* (Cambridge: At the University Press, 1947), pp. 94-95. He uses a similar line of argumentation to distinguish Exodus 21:28-31 from 21:35-36: *ibid.*, pp. 86-87.

10. Cf. Burt Galaway and Joe Hudson (eds.), *Offender Restitution in Theory and Action* (Lexington, Massachusetts: Lexington Books, 1977); Randy E. Barnett and John Hegel III (eds.), *Assessing the Criminal: Restitution, Retribution, and the Legal Process* (Cambridge, Massachusetts: Ballinger, 1977). See the special feature, "Crime and the Victim," in *Trial* (May/June 1972), the national legal news magazine of the American Trial Lawyers Association.

11. *Los Angeles Times* (April 21, 1974).

are covered in some states. In cases of death or permanent disability, maximum payments were anywhere from $10,000 to $50,000. Average payments in 1978 were $3,000 to $4,000 (with the price of gold in the $175-240 per ounce range). Nonviolent crimes were not covered, nor were property losses in violent crimes. Only a small percentage of citizens are aware of these laws; only a small percentage (1% to 3%) of victims received such payments. Also, the states compensated victims from state treasuries; the criminals did not make the payments.[12]

Edward Levi, who served as President Gerald Ford's Attorney General (1974-76), pinpointed the origin of the penitentiary: the ideal of the savior State. "While the existence of jails dates back to medieval times, the idea of penitentiaries is modern — indeed, it is American. Largely it is the product of the Quaker notion that if a wrongdoer were separated from his companions, given a great length of time to think about his misdeeds, and with the help of prayer, he would mend his ways. This late-18th-century concept was the beginning of what has come to be known as the rehabilitative ideal."[13] Here is the great irony: it was Quaker theology that led both to the freeing of the slaves and the imprisoning of criminals whose productivity should be put into service of their victims. Prior to the rise of Quaker jurisprudence, Roger Campbell reports, "Massachusetts law in 1736 provided that a thief should be whipped or fined for his first offense. The second time he was apprehended and proven guilty of that

---

12. *U.S. News and World Report* (July 24, 1978). Predictably, state officials wanted the federal government to fund most of these payments. A bill to pay 90% of such costs through the Law Enforcement Assistance Administration (L.E.A.A.), the Victims of Crime Act, passed the U.S. Senate in 1973, but did not pass the House and was not signed into law. Hearings were held in 1972 and 1973. It was a sufficiently important topic to be included in Major Issues System of the Congressional Research Service of the Library of Congress beginning in 1974: *Crime: Compensation for Victims and Survivors*, Issue Brief 74014.

13. Edward H. Levi, speech at the dedication ceremony for the Federal Bureau of Prisons Detention Center, Chicago, Illinois, October 15, 1975; cited in Roger F. Campbell, *Justice Through Restitution: Making Criminals Pay* (Milford, Michigan: Mott Media, 1977), p. 63. By far, the best historical account of this transition from town punishments to the state penitentiary system is David J. Rothman's prize-winning study, *The Discovery of the Asylum: Social Order and Disorder in the New Republic* (Boston: Little, Brown, 1971).

crime he would be required to pay three times the value of the property stolen to the victim and was forced to sit on the gallows for one hour with a rope around his neck. On the third offence, the trip to the gallows was for real."[14]

Conclusion

The case laws governing restitution indicate a specially protected position for sheep and oxen. This special treatment is unrelated to the costs of producing or replacing them because trained horses and donkeys are not listed as being equally protected. What the traditional commentators have failed to notice is that the Old Testament identifies sheep and oxen as uniquely representative of man, symbolically speaking. The ox represents man in his productive capacity, and the sheep represents man in his state of helplessness. Thus, the covenantally faithful society that specially protects the lives of stolen sheep and oxen will also protect the lives of human beings.

Modern society ignores these laws. The case laws of Exodus are ignored, the Ten Commandments are ignored, and the rights of victims are ignored. Modern man believes that he can impose justice without any reference to the seemingly subtle distinctions of the Bible's case laws, but the result has been tyranny.

There was a time when cattle rustling in the United States was a capital crime. This went too far in the direction of anti-biblical severity. Today, there is nothing special about stealing cattle or sheep; it is just another criminal profession. This goes too far away from anti-biblical leniency. Modern law codes should retain the significant distinctions in penalties for stealing and selling sheep and trained oxen, even if there are few sheep or trained oxen in our society, in order to keep before us the judicial meaning of these biblical symbols: that victims are entitled to protection, especially human victims.

---

14. Campbell, *ibid.*, p. 64.

12

RESTORING FULL VALUE

If a man shall steal an ox, or a sheep, and kill it, or sell it; he shall restore five oxen for an ox, and four sheep for a sheep. . . . If the theft be certainly found in his hand alive, whether it be ox, or ass, or sheep; he shall restore double (Ex. 22:1, 4).

In any attempted explanation of a Bible passage, we must have as our principle of interpretation the Bible's revelation of the theocentric nature of all existence. God created and now sustains all life. Thus, a sin against a person is first and foremost a sin against God. Restitution must always be made to God. God demands the death of the sinner as the only sufficient lawful restitution payment. But God allows a substitute payment, symbolized in the Old Testament economy by the sacrifice of animals. These symbols pointed forward in time to the death of Jesus Christ, which alone serves as the foundation of all of life (Heb. 8). Jesus Christ made a temporary restitution payment to God in the name of mankind in general (temporal life goes on) and a permanent one for His people (eternal life will come).[1] Adam deserved death on the day he rebelled; God gave him extended life on earth because of the atonement of Christ. The same is true for Adam's biological heirs. We live because of Christ's atonement, and only because of it.

Crimes can also be against men. This means that restitution

---

1. Gary North, *Dominion and Common Grace: The Biblical Basis of Progress* (Tyler, Texas: Institute for Christian Economics, 1987), chaps. 3, 6. The Bible passage that indicates these two aspects of salvation is I Timothy 4:10: "For therefore we both labour and suffer reproach, because we trust in the living God, who is the Saviour of all men, specially of those that believe."

must be made to the victim, and not just to God. There is no forgiveness apart from restitution: Christ's primarily, and the criminal's secondarily. As images of God, victims are entitled to restitution payments from criminals. Since crimes differ in terms of their impact on victims, penalties also vary. The biblical principle is a familiar one in Western jurisprudence: the punishment must fit the crime. Since economic restitution is the form that punishment must take in the case of theft, *economic restitution must therefore "fit the crime."* It must fit the crime in at least three ways: first, by restoring to the victim as closely as possible the value of what had been stolen; second, by compensating the victim for his suffering in losing the item or items; third, by compensating the victim for the costs of detecting the thief.

Costs of Retraining: The Traditional Explanation

R. J. Rushdoony's discussion of multiple penalties, which he calls multiple restitution, is important for the light it sheds on the first aspect of restitution, the payment necessary to compensate the victim for the loss he suffered as a result of the theft. Unfortunately, Rushdoony follows rabbinical tradition and introduces an extraneous issue which confuses the discussion, namely, the *use-value of the animals*. He writes: "Multiple restitution rests on the principle of justice. Sheep are capable of a high rate of reproduction and have use, not only as meat, but also by means of their wool, for clothing, as well as other uses. To steal a sheep is to steal the present and future value of a man's property. The ox requires a higher rate of restitution, five-fold, because the ox was trained to pull carts, and to plow, and was used for a variety of farm tasks. The ox therefore had not only the value of its meat and its usefulness, but also the value of its training, in that training an ox for work was a task requiring time and skill. It thus commanded a higher rate of restitution. Clearly, a principle of restitution is in evidence here. Restitution must calculate not only the present and future value of a thing stolen, but also the specialized skills involved in its replacement."[2] Walter Kaiser

---

2. R. J. Rushdoony, *The Institutes of Biblical Law* (Nutley, New Jersey: Craig Press, 1973), pp. 459-60.

agrees.³ The Jewish scholar, Cassuto, argues along similar lines: "*He shall pay five oxen for an ox, and four sheep for a sheep* — less for a sheep than for an ox, possibly because the rearing of a sheep does not require so much, or so prolonged, effort as the rearing of herds."⁴ In fact, this interpretation is quite traditional among Jewish scholars.⁵

This interpretation seems to get support from the laws of at least one nation contemporary with ancient Israel. The Hittites also imposed varying penalties according to which animal had been stolen. Anyone who stole a bull and changed its brand, if discovered, had to repay the owner with seven head of cattle: two three-year-olds, three yearlings, and two weanlings.⁶ A cow received a five-fold restitution payment.⁷ The same penalty was imposed on thieves of stallions and rams.⁸ A plow-ox required a ten-fold restitution (previously 15).⁹ The same was true of a draft horse.¹⁰ Thus, it appears that trained work animals were evaluated as being worth more to replace than the others. Anyone who recovered a stolen horse, mule, or donkey was to receive an additional animal: double restitution.¹¹ The original animal that had received training was returned; thus, the thief did not have to pay multiple restitution.

It seems reasonable to conclude that the Bible's higher payment for a sheep or ox is based on the costs of retraining an equivalent animal. But what seems reasonable at first glance turns out to be mistaken.

---

3. Walter C. Kaiser, Jr., *Toward Old Testament Ethics* (Grand Rapids, Michigan: Zondervan Academie, 1983), p. 105.

4. U. Cassuto, *A Commentary on the Book of Exodus*, translated by Israel Abrahams (Jerusalem: The Magnes Press, The Hebrew University, [1951] 1974), p. 282.

5. See the citations by Nehama Leibowitz, *Studies in Shemot*, Part 2 (Jerusalem: World Zionist Organization, 1976), p. 364.

6. "Hittite Laws," paragraph 60. *Ancient Near Eastern Texts Relating to the Old Testament*, edited by James B. Pritchard (3rd ed.; Princeton, New Jersey: Princeton University Press, 1969), p. 192.

7. *Idem.*, paragraph 67.
8. *Idem.*, paragraphs 61, 62.
9. *Idem.*, paragraph 63.
10. *Idem.*, paragraph 64.
11. *Idem.*, paragraph 70.

Discounted Future Value and Capitalization

We need to consider carefully the argument that the higher restitution penalty is related to the increased difficulty of training domestic animals. No doubt it is true that the owner must go to considerable effort to retrain a work animal. But is a sheep a work animal? Does it need training? Obviously not. This should warn us against adopting such an argument regarding any restitution payment that is greater than two-fold.

It is quite true that the future value of any stolen asset must be paid to the victim by the thief. What is not generally understood by non-economists is that *the present market price of an asset already includes its expected future value.* Modern price theory teaches that the present price of any scarce economic resource reflects the estimated future value of the asset's net output (net stream of income, or net rents), discounted by the market rate of interest for the time period that corresponds to the expected productive life of the asset.[12] For example, if I expect a piece of land to produce a net economic return (rent) equivalent to one ounce of gold per year for a thousand years, I would be foolish to pay a thousand ounces of gold for it today. The present value to me of my thousandth ounce of gold is vastly higher than the present value to me of a thousandth ounce of gold a thousand and one years in the future. When offering to buy the land, I therefore discount that expected income stream of gold by the longest-term interest rate on the market. So do all my potential competitors (other buyers). The cash payment for the land will therefore be substantially less than the expected rental payments of one thousand ounces of gold.

This discounting process is called *capitalization*. When we capitalize something, we pay a cash price – an actual transaction or an imputed estimation – for a future stream of income. Capitalization stems from the fact, as Rothbard argues, that "Rents from any durable good accrue at different points in time, at different dates in the future. The capital value of any good then becomes

---

12. Murray N. Rothbard, *Man, Economy, and State* (New York: New York University Press, [1962] 1979), ch. 7.

the sum of its expected future rents, discounted by the rate of time preference for present over future goods, which is the rate of interest. In short, the capital value of a good is the 'capitalization' of its future rents in accordance with the rate of time preference or interest."[13] This is not a difficult concept to grasp; unfortunately for human freedom and productivity, very few people have ever heard about it.

This process of capitalization means that the higher the prevailing interest rate, the smaller the cash payment that a buyer will offer for a piece of land today: the buyer applies a *higher discount* to its expected stream of income.[14] Always bear in mind, however, that no one knows for certain what the future value of an asset's output will be, nor does anyone know precisely how much the interest rate will fluctuate over the expected productive life of the asset. Obviously, no one is sure just what the productive life of any asset will be. Market forecasting involves a great deal of uncertainty.

What is most important to understand at this point is that this discounting process applies to *all* capital goods (including durable consumer goods) in the market; it is not simply the product of a money economy. Monetary exchanges are as bound by the process of discounting expected future income (rents) as are all other transactions. Put a different way, *the phenomenon of interest is basic to human action; it is not the product of a money economy.*

Uncertainty is the origin of what some economists call en-

---

13. Murray N. Rothbard, Introduction; Frank A. Fetter, *Capital, Interest, and Rent: Essays in the Theory of Distribution* (Kansas City, Kansas: Sheed Andrews and McMeel, 1977), p. 13.

14. If we expect a lower rate of interest in the future than presently prevails, we will be willing to pay the prevailing cash price, since the annual rate of return will be discounted subsequently by a smaller number. Thus, we buy today at a nice, fat "discount for cash," and we will be able to sell the property later on for a smaller discount for cash when the rate of discount (interest) drops. If we expect rates to rise, we will only buy at less than the prevailing cash market price, which means, of course, that we will not be able to buy it, since the owner can sell it for more to someone else. The new buyer will then suffer economic losses, if our expectation is correct. He will get a smaller "discount for cash" when he buys today, and if he wants to sell later on, he will have to accept a larger discount, since the rate of interest will have risen. The market value of his land will drop.

trepreneurial or "pure" profit.[15] When the estimates of the various competing entrepreneurs – market forecasters-investors[16] – are brought to bear in the capital goods markets, the outcome is a price for any capital asset.[17] Today's demand is a composite of demand for present use (shear, kill, and eat a sheep today) and future use (shear a sheep repeatedly over several years and then kill and eat it). Today's price is the product of the competitive interaction between *today's demand* – which includes an estimation of future demand and an estimation of future supply – and *today's supply*.

In short, the present price of any scarce economic resource *already* includes its expected future price, discounted by the applicable period's market rate of interest.[18]

The Economics of Restitution

Having said this, we now consider the economics of restitution. The task of the judges in estimating a morally legitimate restitution payment is easier than it seems. Judges can safely ignore the question of just how much the future value of a stolen

---

15. Frank H. Knight, *Risk, Uncertainty, and Profit* (New York: Harper Torchbooks, [1921] 1965). See also Gary North, *The Dominion Covenant: Genesis* (2nd ed.; Tyler, Texas: Institute for Christian Economics, 1987), ch. 23.

16. Some economists distinguish between the capitalist owner-investor and the future-predicting entrepreneur. I have not found this distinction particularly helpful. A forecaster who does not invest capital is not a participant in the market. If someone invests in terms of what the capital-deficient forecaster has said, then the investor becomes the significant participant. Like the race track tout who refuses to invest his own money, and who therefore has no effect on the odds at the ticket window unless he gets someone to bet in terms of his forecasts, so is the entrepreneur who is not a capitalist. Both are economically irrelevant in practice. I prefer to avoid distinctions that are irrelevant in practice. For examples of this distinction, see Israel Kirzner, *Competition and Entrepreneurship* (University of Chicago Press, 1973), pp. 47-52; Henry Manne, *Insider Trading and the Stock Market* (New York: Free Press, 1966), pp. 117-19.

17. Yes, there can be various prices, depending on market information concerning other buyers and sellers, including substitute producer goods, as well as transportation costs, insurance rates, and so forth. But the tendency of competition is to produce a single market price for a given piece of equipment in a particular geographical region.

18. The prevailing rate of interest for loans of any given duration, like the prevailing price of any asset, is the product of the best guesses of entrepreneurs (speculators) concerning the future of interest rates of that duration.

asset might be. The best experts in forecasting economic value — entrepreneurs — have already provided this information to the judges, all nicely discounted by the market rate of interest. The judges need only use *existing market prices* in order to compute restitution payments.

A restitution payment is normally twice the prevailing market price of the asset. When the stolen ox is returned by the authorities to the owner (the thief neither slaughtered it nor sold it), the thief pays double restitution. "If the theft be certainly found in his hand alive, whether it be ox, or ass, or sheep; he shall restore double" (Ex. 22:4). Rushdoony follows the traditional rabbinical interpretation when he argues that this 100 percent penalty above the market price is the minimum amount by which the thief expected to profit from his action.[19] The thief must return the original beast, plus his expected minimum "profit" from the transaction, namely, the market value of the stolen beast. He forfeits that which he had expected to gain. Maimonides wrote of the requirement that the thief pay double: "He thus loses an amount equal to that of which he wished to deprive another."[20] Akedat Yizhak concurs: "The thief is treated differently from the one who causes damage. The latter who caused damage through his ox or pit did not intend to deprive his fellow of anything. He is therefore only required to make half or total restitution. The thief who deliberately sets out to inflict loss on his fellow deserves to have a taste of his own medicine — to lose the same amount that he deprived his fellow of. This can only be achieved through double restitution."[21] This is analogous to the perjurer who is subject to the judicial penalty which his lie, had it been believed by the judges, would have imposed on the innocent person (Deut. 19:16-21).[22]

---

19. Rushdoony, *Institutes*, p. 460.

20. Moses Maimonides, *The Book of Torts*, vol. 11 of *The Code of Maimonides*, 14 vols. (New Haven, Connecticut: Yale University Press, [1180] 1954), "Laws Concerning Theft," Chapter One, Section Four, p. 60.

21. Cited by Leibowitz, *Studies in Shemot*, p. 362.

22. This section of Deuteronomy is explicitly a case-law application of the "eye for eye" principle.

Victim's Rights

"If a man shall steal an ox, or a sheep, and kill it, or sell it; he shall restore five oxen for an ox, and four sheep for a sheep" (Ex. 22:1). What if a stolen sheep or ox had been sold by the thief? The thief may know where the animal is. If the authorities convict him of the crime, would he be given an opportunity to buy back the stolen animal and return it to the owner, plus the 100 percent penalty, and thereby avoid the four-fold or five-fold restitution penalty? This would seem to violate the third goal of proportional restitution (see pp. 230-31): increasing the risk for thieves who steal sheep or oxen, and who then dispose of the evidence by destroying them or selling them, thereby making it more difficult to convict them in court. The thief would still have to pay the four-fold or five-fold penalty, *unless the victim decides otherwise*. The fundamental judicial principle here is *victim's rights*. The victim decides the penalty, up to the limits of the law.

The victimized original owner should always have the authority to offer the convicted criminal an alternative which is more to the victim's liking. Perhaps he is emotionally attached to the missing ox, especially if he personally trained it. He may even be attached emotionally to the stolen sheep — less likely, I suspect, than attachment to an ox that he had personally trained. What if he offers to accept double restitution if 1) the criminal will tell him where the sold beast is, and 2) the beast is returned to him alive? What if the thief then tells the victim and the civil authorities where the missing beast is? The authorities would then compel the new owner — who, legally speaking, is not truly an owner, as we shall see — to return the animal to the original owner.

The buyer of the stolen beast now has neither beast nor the forfeited purchase price. He has become the thief's victim. The thief therefore owes him some sort of restitution payment. The question is: How much? This is a difficult question to answer. It would be either a 20 percent penalty or a 100 percent penalty. I believe that it is a 20 percent penalty.

Timely Confession Receives Its Appropriate Reward

Here is my reasoning. Say that the convicted thief confesses his crime of having either sold or slaughtered the stolen beast. The court is not sure which he did, but the penalty is the same in either case: four-fold (sheep) or five-fold (ox) restitution. In an attempt to persuade the original owner to accept the return of his animal plus a 100 percent penalty, he now confesses that he sold it. Say that the owner agrees to accept two-fold restitution if the thief can get the animal back. The thief must now return the stolen beast. He goes to the buyer and tells him that the animal was stolen and must be returned to the original owner. He now also owes the victimized buyer the purchase price of the beast, plus a penalty payment of 20 percent (Lev. 6:2-5).

If the initial buyer has already sold the beast, then it is the responsibility of the thief, not the buyer, to trace down its present location. The person who has final possession when the State intervenes and requires him to return it to its original owner is the defrauded buyer to whom the thief owes the restitution payment. Because the "bundle of rights" associated with legal ownership could not be transferred by the thief to the various buyers, the final buyer has no legal claim on the animal. He is in receipt of stolen goods.

By cooperating with the original victim, the thief may be able to reduce his overall liability. Instead of paying the original owner five-fold restitution for an ox, he now pays less. First, the stolen beast is returned to the true owner: basic restitution. Second, the thief then must pay that person the equivalent value of the beast. Third, he also owes the defrauded purchaser the return of his purchase price plus a penalty of 20 percent. Thus, he pays 3.2-fold restitution, plus the cost of locating and transporting the beast, rather than five-fold or four-fold restitution. Obviously, the thief is better off if he cooperates with the true owner, and tells him who bought the stolen ox or sheep from him.

Why assume that the thief only owes the victimized buyer 20 percent? Because biblical law recognizes that thieves have *better information* about what they did than other people do. It is best for the law to offer thieves a reduced penalty for confession in order to elicit better information from them before the costs of the trial must be borne. To encourage the criminal to tell the truth, there has to be a threat hanging over him: the possibility that someone with the missing information will come to the judges and present it. Thus, if the thief remains silent about the person who bought the sheep or ox, he bears greater risk.

The Silent Thief

A silent thief faces an additional threat. Assume that the original owner demands four-fold (sheep) or five-fold (ox) restitution. Still, the thief says nothing because he knows that if he admits that he sold the beast, he will also have to pay the victimized buyer 120 percent, yet the original owner may nevertheless refuse to deal with him, and may demand (as is his legal right) either four-fold or five-fold restitution. Once the thief has sold a stolen sheep or ox, the victim can legally demand the higher penalty payment. The victim is owed the four-fold or five-fold restitution whether or not the thief locates the stolen beast, buys it back, and returns it to its original owner. *The very act of selling a stolen ox or sheep invokes the law's full penalty.* It is very much like the crime of kidnapping; the family of the kidnapped victim or the judge or the jury can legally insist on the death penalty even if the kidnapper offers to identify the person to whom the victim had been sold into bondage.

Why would the thief remain silent about the whereabouts of the stolen animal? One reason might be his fear of revenge from an accomplice in the crime. Laying this motivation aside, let us consider other possible motivations for the thief's remaining silent. First and foremost, the thief may believe that he will not be convicted of the crime. After all, the beast is missing. It is not in the thief's possession. Second, he may believe that the victim is hard-hearted and will insist on the maximum restitution payment even if the thief can get the beast back by identifying the defrauded buyer and paying him the purchase price plus a penalty payment of 20 percent.

He remains silent. He may be convicted anyway. If so, he now faces a new problem: he not only owes four-fold or five-fold restitution to the victim, he could also wind up owing the victimized buyer whatever the buyer paid him for the stolen animal. Why? Because the victimized buyer may later discover that he has purchased a stolen beast. If he then remains silent, he breaks the law. He is a recipient of stolen goods. He has become an accomplice of the thief. His silence condemns him. Additionally, he may feel guilty because he is not its legal owner.

How can the defrauded buyer escape these burdens? He can go to the original owner who has already received full restitution from the thief (or from the person who has purchased the thief as a slave), and offer to sell the animal back to him. Once the victimized buyer identifies himself, the thief now owes restitution to the defrauded buyer: double restitution, minus the purchase price that the defrauded buyer receives from the original owner. The thief has stolen from the buyer through fraud. As is the case with any other victim of unconfessed theft, the defrauded buyer is entitled to double restitution from the thief. Therefore, as soon as the thief gets through paying his debt to the original owner, he then must pay the victimized buyer the penalty payment.

If the original owner declines to buy the beast, the buyer becomes its legal owner. The original owner does not want it back. He has also been paid: restitution from the thief. But the defrauded buyer remains a victim. He keeps the beast, but he is also entitled to restitution from the thief equal to the original purchase price charged by the thief.

If the thief confesses before the trial, he can avoid the risk of the extra payment to the defrauded buyer. Even if the victim demands four-fold or five-fold restitution, by paying it, the thief thereby becomes the owner of the beast. *The criminal's act of timely confession, plus his agreement to pay full restitution to the victim, atones judicially for the theft.*[23]

But what about the defrauding of the buyer? I think the confessed thief would owe the buyer a restitution payment of 20 percent of the purchase price because he had involved the buyer in an illegal transaction. Having repaid both owner and buyer, he has legitimized the new ownership arrangement. The buyer

---

23. Obviously, I am speaking here only of the earthly court. Atonement means "covering."

has gained full legal title to the animal plus restitution, so he is no longer a defrauded buyer. He now has no additional complaint against the thief. He cannot demand any additional restitution payments.

Without confession and restitution, the thief would owe the buyer at least 100 percent restitution if discovered, which is an important economic incentive in getting the buyer to identify himself. Thus, the thief's silence at the trial regarding the existence of a defrauded buyer hangs over him continually.[24]

Let us assume that he is convicted. He pays his maximum restitution to the victim. He still has an economic incentive to confess. He tells the judges that he had sold the animal. He tells them who the defrauded buyer is. He now owes the defrauded buyer the 20 percent restitution payment. This is better than paying the defrauded buyer 100 percent (or two-fold restitution minus any re-purchase price from the original owner), should the buyer learn that the beast was stolen property and decide to confess to the original owner or the judges.

Biblical law puts a premium on timely confession. The criminal who confesses receives a lighter penalty than the criminal who refuses to confess, and who is then subsequently convicted.[25] There is an economic incentive for him to confess. There is also an economic threat if he refuses to confess: the possibility of two-fold restitution provides an incentive for a defrauded buyer to reveal the existence of the stolen animal to the original owner. The Bible's penalty structure for theft provides economic incentives for all parties to present accurate information to the civil authorities. The Bible recognizes that accurate information is not a zero-price resource.

---

24. If the victimized buyer waits for several years before identifying the stolen beast, the court might decide that the stolen beast has aged too much, and that it constitutes half of the payment owed. Still, the thief would have to make the 100% penalty payment to him.

25. In modern U.S. jurisprudence, plea bargaining is used by defense attorneys to reduce their clients' sentences by persuading criminals to confess to milder crimes than they actually committed. In biblical law, the criminal is given an opportunity to escape a heavier sentence by confessing before the trial; the confessed crime, however, remains the same.

Considering an Alternative Arrangement

If there were no risk to the thief attached to remaining silent, what would be the thief's incentive to tell the owner that he knows where the stolen beast is? Assume that the thief owes no mandatory penalty payment to the defrauded buyer once he has paid restitution to the victim. He pays full restitution to the owner, and the defrauded buyer then hears about this, realizes that he has purchased stolen property, and comes to the owner. He offers to sell back the missing beast to the owner at the market price the beast was worth to the owner when the beast was stolen (presumably, the price he paid to the thief). If the thief owes nothing to the defrauded buyer, he is still out only five-fold restitution by having concealed evidence.

What is wrong with this interpretation of the restitution statutes? Answer: the thief has entangled the buyer in an illegal transaction that was inherently filled with uncertainty for the buyer. The latter might have been convicted of being a "fence" — a professional receiver of stolen goods. He has therefore been defrauded by the thief. He deserves restitution.

What if the original owner says that he does not want to buy the beast from the defrauded buyer? The buyer has now in effect purchased the beast from its rightful owner. He now owns the "bundle of rights" associated with true ownership. But the thief has nevertheless exposed him to the discomfort of being involved in an illegal transaction. Shouldn't the thief still owe the seller a 100 percent restitution payment? My assessment of the principle of victim's rights leads me to conclude that biblical law does in principle allow the defrauded buyer to come to the judges and have them compel the thief to pay him 100 percent of the price he had paid the thief. This has nothing to do with whether he has sold the beast to the original owner or whether the owner has allowed him to retain legal possession of it.

Transferring Lawful Title

Why must we regard the sale of the animal as fraudulent? Why can the authorities legitimately demand that the purchaser return the animal to the original owner? Because the thief implicitly and possibly explicitly pretended to be transferring an asset that he did not possess: *lawful title*. The thief did not possess lawful title to the property. This illuminates a fundamental principle of biblical ownership: *whatever someone does not legally own, he cannot legally sell*. Ownership is not simply possession of a thing; it is possession of certain *legal immunities* associated with the thing. It involves above all the *right to exclude*. Writes economist-legal theorist Richard Posner: "A property right, in both law and economics, is a right to exclude everyone else from the use of some scarce resource."[26] This right to exclude was never owned by the thief; therefore, he cannot transfer this bundle of legal immunities to the purchaser. The purchaser can legally demand compensation from the thief, but he does not lawfully own the stolen item. The civil authorities can legitimately compel the buyer to transfer the property back to the thief, who then returns it to the original owner, or else compel him to return it directly to the original owner.

The explicit language of the kidnapping statute provides us with the legal foundation of this conclusion regarding the transfer of ownership. "And he that stealeth a man, and selleth him, or if he be found in his hand, he shall surely be put to death" (Ex. 21:16). Even to have a stolen man in your possession was a capital crime, unless you could prove that you did not know that he or she was stolen. Just because a kidnapper sold you a stolen person as a slave did not mean that this person would remain in your possession as a slave. The same is true of other property.

English common law does not recognize this biblical standard. Receiving stolen goods was not made a crime by statute until the nineteenth century. Common law had recognized no such crime; it took statute law to make it a crime.[27] While it is no doubt true that it is expensive to research every title before making a purchase, especially in a pre-modern society, the responsibility to do so is biblically inescapable if the buyer wishes

---

26. Richard A. Posner, *The Economics of Justice* (Cambridge, Massachusetts: Harvard University Press, 1983), p. 70.

27. Wayne LaFave and Austin Scott, Jr., *Handbook on Criminal Law* (Minneapolis, Minnesota: West, 1972), pp. 681-91: "Receiving Stolen Property." My thanks to Prof. Gary Amos for this reference.

to reduce his risk of purchasing stolen goods — goods that must be returned to the original owner. Not only is the childhood chant of "finders, keepers; losers, weepers" not biblical, neither is common law's "buyers, keepers; victims, weepers." A far better rule is the traditional *caveat emptor*: let the buyer beware.

Conclusion

The traditional explanation of the four-fold penalty for slaughtering or selling a stolen sheep and the five-fold penalty for oxen is based on future costs of retraining the replacement animals. We have already seen that this economic distinction among stolen animals is incorrect. The basis of the distinction of penalties is symbolism, not economics.[28]

In any case, the free market price already contains the extra future costs associated with any item. Prices are set by consumer demand in relation to supply. Added costs of course restrict the supply, but this is already discounted in the existing market price. Thus, judges do not need to take into consideration extra future costs of replacement. All they need to do is use the existing market price of any stolen asset as the base price; double or more restitution is then added to it.

The victim always has the option of making a more acceptable offer to the criminal in order to gain the latter's cooperation. If he wants the return of the original animal or object, he may try to get the thief to agree by offering him a reduced compensation plan if he tells where he sold the stolen item. The buyer will have to return it to the original owner, of course, since the former did not actually receive the rights of ownership when he purchased a stolen item. The thief will then owe the buyer restitution, but this may be lower than what he would owe if he did not cooperate. The point is, the victim sets the penalty, so long as it is not higher than that which God allows in His law.

The modern State acknowledges the validity of this principle of bargaining. Pre-trial plea bargaining, reduced sentences for testifying against accomplices, and other deals are made between prosecutors and criminals. The problem is, these negotiated deals

---

28. Chapter 11: "Protecting the Victims."

are all too often made without the consent of the victims, whose interests are being sacrificed to the career plans of the criminals and the bureaucrats who control the criminal justice system. The Bible teaches that it is always the victim, not the State, whose rights are to be upheld by civil law. He is the one to negotiate any settlement with the criminal, not the State.

13

RESTITUTION AND DETERRENCE

If a man shall steal an ox, or a sheep, and kill it, or sell it; he shall restore five oxen for an ox, and four sheep for a sheep. . . . If the theft be certainly found in his hand alive, whether it be ox, or ass, or sheep; he shall restore double (Ex. 22:1, 4).

We are required by God always to begin our analysis of any problem with the operating presupposition of *the theocentric nature of all existence.* Modern jurisprudence refuses to begin with God. It begins with man and man's needs, and generally progresses to the State and the State's needs. This is why modern jurisprudence is in near-chaos. It is also why the court system is in near-chaos.[1]

Deterring God's Wrath in History

Whenever we speak of deterring crime, we must speak first of the deterrence of God's wrath against the community because of the courts' unwillingness to impose God's justice within the community. The civil government is required by God to seek to deter crimes because all crimes are above all *crimes against God.* An unwillingness on the part of civil magistrates to enforce God's specified sanctions against certain specified public acts calls forth God's specified covenantal cursings against the community. This threat of God's sanctions is the fourth section of God's covenant; without this covenant, either explicit or implicit, no community can exist.[2] Only when we clearly recognize the theocentric nature

---

1. Macklin Fleming, *The Price of Perfect Justice* (New York: Basic Books, 1974).
2. Ray R. Sutton, *That You May Prosper: Dominion By Covenant* (Tyler, Texas: Institute for Christian Economics, 1987), ch. 4.

of deterrence – and when we are ready to seek to have it recognized publicly *in our civil and ecclesiastical statute books* – can we legitimately begin to speak about deterring criminal behavior for the protection of the community.

The Bible does not distinguish between civil law and criminal law. All sins are crimes against God, for they break His law. All public sins must be restrained by one or more of God's covenantal agencies of government: family, church, and State. Certain public transgressions of God's law are specified as acts to be punished by the civil magistrate. In the modern world, we call these acts crimes. (The King James Version uses the word "crime" only twice, and "crimes" only twice.) The civil government enforces biblical laws against such acts. The general guideline for designating a particular public act as a crime is this: if by failing to impose sanctions against certain specified public acts, the whole community could be subsequently threatened by God's non-civil sanctions – war, plague, and famine – then the civil government becomes God's designated agency of enforcement. *The civil government's primary function is to protect the community against the wrath of God* by enforcing His laws against public acts that threaten the survival of the community.

The perverse practice of modern jurisprudence of allowing a person who has been declared legally innocent of a crime to be subsequently sued for damages in civil court by alleged victims cannot be found in the Bible. There is no distinction in the Bible between criminal law and civil law; if the *civil* magistrates are entitled to enforce a rule or law, then this rule or law should be classified in the modern world under a *criminal* statute. Because the State is not omniscient, God allows self-proclaimed victims of lawless behavior to sue other individuals in the presence of a civil magistrate, which we call civil procedure or torts, but if the State is the lawful agency of enforcement, then we are always talking about criminal acts. Continued injustice, *if* it can be biblically defined and publicly identified in advance through statute or judicial precedent, because it goes unpunished by the civil government, calls forth the wrath of God on the community. So, there is ultimately no Bible-based distinction between civil law and criminal law.

The Bible encourages the *legitimate division of labor* in identifying all types of criminal behavior, including such acts of injustice as breaking contracts or polluting the environment. The Bible recognizes that the State is not God. It is not omniscient. The initiation of public sanctions against all criminal acts therefore must not become a monopoly of civil officers. Citizen's arrest and torts — where one person sues another in order to collect damages — are modern examples of the outworking of this biblical principle of the decentralization of law enforcement. All government begins with self-government. The bottom-up, appeals court structure of covenant society (Ex. 18) is protected by not requiring that agents of the civil government initiate all civil government's sanctions against criminal behavior. Nevertheless, all disputes into which the State can legitimately intervene and settle by judicial decision must be regarded in a biblical commonwealth as criminal behavior. There is no biblical distinction between criminal law and civil law.

It is therefore preposterous to argue, as liberal scholar Anthony Phillips argues concerning the Mosaic law, that "A crime is a breach of an obligation imposed by the law which is felt to endanger the community, and which results in the punishment of the offender in the name of the community, but which is not the personal concern of the individual who may have suffered injury, and who has no power to stop the prosecution, nor derives any gain from it."[3] It is preposterous because every transgression of the civil law that goes unpunished by the authorities raises the threat of God's judgment on the community, which is why unsolved murders required expiation in the Old Testament: 1) the sacrifice of a heifer (Deut. 21:1-7); and 2) the elders were required to pray, "Be merciful, O LORD, unto thy people Israel, whom thou hast redeemed, and lay not innocent blood unto thy people of Israel's charge. And the blood shall be forgiven them" (Deut. 21:8). The State must regard as crimes against God all public

---

3. Anthony Phillips, *Ancient Israel's Criminal Law: A New Approach to the Decalogue* (New York: Schocken, 1970), p. 10.

transgressions for which the Bible specifies restitution payments to victims. Such acts are criminal acts against the community. Why? Because if they go unpunished, God threatens to curse the community. Thus, criminal law in the Bible was not enforced "in the name of the community," but *in the name of God*, so as to protect the community from God's wrath.

Restitution to God

Phillips is consistent in his errors, at least; he also argues that Hebrew covenant law was *exclusively* criminal law, meaning that its goal was solely the enforcement of public morals, rather than civil law (torts), in which restitution to the victim was primary.[4] This definition, if correct, would remove from covenant law all biblical statutes that require restitution to victims. What he is trying to do is separate the case laws of Exodus from the Ten Commandments. If believed, this argument would make it far easier for antinomians to reject the continuing validity of the case laws in New Testament times, for the case laws of Exodus and other books rest heavily on the imposition of restitution payments to victims. The antinomians could publicly claim allegiance to the Ten Commandments, but then they could distance themselves from the specific applications of these commandments through the case laws, for they have concluded that the case laws are unconnected to the Decalogue because these are "civil" laws rather than "criminal" laws.[5] Phillips writes: "But it is the contention of this study that Israel herself understood the Decalogue as her criminal law code, and that the law contained in it, and developed from it, was sharply distinguished from her civil law."[6]

If true, then all you need to do to escape from the covenantal, State-enforced requirements of the Decalogue is to make the Ten Commandments appear ridiculous. This he attempts in Chapter Two. "Initially only free adult males were subject to Israel's

---

4. *Ibid.*, pp. 10-11.

5. Phillips says that the "Book of the Covenant," meaning Exodus 21-23, was a product of David's reign, with some of it quite possibly written by David himself. *Ibid.*, ch. 14.

6. *Ibid.*, p. 11.

criminal law, for only they could have entered into the covenant relationship with Yahweh. . . . But women did not enter into the covenant relationship, and were therefore outside the scope of the criminal law. They had no legal status, being the personal property first of their fathers and then of their husbands."[7] The Decalogue is clearly preposterous, he implies. Presto: modern man is freed from *any* covenantal relationship to God. Man is on his own in the cosmos. He is autonomous. He shall be as God.

His case rests, first and foremost, on his distinguishing of criminal law from civil law in terms of the presence of restitution requirements in civil law. Next, he excludes women from the covenant. Then he turns them into chattel slaves. His tactic is obvious: to make God's law appear ridiculous. But it is Phillips who is ridiculous, not the Bible. Like all humanists, he does not begin with the presupposition of a theocentric universe. He therefore does not begin his discussion of crimes and restitution with the understanding that all crimes are ultimately crimes against God, and all restitution payments belong ultimately to God as the ultimate injured party. It does not occur to him that *all of God's curses are His imposition of restitution payments to Himself as the ultimate Victim.* Because covenant-breakers do not voluntarily repay to God what they owe Him as the innocent victim — the ultimate object of their moral rebellion — He therefore repays them with inescapable final judgment. "Vengeance is mine; I will repay, saith the Lord" (Rom. 12:19b).

All sins are crimes against God. All sins are therefore judged by God: "For the wages of sin is death" (Rom. 6:23a). Each person is a sinner in God's eyes, and therefore a criminal. The key question that must be answered during each person's life on earth — acknowledged by him or not — is this one: Will I allow Jesus Christ's payment of the God-imposed eternal penalty to serve as my substitutionary restitution payment to God, or will I

---

7. *Ibid.*, pp. 14, 15. He does say that Deuteronomy later made women full members of the covenant. *Ibid.*, p. 25. This is the standard liberal dismemberment of the Pentateuch into the hypothetical documents of the play-pretend scribes, J, E, D, P, and their as-yet unidentified accomplices. It should be a great comfort for Christians to realize that God will dismember these scholarly covenant-dismemberers throughout eternity.

instead choose to ignore the magnitude of this looming restitution payment and cross death's threshold autonomously? Anyone who makes the second choice will spend eternity in God's non-rehabilitative torture chambers.

"Victimless Crimes" and Civil Judgment

In the ultimate covenantal sense, it is improper to speak of victimless crimes. Every person who entices another to sin is bringing that person under the threat of God's negative sanctions, in time and in eternity. God therefore threatens the whole community for its failure to impose civil sanctions against such crimes. If there were no threat of God's sanctions against the community for the failure of the magistrates to enforce all statutes assigned by the Bible to the civil magistrates for enforcement, then there would be no biblical justification for sanctions against such "victimless crimes" as prostitution, pornography, and drug dealing. Because he rejects the idea of such a covenant, classical liberal economist and legal theorist F. A. Hayek rejects laws against "victimless crimes," saying that they are illegitimate interventions of the civil government, "At least where it is not believed that the whole group may be punished by a supernatural power for the sins of individuals. . . ."[8] But that is the whole point: such a community-threatening God *does* exist.

Many actions that are specified in the Bible as sins are not to be tried and judged by the civil magistrate, but this is not evidence of neglect by God; it is instead *a restraint on the growth of messianic civil government*. The absence of civil penalties against such designated sinful behavior indicates only a postponement of judgment until the sinner's final and eternal restitution payment to God. Through their public enforcement of God's law, civil magistrates warn people of the necessity of obeying God, the cosmic Enforcer: "By the fear of the LORD men depart from evil" (Prov. 16:6b). This legitimate fear is to be both personal and national, for God's punishments in history are imposed on individuals and nations: "If thou wilt not observe to do all the words of this law

---

8. F. A. Hayek, *Law, Legislation and Liberty*, 3 vols. (University of Chicago Press, 1973), I, p. 101.

that are written in this book, that thou mayest fear this glorious and fearful name, THE LORD THY GOD; then the LORD will make thy plagues wonderful, and the plagues of thy seed, even great plagues, and of long continuance, and sore sicknesses, and of long continuance" (Deut. 28:58-59).

The necessity of making restitution reminds the covenanted nation to fear the God who exacts a perfect restitution payment to Himself on judgment day, and who brings His wrath in history as a warning of the final judgment to come. He brings His wrath either through lawfully constituted civil government or, if civil government refuses to honor the terms of His covenant, through such visible judgments as wars, plagues, and famines. This is why the nation was warned to fear God, immediately after the presentation of the Ten Commandments: ". . . God is come to prove you, and that his fear may be before your faces, that ye sin not" (Ex. 20:20b).

Jesus was not departing from the biblical view of judicial sanctions when He warned: "Fear him which is able to destroy both soul and body in hell" (Matt. 10:28b). It is eternal punishment which is to serve as the covenantal foundation of all judicial sanctions. Civil government is supposed to reflect God's government. Public punishments deter evil. They remind men: better temporal punishment that leads to repentance (personal and national) than eternal punishment that does not lead to repentance (personal). Repentance is possible only in history.

Capital Punishment

Phillips is consistently incorrect when he writes: "Modern theories of punishment are therefore totally inapplicable when considering reasons why ancient Israel executed her criminals, for the punishment was not looked at from the criminal's point of view. This extreme penalty was not designed to deter potential criminals, nor as an act of retribution, but as a means of preventing divine action by appeasing Yahweh's wrath."[9] If criminal law was "not looked at from the criminal's point of view," then why does the Bible repeatedly refer to the fear of external punishment

---

9. Phillips, *Ancient Israel's Criminal Law*, p. 12.

by the civil authorities as a means of leading men to fear God and to obey His law? "And all Israel shall hear, and fear, and shall do no more any such wickedness as this is among you" (Deut. 13:11). Deterring future crimes is certainly one of the functions of capital punishment in a biblical law-order. Capital punishment is also an act of retribution and restitution. And, yes, it is also "a means of preventing divine action by appeasing Yahweh's wrath." It is erroneous to argue exclusively in terms of "either-or" when considering the potential social motivations for capital punishment or any other required civil sanction in the Bible.[10]

Capital punishment points to the final judgment as no other civil penalty does. It reminds sinners of the ultimate restitution penalty that God will impose on all those who refuse to accept His Son's payment on their behalf. The civil government acknowledges that its most fearful form of punishment is to speed convicted criminals along into the courtroom of the cosmic Judge. The magistrate announces that there is no way to restore the convicted criminal to fellowship in earthly society. He visibly becomes what he already is in principle: a sinner in the hands of an angry God.

Final Judgment

We see the ultimate example of this two-fold aspect of restitution in the final judgment. Satan and his host, both human and

---

10. I do not want to give the reader an inflated opinion of Phillips's importance. He is just another obscure liberal theologian toiling fruitlessly in the barren wilderness of higher criticism. I have included this brief survey of some of his ideas as an example of just how intellectually sloppy liberal theology can be, not because he is an important thinker. He is simply a convenient foil. He is all too typical of a small army of liberal theologians whose works would be immediately forgotten if they had ever been read in the first place. These scholars will eventually make full restitution to God for their efforts to deceive their readers concerning the Bible.

Liberal scholars are always looking for a new angle to justify the publication of yet another heavily footnoted, utterly boring, totally useless book, especially books like Phillips's, which is a rewritten doctoral dissertation – the most footnoted, boring, and useless academic exercise of all. Doctoral dissertations should be interred quietly, preferably in private, with only the author and close family in attendance. If such interment must be public, then it should be as a summary published in a scholarly journal, where the remains' entombment will seldom be disturbed again. Ashes to ashes, dust to dust.

angelic, pay for their rebellion with their lives. Their leavening power of corruption in history is reduced to zero. Their assets are transferred to God's people, who inherit the earth. From a biblical standpoint, this transfer of legal title to the world was accomplished by Christ at Calvary.[11] Then the rebels are thrown into the lake of fire (Rev. 20:14-15).

This eternal, continual restitution payment honors God, while it simultaneously acts as the perfect deterrent to crime – a covenantal warning that remains before God's servants, both human and angelic, throughout eternity. Resurrected people will never sin again, whether they are covenant-breakers or covenant-keepers. Righteous people will not choose to sin, and resurrected sinners will not be able to. In the lake of fire there is only impotence. The ability to adhere to any of the terms of the dominion covenant cease when grace ceases, and there is no grace in the lake of fire.

Then why speak of the deterrence effect of eternal damnation? Because God's judgment is covenantal: blessings and cursings (point four of the Biblical covenant).[12] There are always conditional aspects to God's covenant promises, as well as unconditional aspects. The promises of God are part of the structure of the covenant. There will be promises and blessings in the post-resurrection new heaven and new earth. Cursing and blessing are eternal, which reminds everyone of the covenant's conditions. Thus, the lake of fire can be spoken of covenantally as a perfect deterrent, for it deters all God-defying behavior forever. It also complements and reinforces the perfect obedience of covenant-keepers who know perfectly well about the perfect torment of covenant-breakers, with their perfect bodies that possess the terrifying ability, like the burning bush that Moses saw, of not being destroyed by a perfect fire. God's perfection is manifested in His perfect wrath.

It is not God's grace that keeps alive covenant-breakers, with their perfect bodies that are so sensitive to every subtle aspect of

---

11. Gary North, *Inherit the Earth: Biblical Blueprints for Economics* (Ft. Worth, Texas: Dominion Press, 1987), ch. 5.

12. Sutton, *That You May Prosper*, ch. 4.

Restitution and Deterrence

their endless torment; it is instead His uncompromising *wrath* that keeps them alive.[13] Covenant promises, conditions, and sanctions are eternally perfect.[14] The soul and body of every covenant-breaker are reunited perfectly at the resurrection, so that each can experience the eternal torments of covenant judgment as unified and fully human. There is no dualism of body and soul in the lake of fire.[15]

Perfect justice brings with it a resurrection life permanently devoid of sin. Furthermore, the punishment perfectly fits the ethi-

---

13. On this point, I disagree with John Calvin's reference to God's grace in keeping souls alive: "And although the soul, after it has departed from the prison of the body, remains alive, yet its doing so does not arise from any inherent power of its own. Were God to withdraw his grace, the soul would be nothing more than a puff or blast, even as the body is dust; and thus there would doubtless be found in the whole man nothing but mere vanity." Calvin, *Commentary on the Book of Psalms* (Grand Rapids, Michigan: Barker Book House, 1979), Baker's volume VI, p. 138: Ps. 103:15. There is no grace shown by God to the souls of covenant-breakers in hell or the lake of fire. Grace is shown only to the souls of covenant-keepers. Calvin's loose language here is misused by Edward William Fudge in his book-long attempt to deny the biblical doctrine of eternal torment: *The Fire That Consumes: A Biblical and Historical Study of Final Punishment* (Houston, Texas: Providential Press, 1982), p. 74.

14. Fudge attempts to trace Protestantism's doctrine of the immortality of the soul to Calvin, and Calvin's doctrine of the immortality of the soul to Plato. This argument is nonsense, though representative of similar arguments used by heretical theologians to reject Bible doctrines in the name of rejecting Greek speculation, when in fact they have adopted some variation of humanist speculation. The Bible's doctrine of the immortality of the soul and also its doctrine of eternal torment of the wicked are both grounded in the doctrine of the covenant. It is not surprising that Fudge finds in the Calvinist tradition the most tenacious die-hard defense of the doctrine of eternal punishment. Fudge, *ibid.*, pp. 26n, 466. There is a reason for this tenacity. Calvinism, more than any other Christian tradition, is grounded in the doctrine of the covenant.

15. Fudge and several of the drifting theologians whom he cites continually refer to the orthodox doctrine of souls in hell as implicitly dualistic. The doctrine of hell is no more dualistic than the traditional doctrine of heaven. The issue is not heaven or hell, for both are temporary way stations for souls until God's final judgment; the issue is the post-resurrection world, where souls and bodies are reunited. Fudge fudges this issue, as he does so many others. He covers his flanks with a whole series of peripheral issues – theological and historical rabbit trails for non-covenant theologians to pursue until exhaustion. The fundamental issue is the covenant: God's eternal dead-end judgment for covenant-breakers. This is the issue Fudge never discusses in chapter 20, "Focusing on the Issue," with its subsection, "Traditional Arguments Summarized." It is not man who is central to discussions of final judgment, but God and His eternal covenant.

cal crime of rebellion against God. It is a punishment whose magnitude God made quite plain from the beginning: "But of the tree of the knowledge of good and evil, thou shalt not eat of it: for in the day that thou eatest thereof thou shalt surely die" (Gen. 2:17). Absolutely proportional restitution at the final judgment creates the conditions necessary to establish a perfect society beyond the final resurrection.

Offsetting Reduced Risks of Detection

The thief who steals a specially protected beast must suffer greater risks for stealing it when compared to any other kind of property. The sheep or ox can easily be slaughtered and eaten. This makes it far more difficult for the civil authorities to discover who the thief is and then prove it in court. Thus, the thief who steals an ox or sheep seems to have a greater likelihood of getting away with the crime. The law therefore imposes far higher penalties in cases of ox-stealing or sheep-stealing. This offsets part of the self-subsidy — the reduction of the risk of detection — that the thief receives when he slaughters the animal, thereby destroying the evidence.

But what about selling the animals? This is the equivalent of kidnapping, for these particular animals represent man. Thus, there is a higher penalty attached to their theft. This higher penalty relates to the *symbolic aspect* of the forbidden act of manstealing. Selling a useful beast that can be taken into a different part of the country makes it easier for the thief to escape detection. The thief does not wear a stolen jewel or use a stolen tool, which would make it easier to detect his crime locally. The animal, which was under the personal protection of its owner, is separated from the owner permanently. Biblical law therefore stipulates that the thief who does sell the beast is placed under greater risk; should he be proven to be the thief, he will be required to pay four-fold or five-fold restitution to the victim.

This explanation may seem strained, but it is necessary if we are to make sense of Exodus 22:9, which regulates property placed in trust with a neighbor. If the neighbor loses the goods, they both must go before the civil magistrates. If the neighbor is found guilty, he pays double restitution. "For all manner of trespass, whether it be for ox, for ass, for sheep, for raiment, or for any manner of lost thing, which another challengeth to be his, the cause of both parties shall come before the judges; and whom the judges shall condemn, he shall pay double unto his neighbour."

Why should the neighbor be required to pay only double restitution for a sheep or ox in this case? What about five-fold and four-fold restitution? My answer: because the neighbor cannot conceal the crime the way that the outsider can when he slaughters or sells the animal. In short, *it is easier for the victimized owner to prove his legal case against a neighbor than it is for him to prove his case against an unknown thief who disposes of the evidence.* Thus, the penalty imposed on the neighbor is double restitution, which is the standard requirement for the theft of all other goods except slaughtered or sold oxen and sheep. Since the owner faces reduced difficulties in recovering his property, and the thief therefore faces increased risk, the penalty payment is reduced.

Conclusion

The primary goal of criminal law is to deter the wrath of God on society. All crimes are primarily crimes against God. Public sins are to be restrained by civil law in order to persuade God not to intervene in history and bring the nation under judgment in the name of the victims. If the authorities do not represent the victims, then God will bring judgment as their representative.

Restitution is made to God by the civil authorities when they enforce His law. This is a public acknowledgment that God is sovereign over society, so His laws must be honored. When the authorities compel criminals to make restitution to their victims, the State is thereby making restitution to God. This is why the civil law of the Old Testament was also criminal law. A State that refuses to enforce God's civil law has become a criminal in the eyes of God.

The modern libertarian concept of "victimless crimes" is in error. Crimes are crimes against God, and if the State does not prohibit them, God threatens judgment in history against that society. Not all sins are crimes, for God has not created a law-order that leads to the creation of a messianic State that polices everything continually. But the State must enforce morality, for all law is legislated morality. The only question is: Whose morality should be legislated, God's or man's?

If laws against criminals are enforced to deter God's wrath against society, then we should not be surprised to learn that these laws are also designed to deter future criminal behavior. God's law is future-oriented as well as past-oriented. It enforces laws that were delivered to man in the past, and whose *works* are written in every human heart (Rom. 2:14-15). It also looks to the future: men are to fear the future judgment of God and His representatives, civil magistrates.

There is a greater penalty for slaughtering or selling stolen oxen or sheep because it is easier for the thief to escape detection. To counter the increased costs of detection, the law specifies four-fold or five-fold restitution for the two symbolic animals, sheep and oxen. The deterrence factor is unquestionably a consideration of biblical justice.

14

GUARDIAN OF THE OATH

And the LORD *spake unto Moses, saying, If a soul sin, and commit a trespass against the* LORD, *and lie unto his neighbour in that which was delivered him to keep, or in fellowship, or in a thing taken away by violence, or hath deceived his neighbour; Or have found that which was lost, and lieth concerning it, and sweareth falsely; in any of all these that a man doeth, sinning therein: Then it shall be, because he hath sinned, and is guilty, that he shall restore that which he took violently away, or the thing which he hath deceitfully gotten, or that which was delivered him to keep, or the lost thing which he found, Or all that about which he hath sworn falsely; he shall even restore it in the principal, and shall add the fifth part more thereto, and give it unto him to whom it appertaineth, in the day of his trespass offering. And he shall bring his trespass offering unto the* LORD, *a ram without blemish out of the flock, with thy estimation, for a trespass offering, unto the priest: And the priest shall make an atonement for him before the* LORD: *and it shall be forgiven him for any thing of all that he hath done in trespassing therein (Lev. 6:1-7).*

This passage appears in the section of Leviticus that presents the laws governing trespasses and guilt offerings. The sin in this instance was intentional. It is said to be a sin against the Lord, yet what is described is a sin against a neighbor.

The question arises: Is keeping an item entrusted for safekeeping, or robbery, or keeping someone's lost item a sin against the Lord, judicially speaking? Theologically speaking, all sin is a sin against the Lord, to be judged in God's final court. The victim of the crime becomes God's legal representative, the earthly target of man's rebellion against God's standards. He is the victim, therefore, of a *boundary violation*. But this passage specifically identifies these transgressions as trespasses against God, whereas other trespasses listed in the Bible are not specifically identified as such. No ram offering was required for those other sins. Why this omission in all the other sins of life if all sin is judicially a trespass against God? Why single out these sins?

The answer lies elsewhere than in the enumerated sins themselves. It was the transgressor's *false verbal testimony* regarding these sins that served as the differentiating factor: lying to the neighbor or swearing falsely to a civil court. Writes Wenham: "By abusing the oath, a person took God's holy name in vain, and trespassed against his holiness. Therefore a reparation offering was required to make amends."[1] The sin was two-fold: a violation of a neighbor's personal property rights (point three of the covenant: boundaries), coupled with a violation of either personal verbal assurances to the victim or the violation of a formal judicial oath (point four: oath).

Because two kinds of sin were involved — one formal-covenantal, one conventional-economic — there had to be two separate acts of restoration. The first act of restoration — the 120 percent restitution payment — was required by God's law to satisfy the earthly victim in his legal capacity as victim. The second act — sacrificing a ram — was necessary to satisfy God in His capacity as high priest of the heavenly court. Both the victim and the priest served as covenantal agents of God: the first civil, the second ecclesiastical.

The lie or false oath had been intended to deflect either the victim or the court from discovering the truth. In this sense, it was an affront to God's kingly justice. It was an attack on the integrity of the heavenly court and His representative earthly civil court. The false testimony may or may not have put someone else under suspicion; we are not told. What we are told is that there were two separate forms of restitution: the return to the victim of the full value of whatever had been stolen, plus a penalty payment

---

1. Gordon J. Wenham, *The Book of Leviticus* (Grand Rapids, Michigan: Eerdmans, 1979), p. 108.

of 20 percent (a double tithe);[2] and a ram to be sacrificed by a priest.

Civil Agents of God's Heavenly Court

The connection between the false oath and the civil court is easy to understand. The court enforces justice in the name of God and on behalf of the victim. It sets things straight judicially and economically. It defends its own integrity. Why, then, is the court not authorized by God to collect for itself the extra 20 percent, or allowed to impose some additional penalty? Why does the entire restitution payment appear to go to the victim, since the false oath was made to impede the proper functioning of the court?

We can find the answer to these questions by first observing that the initial lie was made to the neighbor, not to the court: "If a soul sin, and commit a trespass against the LORD, and lie unto his neighbour in that which was delivered him to keep, or in fellowship, or in a thing taken away by violence, or hath deceived his neighbour; . . ." This preliminary section of the passage does not mention any formal court proceeding, yet the criminal still owed a ram to God. This indicates that the victim, to whom the criminal lied, was in fact an agent of the civil court, even though the court had not been called into session. It was the victim who possessed lawful authority to call the court into session. The victim was gathering facts regarding the violation. He was acting therefore not only on his own behalf but also as an agent of society's primary institution of civil justice, the court. The lie to the neighbor was therefore judicially an oath to a covenantal institution. It had a unique binding character which conventional falsehoods do not possess.

The victim in seeking justice does not represent only himself. Biblical jurisprudence recognizes the earthly victim as a representative of God. A sin against him is always in his legal capacity as God's representative; the ultimate target of the sin is God.[3] The

---

2. Andrew A. Bonar, *A Commentary on Leviticus* (London: Banner of Truth Trust, [1846] 1966), p. 109.

3. Gary North, *Tools of Dominion: The Case Laws of Exodus* (Tyler, Texas: Institute for Christian Economics, 1990), pp. 278-80, 289.

sinner in history attacks various aspects of the creation in his attempt to defy God, since God cannot be attacked directly. He violates earthly boundaries in his rebellion against God. For example, Adam and Eve could not attack God directly; instead, they violated the boundary that God had placed around the forbidden tree.

This leads us to a significant conclusion: *the very existence of an earthly victim calls God's heavenly court of justice into session.* If the existence of a boundary violation becomes known to the victim, this discovery automatically invokes an earthly civil court of justice.[4] This invocation may not be a formal public act, but God, as the sovereign King of the commonwealth, calls it into session historically. When the victim learns of the violation, he is supposed to begin a search for incriminating evidence. Crimes are not to go unpunished in God's social order, for they are inherently attacks on Him. Crimes are to be solved in history if the costs of conviction are not prohibitive, i.e., if too many resources are not drained from the victim or the court in solving a particular crime. The world is under a curse: the curse of scarcity (Gen. 3:17-19). There are limits to anti-crime budgets. In a world of scarcity, including scarcity of accurate knowledge, there cannot be perfect justice. Justice in history is purchased at a price.[5] If the victim thinks it will take too many of his own resources to identify and convict the criminal, or if he thinks his accusation could be turned against him later for lack of evidence gathered by the court, he has the option of refusing to pursue the matter. He can let God settle it in eternity. He can rest confident in God's perfect justice. Rushdoony said it well: "History culminates in Christ's triumph, and eternity settles all scores."[6]

---

4. If someone other than the victim first discovers the violation, he is to inform the victim or the person most likely to be the victim. To fail to do this is judicially to become an accomplice of the criminal.

5. The ultimate price of perfect justice was paid by Jesus Christ's act of comprehensive redemption at Calvary. Without this representative payment, God's perfect justice would have demanded the end of the Adamic race at the conclusion of Adam's trial.

6. R. J. Rushdoony, *The Institutes of Biblical Law* (Nutley, New Jersey: Craig Press, 1973), p. 123.

God nevertheless wants criminals brought to justice in history. The Bible places the responsibility of pursuing justice on the individual who is most likely to want to see the criminal brought to justice: the victim. Because the crime was ultimately against God and His mandated social order, the victim becomes God's primary representative agent in pursuing justice. The victim is also uniquely motivated to begin this search for incriminating evidence, since he is the loser, and he will receive a restitution payment upon confession by, or conviction of, the criminal. As I have argued elsewhere, if he refuses to pursue the criminal or bring charges against him, the civil court is not to intrude on the case, unless he is a minor or legally incompetent.[7] Thus, when he begins his investigation of the crime, he is serving as God's primary covenantal agent. He is officially gathering information to be used in a covenant lawsuit against the criminal. He is acting as an agent of two courts: God's heavenly court and His earthly civil court.

In a sense this does not do full justice to the victim's unique legal position. The civil court is to some degree the agent of the victim, since the victim, in his legal capacity as a victim, is a representative of God. The victim alone determines whether or not to prosecute the covenant lawsuit; the court is to support his decision. If he brings a covenant lawsuit in his own name, he inevitably also brings it in God's name, for God was the primary victim. The civil court is to examine the evidence and announce judgment, but this judgment is made in the name of the two victims: God and the earthly victim. The civil court is an agent of the victim in a way that the ecclesiastical court is not. The civil court acts to defend the victim's rights, whereas the priest acts to defend the civil court's authority.

In a court, there must be interrogation of the suspects. God in the garden publicly interrogated Adam and Eve regarding the facts of the case. It is a crime to testify falsely in God's court or in man's. False testimony is intended to deflect God's justice. Offering it implies that God can be deceived, or at the very least, deterred from bringing negative sanctions in history. It rests on a

---

7. North, *Tools of Dominion*, pp. 279, 294-95.

man's self-confidence in his ability to deceive God's representative agents in history. He believes that he can deflect or delay God's judgment in history by means of misleading information. This faith in false testimony rests on a theology that assumes that God is non-existent, or not omniscient, or not omnipotent, or does not bring significant negative sanctions in history. It assumes that heaven's court is non-existent, or that God is forgetful, or that time apart from restitution covers all sins (universal salvation), i.e., that God does not bring negative sanctions in eternity. It assumes, at the very least, that God's negative sanctions outside the earthly court are minimal compared to the negative sanctions that can be imposed by the court, i.e., double restitution to the victim (Ex. 22:4).

Priestly Agents of God's Heavenly Court

The required animal sacrifice served as an atonement for a crime against God's civil court. This sacrifice covered the sin ritually. It was a public acknowledgment of a transgression against God's civil court. What is significant here is that *an ecclesiastical act was required to cover a civil transgression.* This raises a key question: Why was there a ritual connection between a civil court and the priesthood? Because of the two-fold character of God's judgment. The civil court represents God's heavenly court in a subordinate fashion which is judicially analogous to the victim, who in his legal capacity as a victim represents God subordinately. The civil court acts on behalf of the victim, but only in its judicial capacity as the minister of kingly justice (Rom. 13:4), as the institution that lawfully bears the sword. But God requires more than civil sanctions to placate His wrath against the criminal. He sits on His throne as both high priest and king; on earth, these offices are always divided, except in the person and offices of Jesus Christ. God must be placated in both of His offices. This is why no single earthly court can lawfully offer complete atonement for the criminal.[8] God therefore requires a priestly sacrifice.

---

8. This is surely the biblical legal basis for the tax-financed office of prison chaplain. This is why he is on call for the prisoners, especially immediately prior to an execution. The office of chaplain of the two houses of Congress, where laws are

In the New Testament, this priestly sacrifice was made by Jesus Christ at Calvary. The various animal sacrifices in the Old Testament representationally prefigured this ultimate sacrifice (Heb. 9). A question legitimately can be raised: Is any post-Calvary public mark of contrition lawfully imposed by the church on the perjurer? If so, on what basis?

If the perjurer is a church member, he has partaken of the Lord's Supper throughout the period following his false testimony to the court. This placed him in jeopardy of God's negative sanctions (I Cor. 11:30). He ignored this threat, thereby implicitly adopting the same false theology of God's minimal sanctions, previously described. The church's officers deserve to know of the transgression, and can lawfully assign a penalty. This penalty should not exceed the value of a ram in the Old Testament economy.

If the perjurer is not a church member, he is still dependent on the continuing faithfulness of the church to preserve God's common grace in history. The State can lawfully function in non-Christian environments, but only because of the common grace of God mediated through His church and its sacraments. Offering these representative sacrifices in the Old Covenant was the permanent responsibility of God's church. This is why Israel had to offer 70 bullocks annually as sacrifices for the symbolic 70 pagan nations of the world (Num. 29:12-32), plus a single bullock for herself on the eighth day (Num. 29:36).[9]

What this means is that *the church is the guardian of the covenantal oath*. This is an inescapable conclusion from the fact that only the church has the authority to accept the perjurer's sacrifice in atonement for the false oath. The State cannot offer this release from guilt. The oath involves the formal calling down of God's negative covenant sanctions on the oath-taker. He who uses God's name

---

offered for consideration by the legislative representatives of the people, has remained immune to American Civil Liberties Union protests; so has the office of prison chaplain, where the law's negative sanctions are imposed.

9. When Israel fell in A.D. 70, she had become like all the other pagan nations. She could no longer offer efficacious sacrifices for them or for herself. From that point on, only the church's offering of bread and wine could serve as a representative covering for the world.

in vain in a formal judicial conflict must then seek legal covering by the church. The reason why the oath is guarded by the church is that the church alone can lawfully invoke the eternal negative sanctions of God against an individual.[10] Thus, by invoking the oath in court, the criminal necessarily brings himself under the authority of the church.

The modern practice of allowing atheists to affirm to tell the truth in court, but not to swear on the Bible or in God's name, is a direct affront against God and against the church as the guardian of the oath. It is also inevitably an act of divinizing the State by default. The State becomes the sole enforcer of the affirmation. In such a worldview, there is no appeal beyond the State and its sanctions. The atheist's affirmation is therefore a judicial act demanding the removal of God from the courtroom. Thus, it requires the creation of a new oath system, with the State as the guardian of the oath. The State acts not in God's name but in its own. Rushdoony's comments are on target: "If a witness is asked to swear to tell the whole truth and nothing but the truth without any reference to God, truth can be and is commonly redefined in terms of himself. The oath in God's name is the 'legal recognition of God'[11] as the source of all things and the only ground of true being. It establishes the state under God and under His law. The removal of God from oaths, and the light and dishonest use of oaths, is a declaration of independence from Him, and it is warfare against God in the name of new gods, apostate man and his totalitarian state."[12]

Conclusion

The biblical State can lawfully impose negative sanctions against a perjurer, but only on behalf of the victim. The State cannot lawfully pronounce the eternal negative sanctions of the oath against anyone. The State can lawfully require an oath, but

---

10. Gary North, *The Sinai Strategy: Economics and the Ten Commandments* (Tyler, Texas: Institute for Christian Economics, 1986), pp. 52-56.

11. T. Robert Ingram, *The World Under God's Law* (Houston, Texas: St. Thomas Press, 1962), p. 46.

12. Rushdoony, *Institutes of Biblical Law*, p. 115.

Guardian of the Oath

it is not the sole institutional enforcer of this oath. The presence of the oath to God is a public acknowledgment of the non-autonomy of the State. God is above the State, and the church stands next to it as the guardian of the oath.[13]

This means that theocracy is required by God's civil law. Without the God-given authority to require an oath, the State would lose its covenantal status as a lawful monopolistic institution with the authority to enforce physical sanctions against evildoers. It would lose its status as a covenantal institution. Yet by imposing an oath, it inevitably places itself under the protection of the church, for the church is the defender of the oath. As the great seventeenth-century jurist Sir Edward Coke put it, "protection draws allegiance, and allegiance draws protection."[14]

To argue that the State imposes the oath as an agency under God apart from the church is to make the State an ecclesiastical intermediary between God and man, an institution possessing the power to declare God's negative eternal sanctions. An oath is always self-maledictory: it calls down God's negative sanctions on the oath-taker. This has to include eternal negative sanctions. Thus, the State cannot lawfully act as an autonomous intermediary between God and man; it acts only on behalf of victims: God's primary representatives in criminal cases.

---

13. The State, in turn, is responsible for the preservation of the legal environment that protects the church. The church is not institutionally autonomous, either.

14. Cited by Rebecca West, *The New Meaning of Treason* (New York: Viking Press, 1964), p. 12; in Rushdoony, *Institutes*, p. 118.

15

PERSONAL RESPONSIBILITY AND PERSONAL LIBERTY

If a man shall cause a field or vineyard to be eaten, and shall put in his beast, and shall feed in another man's field; of the best of his own field, and of the best of his own vineyard, shall he make restitution. If fire break out, and catch in thorns, so that the stacks of corn, or the standing corn, or the field, be consumed therewith; he that kindled the fire shall surely make restitution (Ex. 22:5-6).

The theocentric issue raised by this passage is the question of each person's legal obligations as a responsible steward over private property in a world in which God is the absolute owner of the world. As part of His providential administration over the world, God establishes boundaries in life. These boundaries are ultimately ethical: the boundaries between covenant-keepers and covenant-breakers. The existence of these ethical boundaries is reflected in every area of life. Man cannot think or act apart from boundaries of various kinds. Among these ethical boundaries are legal boundaries separating the use of property. Boundaries are therefore inescapably tied to the legal issue of personal responsibility before God and man.

God parcels out property to his subordinates. The very phrase, *parcels out*, reflects the noun, a parcel. God places specified units of land under the administration of specific individuals, families, and institutions. This division of authority is an aspect of God's overall system of the division of labor. Responsibility for the administration of specific property units can therefore be specified by law. The allocation of legal responsibility matches the allocation of property. God holds specific people responsible for their stewardship over specific pieces of property. This enables owners to evaluate their own performance as stewards, and it also allows the free market and God-ordained govemmantal authorities to evaluate owners' specific performance. The ultimate issue is each person's stewardship in history and God's judicial response, in history and at the final judgment. The temporal institutional issues of ownership-stewardship are covenantally related to this ultimate issue.

These verses make plain at least three facts. First, the Bible affirms the moral and legal legitimacy of the private ownership of the means of production. Fields and cattle and crops are owned by private individuals. Second, private property rights (legal immunities from action by others) are to be defended by the civil government. The State can and must require those people whose activities injure their neighbor or their neighbor's property to make restitution payments to those injured. Third, owners are therefore responsible for their own actions and for the actions of their subordinates, including wandering beasts.[1]

This combination of 1) privately owned property, 2) personal liability, and 3) predictable court enforcement of private property rights is the foundation of capitalism. It surely was a major aspect of the West's long-term economic growth.[2]

The Wandering Animal

We begin with the case of the wandering animal. It wanders from its property and invades another man's corn field. It eats some of this corn. The owner of the beast owes the victimized

---

1. Hammurabi's Code penalized a man who neglected to repair a dike on his property, which in turn broke and allowed his neighbor's property to be flooded: CH, paragraph 53. If he allowed water to flow through his canal and onto his neighbor's property, he was liable: CH, paragraph 55. *Ancient Near Eastern Texts Relating to the Old Testament*, edited by James B. Pritchard (3rd ed.; Princeton, New Jersey: Princeton University Press, 1969), p. 168.

2. Nathan Rosenberg and L. E. Birdsell, Jr., *How the West Grew Rich: The Economic Transformation of the Industrial World* (New York: Basic Books, 1986), ch. 4: "The Evolution of Institutions Favorable to Commerce."

neighbor the equivalent of whatever has been destroyed.[3] The owner of the beast must not short-change the victim; he pays from the best of his field.

There is an additional theocentric principle involved here. The legal principle is this: the injured party is entitled to the replacement of his damaged goods by the best of the responsible party's possessions. What is the theocentric principle that this legal principle reflects? It is this: *God, in imposing an appropriate restitution payment from rebellious mankind, is entitled to the best that man has to offer.* This is why man was not allowed under the Old Covenant to bring to God's sacrificial altar any injured or blemished animal (Lev. 1:10). "Cursed be the deceiver, which hath in his flock a male, and voweth, and sacrificeth unto the Lord a corrupt thing" (Mal. 1:14a). When Ananias and Sapphira brought only part of their pledged money to the church, but claimed that they were bringing in all of it, God killed them (Acts 5:1-10). They had violated a fundamental biblical principle. They became publicly cursed deceivers. "And great fear came upon all the church, and upon as many as heard these things" (Acts 5:11).

This theocentric principle governing restitution to God points to the ultimate principle governing the atonement: *only a perfect offering for sin can placate the God of perfect wrath.* Anyone who attempts to bring a blemished sacrifice to the altar of God will be destroyed. This, of course, is the underlying soteriological requirement that made necessary the incarnation, death, resurrection, and ascension of Jesus Christ. Only a perfect man, God's own Son, can serve as an acceptable sacrifice for sinful mankind (Heb. 2:14-18; 9:12-14). A sinful man will perish eternally if he attempts to short-change God by offering anything on judgment day in place of exclusive faith in the true mediator and high

---

3. Maimonides made this peculiar exception: "If an animal eats foodstuffs harmful to it, such as wheat, the owner is exempt because it has not benefited." Moses Maimonides, *The Book of Torts*, vol. 11 of *The Code of Maimonides*, 14 vols. (New Haven, Connecticut: Yale University Press, [1180] 1954), Chapter Three, Section Three, p. 12. That the victim must suffer an economic loss just because his neighbor's animal did not profit biologically from its invasion of the former's property is a principle of justice that needs a great deal of explaining. Maimonides provided no further discussion; he just laid down this principle of Jewish law, and went on.

priest, Jesus Christ.

Fences Reduce Conflicts

The Bible affirms that those who violate fences or property lines must make full restitution to the economically injured neighbor. The assessment of harm is easier to make than under common ownership. "*His* cows ate *this* row of corn in *my* cornfield." The owner of the damage-producing animals is responsible. Responsibility and ownership are directly linked under a system of private property rights. Under a system of private ownership, *property lines* are in effect *cost-cutting devices*, for they serve as *cost-assessing devices*. Without clearly defined property rights for men, and therefore clearly defined responsibilities, the rights of "property" – God's living creatures and a created environment under man's dominion (Gen. 9:1-17)[4] – will be sacrificed.

Carefully defined property rights also help to reduce social conflicts. Dales writes: "Unrestricted common property rights are bound to lead to all sorts of social, political, and economic friction, especially as population pressure increases, because, in the nature of the case, individuals have no legal rights with respect to the property when its government owner follows a policy of 'anything goes.' Notice, too, that such a policy, though apparently neutral as between conflicting interests, in fact always favours one party against the other. Technologically, swimmers cannot harm the polluters, but the polluters can harm the swimmers; when property rights are undefined, those who wish to use the property in ways that deteriorate it will inevitably triumph every time over those who wish to use it in ways that do not deteriorate it."[5] Common ownership of large bodies of water, when coupled with an opportunity to pass on private costs of polluted production, increases the extent of water pollution. It is a bad system for the swimmers of this world.

In questions of legal responsibility, there can be no neutrality.

---

4. Gary North, *The Dominion Covenant: Genesis* (2nd ed.; Tyler, Texas: Institute for Christian Economics, 1987), ch. 14: "The Ecological Covenant."

5. J. H. Dales, *Pollution, Property, and Prices: An Essay in Policy-Making and Economics* (Toronto: University of Toronto Press, 1968), p. 67.

It is the task of biblical exegesis to establish the ethical and legal foundations that enable civil judges to do the following: 1) identify the winners and the losers; 2) adjudicate cases properly in the sight of God; and 3) determine what is fair compensation to the losers from any unauthorized winners. One thing is certain: we cannot hope to attain a perfectly safe world. There are always risks in life. We are mortal. We are not omniscient.

Transferring Risk

Each owner is also responsible for whatever actions his animate or inanimate objects do that injure others. A fire that a man kindles on his land must be kept restrained to his property. If the fire spreads to his neighbor's field, he is fully accountable for all the damages. Men therefore have an incentive to take greater care when using potentially dangerous tools or techniques.

The problem of pollution should be subsumed under the general principle of responsibility for fire. A fire is a physical cause of physical damage. From the case-law example in Exodus 22:5, it is clear that the fire which a man starts is his responsibility. *He cannot legally transfer risks to his neighbor without his neighbor's consent.*

The Bible is not talking here about some shared project in which both men expect to profit, such as burning fields to get rid of weeds or unwanted grass. In such a mutually shared project, the case-law example of the man who rents his work animal to a neighbor, but who stays with the animal the whole time, is applicable. The neighbor is not required to pay anything beyond the hiring fee to the owner (Ex. 22:14-15). If the animal is hurt or killed, the neighbor owes nothing.

There is no doubt that the fire-starter is responsible for all subsequent fires that his original fire starts. Sparks from a fire can spread anywhere. A fire beginning on one man's farm can spread over thousands of acres. Fire is therefore essentially unpredictable. Its effects on specific people living nearby cannot be known with precision. The *uncertainty*, meaning the statistical unpredictability, of specific, individual consequences is the factor that governs the rule of restitution for damage-producing fires, as well as laws relating to the regulation of fire hazards.

Insurable Risk

The existence of fire insurance does not invalidate this analysis of "the economics of specific effects." While it is sometimes possible for a person to buy fire insurance, the reason why fire insurance is available at all is because companies insure many different regions, thereby taking advantage of "the law of large numbers." They can insure specific properties economically only because fires have known effects in the aggregate. If there were no known statistical pattern to fires in general, insurers would not insure specific properties against fire damage.

This is not to say that the following arrangement should be prohibited by law. A person who wishes to begin a business which is known to be dangerous approaches others who could be affected. "I'll make you a deal," he says. "I will pay for all increases in your insurance coverage if you let me begin this business in the neighborhood." If they agree, and if the insurance companies agree to write the policies, then he has met his obligations. He has made himself economically responsible for subsequent damages. Instead of paying for damages after the fact, he has paid in advance by providing the added insurance premiums necessary to buy the insurance.

What if some resident says "no"? The prospective producer of danger can then offer to buy him out by buying his property. If the offer is accepted, the prospective danger-producer can then either keep the property or sell it to someone who is willing to live with the risk, if the discount on the land's selling price is sufficiently large. But if the original owner refuses to sell, and also refuses to accept the offer regarding insurance premiums, then the first man should not be allowed to force out the original owner. If he begins the dangerous production process, the existing property owner can legitimately sue for damages. The court may require a money payment from the danger-producer to the potential victim. The court need not necessarily prohibit the activity altogether.

This decision by the judges requires that judges do the best they can in estimating the costs and benefits to the community, *including the perceived value to citizens everywhere of the preservation by the*

State of private property rights. They cannot estimate perfectly, for they cannot know the psychic costs and benefits involved in the minds of the conflicting parties. But they can make general, "unscientific" estimations, given the image of God in all men, and given the created environment in which all men live. This is an important application of biblical revelation to economics: if there is no universal humanity — no universal human nature — and no Creator who serves as the basis for man's image, and no creation governed by the Creator in terms of His value and His laws, then it is impossible for the judges legitimately to have confidence in their estimation of social costs, social benefits, private costs, and private benefits. Without our knowledge of objective economic value provided by God's plan and His image in man, objective economic value becomes epistemologically impossible.[6] Judges would then be blind in a sea of exclusively subjective economic values, a world in which it is philosophically impossible for men to make interpersonal comparisons of subjective utility.[7]

The Principle of the Fire Code

In the case of a single violator or a few potential violators, there are two reasons justifying the coercive intervention of the civil government. *First,* to use the biblical example of fire, a man who permits a fire to get out of control may see an entire town burned to the ground. There is no way, economically, that he can make full restitution. In fact, it would be almost impossibly expensive to estimate the value of the destroyed physical property, let alone the loss of life, or the psychological anguish of the victims. Therefore, in high-risk situations, the civil government can legitimately establish minimum fire prevention standards. (Analogously, the civil government can also legitimately establish medical quarantines to protect public health: Lev. 13, 14.)

Carl Bridenbaugh, in his study of urban life in seventeenth- and early eighteenth-century colonial America, discusses this prob-

---

6. North, *Dominion Covenant: Genesis,* ch. 4: "Economic Value: Objective and Subjective."

7. Gary North, *Tools of Dominion: The Case Laws of Exodus* (Tyler, Texas: Institute for Christian Economics, 1990), Appendix D: "The Epistemological Problem of Social Cost."

lem in detail. "The specter of fire has ever haunted the town-dweller. This necessary servant may, amidst crowded town conditions, buildings of inflammable construction, and the combustible materials of daily housekeeping and commerce, become his deadly enemy. Even in Europe the means of fighting fire were very crude in the seventeenth century, and only towards its close did the great cities, driven by a series of disasters, begin to evolve a system for combatting it."[8]

Massachusetts passed laws in 1638 and 1646 that forbade smoking tobacco out of doors, not because of Puritan prudery, but because of the fear of fire.[9] A similar law was passed in non-Puritan Philadelphia in 1701.[10] English curfew laws were passed, not to keep people off the streets at night (as they have been used against juveniles and rioters in American cities in the twentieth century) but to stop people from keeping fires burning in their homes at night. Boston passed such a law in 1649. A bell-ringer was hired to ring the bell at 9 p.m. and 4:30 a.m. Fires were not permitted in homes between these hours, unless they were covered. New Amsterdam (which later became New York City) passed a similar law in 1647.[11] Building codes were established, as well as local fire departments, yet a series of devastating fires swept through Boston in the seventeenth century (1653, 1676, 1679, 1682, and 1691). The city was struck again in 1711, the worst fire ever known in the colonies, when 100 homes were burned, and others were deliberately blown up with gunpowder to keep the fire from spreading.[12] The great problem was to protect movable property from thieves, and Boston subsequently established firewardens who had legal authority to remove personal property from burning buildings to a safe place.

Charles Town (Charleston), South Carolina, was devastated by fires in 1698, 1700, and 1740.[13] Only Philadelphia, a city of

---

8. Carl Bridenbaugh, *Cities in the Wilderness: The First Century of Urban Life in America, 1625-1742* (New York: Capricorn, [1938] 1964), p. 55.
9. *Ibid.*, p. 56.
10. *Ibid.*, p. 209.
11. *Idem.*
12. *Ibid.*, pp. 208-10.
13. *Ibid.*, pp. 212, 372.

brick houses, was spared.[14] Other towns adopted "brick-only" building codes for chimneys (and even for entire homes in the eighteenth century). Publicly financed chimney sweeps inspected chimneys, the single greatest cause of fires in these years.[15] New York had weekly chimney inspections for twenty years, beginning in 1697, and the city experienced no major fires.[16] Such measures represented an infringement on personal freedom, and they increased costs to taxpayers, but they were necessary to help protect people from each other's mistakes — mistakes for which the person responsible could not have afforded to pay.

No Omniscience

Men are not omniscient; therefore, information must be paid for. Accurate information is even more expensive. Any approach to economics that does not honor this principle from start to finish will be filled with errors.[17]

Individual sparks from a fire are unpredictable in their effects. We can make guesses about the overall effects of a fire, but an area of uncertainty is inescapable. Living next door to a firestarter may be tolerable. Farmers start fires to burn grasses or timber, for example. We do not call for a complete banning of all open fires. We do make people responsible for damage produced by fires that they start. The greater the danger of fire, the more concerned nearby residents must be. Sometimes, the public bans fires altogether.

Because no one can know everything, it is impossible to preserve life by eliminating every possible danger before any action can be taken. It would make human action impossible. We are not God; society must not expect people to perform as if they were God. Thus, there must always be limited legal liability in life. Nevertheless, for those actions that are known to be dangerous, people must be made legally responsible for their actions. This does not justify holding people fully responsible for actions

---

14. *Ibid.*, p. 61.
15. *Ibid.*, p. 56.
16. *Ibid.*, p. 207.
17. Thomas Sowell, *Knowledge and Decisions* (New York: Basic Books, 1980).

made in terms of earlier knowledge. With greater knowledge comes greater responsibility (Luke 12:47-48). If society tries to impose damages retroactively on actions that were taken yesterday based on yesterday's information, it would destroy the legal foundation of progress.

There can be no life without risk and uncertainty. We must not strive to build a zero-risk world. What we must do is to restrain those who would impose added known risks in the lives of neighbors without the latter's permission. We find the legal rule that provides this restraint in Exodus 22:5-6.

Externalities

A man should not be prosecuted for polluting, defacing, or otherwise lowering the value of his own land, so long as his actions do not have measurable physical effects on anyone else's life, health, or property. Because it is his own land, *he has internalized the costs of operation.* (By "internalize," I do not mean simply a mental calculation; I mean that *his property alone* suffers from his mistakes.) He risks starting a fire on his own property, or he runs a herd of cattle on his own property. The man making the estimate of benefits is the same person who makes the estimate of costs; it is the same man who will reap what he sows.

Once he sells a section of his land, he no longer internalizes costs and benefits on the section that was sold. Another person is now involved: his neighbor. The first man must not be allowed to pass on to his neighbor the risks of living next door to a person who sets fire on his property. The fire-starter cannot legally transfer to his neighbor the *generally known* but highly unpredictable *specific, individual* production costs of fire. *Economic analysis must begin with the Bible's assessment of personal responsibility for a man's actions.* It must begin with the presupposition of the rights (legal immunities) of private property. These rights must be protected by civil law and custom.

Conclusion

By assigning to individuals the economic and legal responsibilities of ownership, God imposes on individuals the burden of assessing the costs and benefits of their actions. There is no escape from this economic responsibility. "No decision" is still a decision. If an asset is squandered, the owner loses.

The chief failure of what is commonly referred to as collective ownership is that no individual can be sure that his assessment of the costs and benefits of a particular use of any asset is the same assessment that those whom he represents would make. The tendency is for individuals who are legally empowered to make these representative decisions to decide in terms of what is best for them as individuals. There is also a tendency for the decision-maker to make mistakes, since he cannot know the minds and desires of the community as a whole.

The common property tends to be wasted unless restraints on its use are imposed by the civil government. The "positive feedback" signals of high profits for the users are not offset by equally constraining "negative feedback" signals. Users of a scarce economic resource benefit highly as immediate users, yet they bear few costs as diluted-responsibility collective owners. Thus, in order to "save the property from exploitation," the civil government steps in and regulates users. This leads to political conflicts.

The biblical solution to this problem is to establish clear ownership rights (legal immunities) for property. The individual assesses costs and benefits in terms of his scale of values. He represents the consumer as an *economic agent* only because he has exclusive use of the property as *legal agent*. He produces profits or losses with these assets in terms of his abilities as an economic steward. The market tells him whether he is an effective agent of the competing consumers.

The legal system simultaneously assigns responsibility for the administration of these privately owned assets to the legal owners. It becomes the owners' legal responsibility to avoid damaging their neighbors through the use of their privately held property.

16

BINDING THE STATE

Ye shall observe to do therefore as the LORD your God hath commanded you: ye shall not turn aside to the right hand or to the left (Deut. 5:32).

This law was given to all of Israel: to resident aliens, members of the civil covenant, and judges. There is to be no wavering in obedience to God's law. Biblical law is clear; its punishments are clear. God restrains evil men through the lawful sanctions specified in His law; men are supposed to restrain themselves in terms of the specifics and principles of God's law. The "strait and narrow gate" (Matt. 7:13-14) is the gate of God's revealed law; men are not to depart from it. This restriction applies above all to law-enforcement officers, who represent God judicially to mankind in their capacity as civil magistrates. They must judge righteously, meaning in terms of His law, precisely because they are God's ministers (Rom. 13:4).[1]

The State's authority to impose vengeance is limited. This authority is too easily abused, for the State has a legal monopoly of violence. All monopolies are easy to abuse; the legal monopoly of violence is the easiest to violate. The officers of the civil government, fearing no one below them, readily overstep their authority.

The State has often been seen as divine because it possesses the legal authority and ability to impose the death penalty and other major punishments. What the Bible presents as a limited,

---
1. Greg L. Bahnsen, *By This Standard: The Authority of God's Law Today* (Tyler, Texas: Institute for Christian Economics, 1985), ch. 25: "Law and Politics in the New Testament."

derived sovereignty, men have defined as an ultimate, original sovereignty. To combat this false interpretation, biblical law restrains the officers of the State by imposing strict limitations on their enforcement of law. It is God's law that must be enforced, and this law establishes criteria of evidence and a standard of justice. This standard is "an eye for an eye." A popular slogan in the modern world promotes a parallel juridical principle: "The punishment should fit the crime."

The Punishment Should Fit the Crime

Why should the punishment fit the crime? What ethical principle leads Western people to believe that the Islamic judicial practice of cutting off a pickpocket's hand is too severe a punishment? After all, this will make future pickpocketing by the man far less likely. Why not cut off his other hand if he is caught and convicted again? People who have grown up in the West are repelled by the realization that such punishments have been imposed in the past, and are still imposed in Muslim societies.[2] Why this repulsion? Because they are convinced that the punishment exceeds the severity of the loss imposed on the victim by the thief.

Proportional Restitution

The Bible teaches that the victim must have his goods restored two-fold (Ex. 22:4,7), four-fold (for stealing a sheep), or five-fold (for stealing an ox) (Ex. 22:1). The seven-fold restitution of Proverbs 6:31 appears to be a *symbolic statement* regarding the comprehensive nature of restitution. The hungry thief who is destitute and who steals food must repay "all the substance of his house," meaning that what little he owns is forfeited when the normal two-fold restitution payment is imposed. A rich man who

---

2. This is Islam's *Shari'a* law. It is officially the civil law in Mauritania, where such amputations are still imposed: Roger Sawyer, *Slavery in the Twentieth Century* (London: Routledge and Kegan Paul, 1986), p. 15. *Shari'a* was reimposed in Sudan in 1988. Complains M. Ismail of Arlington, Virginia in a letter to the editor: "As a Sudanese, I feel that the previous legal code, which was an adoption of the British secular code, was a colonial yoke that disfigured our national independence." *Washington Times* (Oct. 3, 1988). Better to disfigure pickpockets than Sudan's national independence, Mr. Ismail is saying.

steals bread would not be made destitute by a two-fold payment. The poor thief has to pay to the limits of his wealth, despite his "extenuating circumstances," while the rich thief who steals for the love of evil-doing is barely touched financially. In short, the law plays no favorites. It does not respect persons. The perverse rich thief is not required to pay any greater percentage than the impoverished thief.

The seven-fold vengeance of God against anyone who might persecute Cain is another example of the language of fullness (Gen. 4:15). It means full judgment. Christ's words in Matthew 18 also indicate fullness: "Then came Peter unto him, and said, Lord, how oft shall my brother sin against me, and I forgive him? Till seven times? Jesus saith unto him, I say not unto thee, Until seven times: but, Until seventy times seven" (vv. 21-22). "Seventy times seven" is hyperbolic language; seventy times "fullness" means totality. Such forgiveness is not to be forgiveness apart from biblical restitution, however; the principle of forgiveness is not to be used to subsidize evil.[3]

The passage on restitution in Leviticus 6 indicates that if the thief turns himself in before the authorities identify him as the thief, he must restore the principal (Lev. 6:4), and must also add a 20 percent payment – a double tithe – presumably because of the false oath (Lev. 6:5). The restitution is equal to the value of the item stolen, and the penalty is one-fifth of this.[4]

Productivity and Dominion

The Bible does not teach that a convicted man's future productivity should be utterly destroyed by the judges, except in the case of capital crimes. The dominion covenant imposes a moral obligation on all men to labor to subdue the earth to the glory of God. A man whose body has been deliberately mutilated probably

---

3. R. J. Rushdoony, *The Institutes of Biblical Law* (Nutley, New Jersey: Craig Press, 1973), p. 463.

4. The King James translation reads: "he shall even restore it in the principal, and shall add the fifth part more thereto" (6:5). The New English Bible is clearer: "He shall make full restitution, adding one fifth to it." The New American Standard reads: "[H]e shall make restitution for it in full, and add to it one-fifth more." The restitution payment would appear to be the penalty payment equal to the item stolen.

will become a less productive worker. He may find it difficult to earn enough wealth to repay his debt to the victim. By cutting off the pickpocket's hand, the State is saying that there is no effective regeneration in life, that God cannot restore to wholeness a sinner's soul and his calling. Because he is a convicted pickpocket, he must be assumed to be a perpetual thief by nature; therefore, the State must make his future labor in his illegal calling less efficient. His hand is not being cut off because his victim lost a hand; it is being cut off simply as *an assertion of State power*, and as a deterrent against crime.

The liberal Bible scholar Hans Jochen Boecker correctly observes that "The intention of the talion was not, therefore, to *inflict* injury — as it might sound to us today — but to *limit* injury."[5] But then he gets everything confused. He says that this law restrained the institution of blood revenge.[6] He never bothers to apply this principle of restraint to the modern State. The Bible teaches that excessive penalties imposed by the State violate a fundamental principle of biblical obedience, both personal and civil: "Ye shall observe to do therefore as the LORD your God hath commanded you: ye shall not turn aside to the right hand or to the left" (Deut. 5:32). Conclusion: neither is the State to *cut off* the pickpocket's right hand or his left.[7]

The Punishment Should Benefit the Victim

Societies that are not governed by biblical law do not place the proper emphasis on the principle of economic restitution. The concern of the judicial system becomes *punishment of the criminal* rather than *restitution to the victim*. W. Cleon Skousen, a lawyer and former law enforcement official, has described the prevailing situ-

---

5. Hans Jochen Boecker, *Law and the Administration of Justice in the Old Testament and Ancient East*, translated by Jeremy Moiser (Minneapolis, Minnesota: Augsburg, [1976] 1980), p. 174.

6. *Ibid.*, pp. 174-75.

7. The Hammurabi Code specified death for any thief who had taken an oath that he had not stolen: CH, paragraphs 9-10. There was a 30-fold restitution for stealing animals belonging to the State: paragraph 8. *Ancient Near Eastern Texts Relating to the Old Testament*, edited by James B. Pritchard (3rd ed.; Princeton, New Jersey: Princeton University Press, 1969), p. 166.

ation: "Under modern law, fines are almost invariably paid to the city, county or federal government. If the victim wants any remedy he must sue for damages in a civil court. However, as everyone knows, by the time a criminal has paid his fines to the court, he is usually depleted of funds or consigned to prison where he is earning nothing and therefore could not pay damages even if his victim went to the expense of filing a suit and getting a judgment. As a result, modern justice penalizes the offender, but does virtually nothing for the victim."[8] In later stages of the development of humanism, State officials begin to substitute the shibboleth of "rehabilitation" for punishment, although the form this "rehabilitation" takes makes the State's officers even more arbitrary than before.

Biblical law restrains the arbitrariness of the State's officers. If the punishment must fit the crime, then the judges do not have the authority to impose lighter judgments or heavier judgments on the criminal. The victim decides the penalty, not the judges.[9] The criminal is to be given sufficient freedom to repay the victim, even if he must be sold into indentured servitude for a specific period of time in order to raise sufficient funds to pay off the victim. As a servant, he learns the discipline of work, and perhaps sufficient skills to give him a new calling and a new life when his debt is paid. But the debt is always to a private party: to the victim originally, and the slave-owner secondarily. Where a specific victim is involved and can be identified, the debt is not owed as a fine to the State. It is owed to the victim. The man who causes a premature birth in which the baby is not harmed nevertheless pays a fine to the family because of the risk to which he subjected the pregnant woman and her child.

Fines Should Compensate Victims

This should not be understood as an argument against fines

---

8. W. Cleon Skousen, *The Third Thousand Years* (Salt Lake City, Utah: Bookcraft, 1964), p. 354. Skousen served in the Federal Bureau of Investigation (FBI) for 16 years and also served as Chief of Police in Salt Lake City in 1956. He became Editorial Director of *Law and Order* in 1960, the leading professional law enforcement journal in the United States.

9. See above, Chapter 6: "The Ransom for an Eye."

to the civil government for so-called "victimless crimes." For example, a person is prohibited from driving a car at 70 miles an hour through a residential district or school zone. There are potential victims who deserve legal protection. The speeding driver is subjecting them to added risk of injury or death. Clearly, it is more dangerous statistically for children to attend a school located near an unfenced street on which drivers are travelling at 70 miles an hour rather than 25. The imposition of a fine helps to reduce the number of speeding drivers. Because they increase risks to families, drivers who exceed the speed limit can legitimately be fined, since the victims of this increased statistical risk cannot be specified. These fines should be imposed locally: to be used to indemnify future local victims of unsolved hit and run incidents.

The State is not to use fines to increase its operating budget or increase its control over the lives of innocent citizens. The State is to be supported by tax levies, so that no conflict of interest should occur between honest judgment and the desire to increase the State's budget. The proper use of fines is the establishment of a *restitution fund for victims of crimes whose perpetrators cannot be located or convicted*, analogous to the Old Testament sacrifice of the heifer when a murderer could not be found (Deut. 21:1-9). Such a fund is a valid use of the civil law. Even if law enforcement authorities are unable to locate and convict a criminal, the victim still deserves restitution, just as God deserved restitution for an unsolved murder in Israel in the form of a sacrificed heifer. A reasonable way of funding such a restitution program is to collect money from those who have been successfully convicted by law enforcement authorities.

Hayek's Three Principles

Lex talionis binds the State. This so-called "primitive" principle keeps the State from becoming arbitrary in its imposition of penalties. *Citizens can better predict in advance what the penalty will be for a specific crime.* This is extremely important for maintaining a free society. The three legal foundations for a free society, Hayek argues, are known general rules, certainty of enforcement, and equality before the law. I argue that the principle of "eye for eye" preserves all three.

1. General Rules

First, with respect to general rules, Hayek writes that these rules must distinguish private spheres of action from public spheres, which is crucial in maintaining freedom: "What distinguishes a free from an unfree society is that in the former each individual has a recognized private sphere clearly distinct from the public sphere, and the private individual cannot be ordered about but is expected to obey only the rules which are equally applicable to all. It used to be the boast of free men that, so long as they kept within the bounds of the known law, there was no need to ask anybody's permission or to obey anybody's orders. It is doubtful whether any of us can make this claim today."[10] If men must ask permission before they act, society then becomes a *top-down bureaucratic order*, which is an appropriate structure only for the military and the police force (the "sword").[11] The Bible specifies that the proper hierarchical structure in a biblical covenant is a bottom-up appeals court structure (Ex. 18).[12]

Adam was allowed to do anything he wanted to do in the garden, with only one exception. He had to avoid touching or eating the forbidden fruit. He did not have to ask permission to do anything else. He was free to choose.[13] This biblical principle of legal freedom is to govern all our decisions.[14] This is stated clearly in Jesus' parable of the laborers who all received the same wage. Those who had worked all day complained to the owner of the field. The owner responded: "Friend, I do thee no wrong: didst not thou agree with me for a penny? Take that thine is, and

---

10. F. A. Hayek, *The Constitution of Liberty* (University of Chicago Press, 1960), pp. 207-8.

11. Ludwig von Mises, *Bureaucracy* (Cedar Falls, Iowa: Center for Futures Education, [1944] 1983), ch. 2. Distributed by Libertarian Press, Spring Mills, Pennsylvania.

12. Ray R. Sutton, *That You May Prosper: Dominion By Covenant* (Tyler, Texas: Institute for Christian Economics, 1987), ch. 2.

13. Milton and Rose Friedman, *Free to Choose: A Personal Statement* (New York: Harcourt Brace Jovanovich, 1980).

14. Grace Hopper, who developed the computer language Cobol, and who served as an officer in the U.S. Navy until she was well into her seventies, offered this theory of leadership: "It's easier to say you're sorry than it is to ask permission."

go thy way: I will give unto this last, even as unto thee. Is it not lawful for me to do what I will with mine own? Is thine eye evil, because I am good?" (Matt. 20:13-15). Neither the owner nor the workers had to get permission in advance from some government agency. God leaves both sides free to choose the terms of labor and payment.

Because God alone is omniscient, He controls the world perfectly. Men, not being omniscient, must accept judicial restrictions on their own legitimate spheres of action. In doing so, they acknowledge their position as creatures under God. They must face the reality of their own limitations as creatures. They must not pretend that they can foresee the complex outcome of every activity of every person in society. The complexity of life is too great. Men can only make guesses about the consequences of human action. *To bring the greatest quantity of accurate knowledge to bear on society at any point in time, men must be allowed great latitude in their personal decision-making.* This division of intellectual labor is what provides society with the best available knowledge at a price people are willing to pay.[15] If men pretend that a committee of experts can plan for an entire economy, they have pretended to be Divine. Hayek is correct: ". . . the demand for conscious control is therefore equivalent to the demand for control by a single mind."[16] He goes on to argue: "Indeed, any social processes which deserve to be called 'social' in distinction from the action of individuals are almost *ex definitione* not conscious. Insofar as such processes are capable of producing a useful order which could not have been produced by conscious direction, any attempt to make them subject to such direction would necessarily mean that we restrict what social activity can achieve to the inferior capacity of the individual mind."[17] Worse; in a socialist society, we restrict what social activity can achieve to what a responsibility-avoiding, government-protected committee can achieve.

---

15. Hayek, *Individualism and Economic Order* (University of Chicago Press, 1948), ch. 4: "The Use of Knowledge in Society."

16. Hayek, *The Counter-Revolution in Science: Studies on the Abuse of Reason* (Indianapolis, Indiana: Liberty Press, [1952] 1979), p. 153.

17. *Ibid.*, p. 154.

By decentralizing decision-making within a system of known rules, and by allowing a competitive system of market-imposed rewards and punishments, society preserves individual freedom, individual and corporate productivity, and personal responsibility. This decentralized decision-making process is what is established by the profit management system.[18]

The principle of "eye for eye" is easily understood. It allows people to evaluate in advance their potential liabilities for actions that inflict physical harm on others. This encourages personal responsibility. It also encourages people to make accurate assessments of potential costs and benefits of their actions. This is the biblical principle of *counting the cost* (Luke 14:28-30). It is basic to biblical liberty that individuals count the costs of their behavior.

2. Legal Predictability

Second, there is the crucial issue of legal predictability. "There is probably no single factor which has contributed more to the prosperity of the West than the relative certainty of the law which has prevailed here."[19] He makes a very important point in this regard. The certainty of law is important, not just in cases that come before the courts, but also in those cases that do not lead to formal litigation because the outcome is so certain. "It is the cases that never come before the courts, not those that do, that are the measure of the certainty of the law."[20] In the United States, there is seemingly endless litigation, precisely because of the unpredictability of the courts.[21] Men go into the courts seeking justice because they do not know what to expect from the courts. If they knew what to expect, fewer people would bother to litigate. They would settle out of court or perhaps even avoid the original infraction.

The law of God establishes the "eye for eye" principle. Men can assess, in advance, what their punishment is likely to be if they transgress the law. They can count the potential cost of

---

18. Mises, *Bureaucracy*, ch. 1.
19. Hayek, *Constitution of Liberty*, p. 208.
20. *Idem.*
21. Macklin Fleming, *The Price of Perfect Justice* (New York: Basic Books, 1974).

violence. This is a restraining factor on all sin. A person can imagine the costs to his potential victim of losing an eye or a tooth. If convicted, the criminal will bear a comparable cost.

Rulers must be aware that the *lex talionis* principle is not simply limited to crimes by private citizens. Judgments fall on nations, both blessings and cursings (Judges, Jonah, Lamentations). The list of promised *national* cursings in Deuteronomy 28:15-68 is a detailed extension of the list of promised blessings in verses 1-14. When nations defy God in specific ways, they will be judged in specific ways — mirror images of the promised blessings to covenantally faithful nations. Instead of going out in war (a national endeavor, not private) and scattering their enemies, they will go out to war and be scattered by their enemies. Instead of lending to their enemies, they will become debtors to their enemies. The principle of "eye for eye" is essential to all of life. From him to whom much has been given, much is expected (Luke 12:47-48).

3. Equality Before the Law

"The third requirement of true law is equality."[22] Equality before the law, as Albright has said, is reinforced by the "eye for eye" principle.[23] The rich man, as well as the poor man, wants to avoid the loss of an eye or a tooth. Therefore, the rich man, like the poor man, must avoid inflicting such injuries on other people. There must be equality before the law (Lev. 19:15). The judges must not impose a tooth's worth of punishment for an eye's worth of damage just because the convicted person is rich or famous. People can then trust the law and the courts, for they know that the law is being enforced because God is sovereign over the affairs of men. The law does not become a weapon of oppression to be used by one class over another. The law, to use Marx's terminology, is not to become a superstructure which is

---

22. Hayek, *Constitution of Liberty*, p. 209.

23. "So the *lex talionis* (is) . . . the principle of equal justice for all!" W. F. Albright, *History, Archaeology, and Christian Humanism*, p. 74, cited by Shalom Paul, *Studies in the Book of the Covenant in the Light of Cuneiform and Biblical Law* (Leiden: E. J. Brill, 1970), p. 77.

built on the foundation of an economic substructure. The law of God is the substructure in terms of which the economy, the political order, and the pattern of society develop.

Thus, the general legal principle of "eye for eye" in the imposition of civil punishments is a crucial foundation of human freedom, for it binds the civil government in advance. Hayek's discussion is very useful for understanding the State-binding purposes of the *lex talionis*. There are three legal principles that undergird a free society, he argues: general legal rules that 1) distinguish private from public spheres of action; 2) provide legal predictability; and 3) provide equality before the law. The judicial principle of *lex talionis* supports all three.

Conclusion

The biblical principle of an eye for an eye protects society from a lawless State which recognizes no limitations on its power. This law establishes the fundamental judicial principle that the punishment should fit the crime. This principle, sometimes called *lex talionis*, requires that the criminal *pay back* to the victim whatever was stolen, and in some cases an additional penalty payment is required.

There is no doubt that this law is based on vengeance, but vengeance is a basic principle of biblical law. God extracts a vengeance payment from evil-doers: perfect vengeance at the day of judgment and imperfect vengeance through the civil government. Vengeance is a form of restitution to God.

The fundamental goal of biblical law is *restoration*. Evil people are to be restored by God to righteousness. The State cannot save mankind, but it can impose external punishments that make social and economic restoration possible. Restitution by the criminal to the victim is an effective way of restoring wholeness to both parties. It upholds a basic principle of civil law: the punishment should benefit the victim.

Prisons are a second-best system of punishment. They keep hardened criminals off the street, but they do very little for the past victims. While they should eventually be emptied, except for holding suspects for trial at the local level, this would be too risky before all three biblical sanctions are restored to civil law: the death penalty, corporal punishment, and economic restitution.

17

EMPTYING THE PRISONS, SLOWLY

Then his lord, after that he had called him, said unto him, O thou wicked servant, I forgave thee all that debt, because thou desiredst me. Shouldest not thou also have had compassion on thy fellowservant, even as I had pity on thee? And his lord was wroth, and delivered him to the tormenters, till he should pay all that was due unto him. So likewise shall my heavenly Father do also unto you, if ye from your hearts forgive not every one his brother their trespasses (Matt. 18:32-35).

Debtors prison: one of the horrors of any humanist age. The governments of the West closed them only in the final third of the nineteenth century. They had obviously existed as early as Jesus' era. But they did not exist in the Old Testament.

Why did Jesus use the debtor's prison as His example of God's eternal punishment? Was He sanctioning the creation of an institution unknown to Old Testament Israel? No. On the contrary, He was demonstrating that until the day of judgment, God is merciful to men, allowing them to make restitution to their victims and to God for their sins. God keeps open the door for men to affirm the only restitution payment suitable in God's court of final judgment: personal faith in the atoning (restitution-paying) work of Jesus Christ on Calvary. Just as the rich lord allowed his servant time to pay off his enormous debt, so should this servant have allowed his debtor time to pay off a much smaller debt.

There is no doubt what this passage teaches: once you are thrown into the cosmic debtor's prison of hell, there is no escape.

Each person's debts are too large. There is only one way to get them paid off: payment by one's kinsman-redeemer. But this is available only while a person is alive in this world. Thus, the imagery of the Old Testament's kinsman-redeemer who bought his kinsman out of servitude (Lev. 25:47-49) was basic to Christ's message regarding His own role in history.

In Israel, there was no prison system. Egypt had prisons; Israel did not.[1] Why not? Because prisons do not offer adequate opportunities for criminals to repay their victims. *A prison restricts the criminal's ability to make restitution, and restitution is the very essence of biblical punishment.* Prisons restrict men's ability to repay; they also make it difficult for men to exercise dominion over nature.

There is no restitution to victims by those in hell or in the lake of fire. *There is permanent restitution to God, but not to man.* In this sense, hell is outside history and the process of restitution and restoration. The debtor of the parable is cast into prison until every last payment is made. The debtor could get out only if someone else paid his obligations. Clearly, this is a picture of Christ's payment of His people's ethical debts to God, as kinsman-redeemer. This substitute payment is available to mankind only in history. *Thus, the prison is illegitimate because it represents a denial of history and the opportunities of history.* That Egypt should have prisons is understandable; Egyptians had a static view of time. Israel did not.

The parable should have taught men not to construct debtors prisons, but men generally refuse to listen carefully to Christ's parables. They went on building them until very recent times. Instead of debtors prisons, the Old Testament created a system of lifetime servitude or slavery. Victims could get immediate cash when the court sold the thief into slavery. Convicted criminals were allowed to work off their obligations; when the debt was paid to the buyer, the criminal went free. Unlike the debtor in prison who had no work and hoped only in the rich relative who might pay his debt, the criminal in the Old Testament had hope in the possibility of buying his way out of slavery by hard work. He

---

1. R. J. Rushdoony, *The Institutes of Biblical Law* (Nutley, New Jersey: Craig Press, 1973), pp. 514-16.

learned the skills of liberty and prosperity in the very bondage of punishment.

But modern man believes that he is wiser than God. He has become the classic wise guy. He sees slavery as a terrible evil. So he relies on prisons to do the work of restoration.

A Recent Invention

The prison as a correctional and rehabilitative institution was the invention of the early nineteenth-century reform movement in the United States. Visitors from all over Europe came to see these correctional "wonders." The most famous of these visitors was Alexis de Tocqueville, who came from France in 1831 to see our prisons, and who then wrote the most insightful study of American institutions in the nineteenth century, which also became the earliest major work in the discipline of sociology, *Democracy in America* (1835, 1840). He and his colleague Gustave de Beaumont produced a famous report on their observations, *On the Penitentiary System in the United States* (1833). Parallel tax-supported institutions were developed during this same era: the insane asylum, the orphanage, the reformatory for youthful delinquents, and the large-scale public almshouse. It was also the era of the first "religiously neutral" (humanistic) tax-supported day schools in the United States.[2]

David Rothman writes: "Americans in the colonial period had followed very different procedures. They relieved the poor at home or with relatives or neighbors; they did not remove them to almshouses. They fined or whipped criminals or put them in stocks or, if the crime was serious enough, hung them; they did not conceive of imprisoning them for specific periods of time. The colonists left the insane in the care of their families, supporting them, in case of need, as one of the poor. They did not erect special buildings for incarcerating the mentally ill. Similarly, homeless children lived with neighbors, not in orphan asylums. . . .

---

2. The two major leaders in this self-consciously anti-Christian public school movement were Horace Mann and James G. Carter. See R. J. Rushdoony, *The Messianic Character of American Education: Studies in the History of the Philosophy of Education* (Nutley, New Jersey: Craig Press, 1963), chaps. 3, 4.

The few institutions that existed in the eighteenth century were clearly places of last resort. Americans in the Jacksonian period reversed these practices. Institutions became places of first resort, the preferred solution to the problems of poverty, crime, delinquency, and insanity."[3]

Western Europe abandoned debtors prison during the decade 1867-77.[4] Legislators at last recognized that it did victims no good to see a debtor cast into prison until he paid, since he could not earn his way out. It is not coincidental that Europe passed such legislation in the same era that the United States and Russia abolished slavery, another system that also did not provide a way for people to buy their way out.

The Concentration Camp

The ultimate earthly prison is the concentration camp. While the modern Soviet camp has economic functions, the cruelty of long sentences is obvious. Under Stalin, these sentences were incredibly grotesque. As many as 30 million people were sent into the camps, never to return.[5] The magnitude of the crime against humanity seems irrationally cruel.[6] They were irrational, according to Solzhenitsyn. The first thought of the arrested person was always, "Me? What for?"[7] From 1934 on, a soldier captured in wartime was given a ten-year sentence upon being freed from the enemy.[8] Encircled military units got ten year sentences after 1941.[9] Failure to denounce specified evil acts carried an indeterminate

---

3. David J. Rothman, *The Discovery of the Asylum: Social Order and Disorder in the New Republic* (Boston: Little, Brown, 1971), p. xiii.

4. France abolished debtors prison in 1867; England abolished it by the Debtors Act of 1869. Ireland followed in 1872, Scotland in 1880. Switzerland and Norway abolished it in 1874, Italy in 1877. "Debt," *Encyclopaedia Britannica* (11th ed.; New York: Encyclopaedia Britannica, Inc., 1910), VII, p. 906.

5. Robert Conquest, *The Great Terror: Stalin's Purges of the Thirties* (rev. ed.; New York: Collier, 1973), p. 710.

6. Ernest van den Haag, *Punishing Criminals: Concerning a Very Old and Painful Question* (New York: Basic Books, 1975), p. 43.

7. Aleksandr Solzhenitsyn, *The Gulag Archipelago, 1918-1956: An Experiment in Literary Investigation, I-II* (New York: Harper & Row, 1974), p. 4.

8. *Ibid.*, p. 61.

9. *Ibid.*, p. 79.

sentence.[10] Quotas for arrests made the diversity of the camps fantastic, he says; there was no logic to them.[11] A chance meeting with a condemned man could get you ten years.[12] Owning a radio tube was worth ten years.[13] In 1948, the average sentence increased to 25 years; juveniles received ten.[14]

The classic story he tells was of a district Party conference in Moscow Province. At the end of the conference, someone called for a tribute to Stalin. A wave of applause began and continued. Everyone was afraid to be the first person to stop clapping, for fear of being arrested. It went on for eleven minutes. Finally, one man, a factory director, stopped clapping and sat down, then the whole group immediately stopped and sat down. That night the man was arrested and given a ten-year sentence.[15]

There is only one way to explain this: *the desire of the State to become God and to impose hell on earth.* It became a goal of State policy to destroy men's lives, to leave them without earthly hope in the future. It was easy to go to jail without a trial. The Special Boards attached to the secret police, the OSO's,[16] handed down "administrative penalties," not sentences. "The OSO enjoyed another important advantage in that its penalty could not be appealed. There was nowhere to appeal to. There was no appeals jurisdiction above it, and no jurisdiction beneath it. It was subordinate only to the Minister of Internal Affairs, to Stalin, and to Satan."[17] It is not surprising that the camps became hell on earth.

The Chamber of Horrors

The prison also creates other horrors, such as homosexuality and training in criminal behavior for the younger inmates by the "skilled" older inmates. It puts too much power in the hands of

---

10. *Ibid.*, pp. 67, 363.
11. *Ibid.*, p. 71.
12. *Ibid.*, p. 75.
13. *Ibid.*, p. 78.
14. *Ibid.*, p. 91.
15. *Ibid.*, pp. 69-70.
16. *Ibid.*, p. 275.
17. *Ibid.*, p. 285.

guards, who can then indulge their tastes in brutality. It puts too much power in the hands of parole boards, who can shorten a man's sentence irrespective of the crime, thereby making the punishment fit the board's assessment of the criminal, not the judge's assessment of the effects of the crime — or more to the point, making the punishment fit the latest humanistic theory of criminal behavior and social responsibility, not the crime.

Left-wing humanists have begun to see the threat to justice posed by the indeterminate sentence.[18] Mitford has described the indeterminate sentence as "a potent psychological instrument for inmate manipulation and control, the 'uncertainty' ever nagging in the prisoner's mind a far more effective weapon than the cruder ones then [in the 1870's] in vogue: the club, the starvation regime, the iron shackle."[19] Because of doubts regarding the prison as a means of correcting evil behavior, we have seen an increasing resistance by juries and judges to send first offenders or minor offenders to prison. But because restitution has not yet become a common means of punishing criminals, these "minor" criminals receive no punishment, other than having to report occasionally to an overburdened probation or parole officer.

A good example of the failure of the parole system is the case of Charles Manson. Manson led the "family" (gang) of murderers who killed actress Sharon Tate and several others in 1969. He was on parole from prison at the time. Others in his "family" were also on probation. As the prosecuting attorney later wrote: "Manson associated with ex-cons,[20] known narcotics users, and minor girls. He failed to report his whereabouts, made few attempts to obtain employment, repeatedly lied regarding his activities. During the first six months of 1969 alone, he had been charged, among other things, with grand theft auto, narcotics possession, rape, contributing to the delinquency of a minor. There

---

18. Jessica Mitford, *Kind and Usual Punishment: The Prison Business* (New York: Knopf, 1973), ch. 6. Those who have opposed capital punishment have denounced it as cruel and unusual. Mitford's attack implies that imprisonment is, too. What, then, is legitimate punishment? The Bible gives us guidelines; few humanists do.

19. *Ibid.*, p. 82.

20. That is, former convicts.

was more than ample reason for parole revocation."[21] Manson's parole officer stated in court that he could not remember whether Manson had been on probation or parole; the man was responsible for overseeing 150 persons.[22] Manson had actually begged to be allowed to remain in jail when they released him in 1967; at that time, he was 32 years old, and had spent 17 years in penal and reform institutions.[23]

Humanists look at the "eye for eye" principle, and react in horror. They do not react with equal consternation when they confront the problem of the late twentieth century's increase in violent crime. Statistics on crime for the United States are readily available and comprehensive, and I am including a brief survey of this material in order to present an overview of the crisis facing Western, humanist culture. At the end of an age, we expect to see an increase in criminal behavior, as lawlessness becomes a way of life for a dedicated, pathological minority, while religious and cultural relativism and self-doubt render citizens and their elected authorities helpless to stem this tide of consistent lawlessness. Gilbert Murray, the great student of Greek civilization, characterized the last days of Greek religion as "the failure of nerve."[24] This seems to fit late-twentieth-century Western humanism quite well.

The prison is a bureaucracy, not a market-oriented institution. It is run by the State through taxes; it is a bureaucratic management system, not a profit management system.[25] Men are trained to follow orders, not to innovate, take risks, and meet market demand. There are many arguments against prisons, as revealed by an enormous bibliography on alternatives to pris-

---

21. Vincent Bugliosi, *Helter Skelter: The True Story of the Manson Murders* (New York: Norton, 1974), p. 420.

22. *Ibid.*, p. 419.

23. *Ibid.*, p. 146.

24. Gilbert Murray, *The Five Stages of Greek Religion* (1925 edition), reprinted by AMS Press and Greenwood Press.

25. See Gary North, "Statist Bureaucracy in the Modern Economy," in North, *An Introduction to Christian Economics* (Nutley, New Jersey: Craig Press, 1973), ch. 20. See also Ludwig von Mises, *Bureaucracy* (Spring Mills, Pennsylvania: Libertarian Press, [1944] 1983).

ons,[26] but the most important one is that they thwart the biblical principle of restitution.

Emptying Prisons and Stoning Sons

Prisons need to be emptied. The biblical way to accomplish this is to revive the biblical practices of execution for habitual criminals (Deut. 21:18), corporal punishment (Deut. 25:1-3), and restitution. It is interesting that the justification for executing habitual criminals rests on that bugaboo of all pietism, the execution of the rebellious son. It is a case of "if *this*, then how much more *that*." If it is mandatory that a man bring his incorrigible adult son before the elders for gluttony, drunkenness,[27] and verbal rebellion, how much more ready will a society be to execute repeatedly violent individuals or members of a professional criminal class! Remove from the law books the law regarding the civic execution of the rebellious son, and you thereby remove the one *and only* biblical sanction for executing professional criminals. The "three-time loser" penalty of American jurisprudence[28] has disappeared; in its place has come a criminal class of far more than three felony convictions — and most of these professionals are paroled early.

Incorrigible sons and incorrigible criminals are to be removed from society: ". . . so shalt thou put evil away from among you; and all Israel shall hear, and fear" (Deut. 21:21b). Rushdoony has identified the importance of this law for society: "Such persons were thus blotted out of the commonwealth. When and if this law is observed, ungodly families who are given to lawlessness are denied a place in the nation. The law thus clearly works to eliminate all but godly families."[29]

---

26. James R. Brantley and Marjorie Kravitz (eds.), *Alternatives to Institutionalization: A Definitive Bibliography*, published by the National Criminal Justice Reference Service of the National Institute of Law Enforcement and Criminal Justice, a division of the Law Enforcement Assistance Administration, U.S. Department of Justice (May 1979), 240 pages.

27. Seven-year-olds are not drunkards; this verse deals with adult rebels.

28. A man convicted of a felony for the third time used to receive life imprisonment without possibility of parole.

29. Rushdoony, *Institutes*, p. 380.

What we find in our day is that Christians despise biblical law almost as much as secular humanists do. They attack the very thought that the stoning of drunken, gluttonous sons — not young children, but adult sons who are living at home with their parents, debauching themselves — as some sort of "crime against humanity," when stoning them is specifically a civil sanction required by God (Deut. 21:18-21).[30] The very idea of execution by public stoning embarrasses Christians, despite the fact that public stoning is by far the most covenantally valid form of execution, for God's law requires the witnesses to cast the first stones, and it also requires representatives of the entire covenantal community to participate directly, rather than hiding the act in a sanitary room in some distant prison. The Bible is clear: "The hands of the witnesses shall be first upon him to put him to death, and afterward the hands of all the people. So thou shalt put the evil away from among you" (Deut. 17:7).

The Evil of Modern Impersonalism

Stoning was a communal activity, an aspect of the civil covenant: sanctions. It took place outside the town (Lev. 24:14; Num. 15:35-36; I Ki. 21:13). "If sentence was passed with the help of eye-witnesses, the witnesses had to begin the execution (Deut. 17:7). This was to discourage frivolous testimony in court."[31] Boecker argues that it was a form of excommunication, and that those stoned were not entitled to burial in the family plot, but he cites no Scriptural evidence. "For the ancients, the criminal was possessed of a real guilt which jeopardized the community. By covering the evil-doer with stones outside the town, the evil that he could spread was banished."[32] This argument is ridiculous, a liberal's self-conscious attempt to reinterpret the Bible's covenantal concepts as magical. The execution of the evil-doer was suffi-

---

30. Ed Dobson and Ed Hindson, "Apocalypse Now?", *Policy Review* (Fall 1986), p. 20.

31. Hans Jochen Boecker, *Law and the Administration of Justice in the Old Testament and Ancient East*, translated by Jeremy Moiser (Minneapolis, Minnesota: Augsburg, [1976] 1980), p. 40.

32. *Idem.*

cient to stop the spread of his evil. The pile of stones was intended rather to serve as a covenantal reminder. Each pile of stones testified to the reality of covenant sanctions, a monument to God's judgment of cursing in history, just as the stones from the River Jordan were made into a memorial of God's judgment of the deliverance of Israel (Josh. 4:7-8).

Public stoning forces citizens to face the reality of the ultimate civil sanction, execution, which in turn points to God's ultimate sanction at judgment day. Stoning also faithfully images the promised judgment against Satan: the crushing of his head by the promised Seed (Gen. 3:15). Because most people, including Christians, do not want to think about God's final judgment, they prefer to assign to distant unknown executioners the grim task of carrying out God's judgment in private. This privatization of execution is immoral; it is itself criminal. It is unjust to the convicted criminal, and it is unjust to the surviving victims, who do not see God's justice done in public. The *systematic impersonalism of capital punishment* is the problem, not capital punishment as such. This deliberate impersonalism has corrupted the entire penal system today.

Public stoning would allow a condemned man to confront the witnesses and his executioners. The idea of a private execution where the condemned person cannot have a final word to those who have condemned him is anything but liberal-minded. It was long considered a basic legal privilege in the West for a condemned person to have this final opportunity to speak his mind. The sign of the intolerance of the "liberal" French Revolutionaries was their unwillingness to allow King Louis XVI to speak to the crowd at his execution. The judges had ordered drummers to begin drumming the moment he began to speak, which they did.[33]

Whereas men used to be flogged in public or put in the stocks for a few days, we now put them in hidden jails that are filled with a professional criminal class, as well as with AIDS-carrying homosexual rapists. This impersonalism of punishment has been paralleled by a steady bureaucratization and institutionalization

---

33. Leo Gershoy, *The French Revolution and Napoleon* (New York: Appleton-Century-Crofts, 1933), p. 238.

of the penal system. The guards in prisons tend to become as impersonal and callous as their prisoners. Bukovsky writes of Soviet prisons: "There's no real difference between the criminals and the guards. Except for the uniforms. The slang is the same, the manners, concepts, psychology. It's all the same criminal world, all joined by an unbreakable chain."[34]

The growth of impersonalism has been a problem for the West from the beginning. Even in the days of public executions, several centuries ago, the axeman wore a face mask. The Bible does not allow the establishment of a professional, taxpayer-financed guild of faceless executioners who, over time, inevitably either grow callous and impersonal toward their awful (full of awe) task, or else grow sadistic. Instead, the Bible imposes personal responsibility on members of society at large for enforcing this ultimate sanction. But people in the Christian West have always refused to accept this God-imposed personal responsibility. They prefer to make a lone executioner psychologically responsible for carrying out the sentence rather than participate in this covenantal responsibility, as God requires. This refusal to accept personal responsibility by citizens has led to a crisis in Western jurisprudence in the twentieth century. Decade by decade, the more consistent haters of God's law have become politically dominant. They have used the same kinds of arguments against capital punishment in general that embarrassed Christians had accepted in their rejection of public stoning. Step by step, society eliminates capital punishment. Men's hatred of God's law is steadily manifested covenantally in modern civil law.

Conclusion

The prison is a second-best device. It does keep some habitual criminals locked up for part of their lives. It is sometimes argued that by keeping them out of circulation, the overall crime rate drops, but only if they are kept in prison, and even in this case, there is only spotty evidence. The problem is this: when one

---

34. Vladimir Bukovsky, *To Build a Castle – My Life as a Dissenter* (New York: Viking, 1978), p. 334.

criminal is locked up, others move in to the "vacuum" of crime.[35] It may take time for the new entrants to become equally skilled, however.

Still, prison is a threat. If a society refuses to execute professional criminals, then it must impose some kind of sanctions if evil is not to be indirectly subsidized. In short, biblical law is a package deal. It will not suffice to empty the prisons until the whole of biblical criminal law is on the law books and enforced, especially the death penalty against rebellious sons. Those who are appalled by this law are not sufficiently appalled by professional criminal behavior.

The problem modern society faces is that we no longer honor the three biblical civil sanctions against crime: restitution to victims, flogging, and capital punishment. We no longer think it is moral to sell a criminal into slavery in order to raise money to repay his victims. We no longer believe that such "harsh" penalties are morally valid. But God is not mocked. The result of this hostility to biblical law is a subsidy to the criminal paid for by his victims and potential victims. Taxpayers pay to keep criminals in prison for brief periods, and criminals have learned that in the modern humanist West, *crime pays*. Few get caught for any given crime, few who are caught are convicted, and few who are convicted receive stiff sentences. We have created a system of temporary free housing for criminals.

Dallas County in Texas is a good example. More people move through the Dallas County criminal justice system than in any other county except California's Los Angeles. Each month, twelve thousand people go into the four county jails, and the same number are released. Over 80% of them are former occupants of the jail system. They seldom serve more than three months for their two-year to ten-year sentences.[36] Yet all this goes on, decade after decade. Nothing changes. Nothing will, except to get worse, unless we return to biblical law. We will see either the tyranny of a political backlash or the ever more lenient

---

35. Van den Haag, *Punishing Criminals*, pp. 53-60.

36. Laura Miller, "Inmates laugh at joke called prison system," *Dallas Times Herald* (Feb. 19, 1988), Sect. B, p. 1.

handling of prisoners.

What we have is a universally acknowledged failure, the prison system. But men prefer failure to biblical law. This is as true of Christians as it is of humanists. They hate biblical law, so they have become the criminals' potential victim. They prefer it this way.

CONCLUSION

> *Blessed are the undefiled in the way, who walk in the law of the* LORD. *Blessed are they that keep his testimonies, and that seek him with the whole heart. They also do no iniquity: they walk in his ways. Thou hast commanded us to keep thy precepts diligently. O that my ways were directed to keep thy statutes! Then shall I not be ashamed, when I have respect unto all thy commandments (Ps. 119:1-6).*

These words of the Psalmist do not express the sentiments of modern man. Modern man despises biblical law, for it threatens to restrain him and the vain works of his imagination. Biblical law places restraints on the State as well as on individual evil-doers. It defines evil in terms of the revealed laws of a God who threatens covenant-breakers with eternal torture, a God who knows the hearts and minds of every person, and who judges them accordingly. Modern man does not want to be reminded of such a God or the judgment to come, so he renounces biblical law. He correctly sees biblical law as a curse on his dreams of autonomy.

A society that renounces biblical law has two choices: to attempt to construct a legal order that is either more rigorous than biblical law or more lenient. Such a society inevitably turns aside from God's law. It violates God's commandment: "Ye shall observe to do therefore as the LORD your God hath commanded you: ye shall not turn aside to the right hand or to the left" (Deut. 5:32). Anarchism beckons on one side, while a one-world socialist State beckons on the other.

If covenant-breaking man identifies with the criminal, he will prefer judicial leniency. He knows what is coming for him in eternity if God's word is true, so he sides ethically, emotionally, and philosophically with the criminal, in whose camp God also places him: *covenant-breaker*. On the other hand, covenant-breaking man may choose to imitate God, to become part of a messianic political movement that uses State power in a program to redeem some men and to crush all opposition. In this case, he will seek to make civil law more rigorous and more harsh than Old Testament law.

Or he may hold both positions at once, as the modern humanist liberal has done, by condemning the West's criminal justice system as being far too harsh, while praising Communist "re-education camps" as being truly (or at least necessarily) progressive. He rejects the West as too severe judicially, yet praises the Communists for being realistic in setting up slave labor camps. As is so often the case, Malcolm Muggeridge has magnificently described this schizophrenic liberal mentality and the effective use that the Communists have made of it: ". . . I have seen many Soviet frontiers, with barbed-wire, and land-mines, and dogs; with armed sentries in watch-towers ready to shoot on sight, like prison guards. All designed, not so much to bar people from coming in, as to prevent those inside from getting out. How strange, I have often reflected, that a régime which needs thus to pen up its citizens should nonetheless be able to make itself seem desirable to admirers outside. As though the purpose in taking the Bastille should have been to gain admission there and do a stretch."[1]

Spiritual Schizophrenia

There are millions of Christians today who suffer from a similar kind of intellectual schizophrenia. They contemptuously reject the Old Testament's legal system, claiming that any attempt to revive it would be a sure road to tyranny. They ignore the obvious fact that the Bible clearly reveals that Israel's rival kingdoms in the ancient Near East were the tyrannies, for those cultures were in bondage to false gods. But without biblical law to guide them in the reconstruction of the visibly corrupt societies and institutions of the modern world, what Bible-based alternative can they offer? None.

---

1. Malcolm Muggeridge, *Chronicles of Wasted Time: The Green Stick* (New York: William Morrow, 1973), p. 267.

Perceiving this to be their dilemma, Christians then express complete satisfaction that "we Christians can live faithfully under any kind of political or economic system," meaning that it makes no difference if God's people "return to Egypt, Assyria, and Babylon." In the very next breath they condemn Old Testament law as morally questionable and politically intolerable. Somehow, it seems that Christians can live faithfully under any legal order except the one that God established for His covenant people, Israel. Marx is tolerable; Moses is not.

Christians, especially college classroom Christians, proclaim confidently that the Bible does not offer judicial blueprints for social reform. This viewpoint leads to one of three conclusions: 1) there are no biblical standards of social reform, and therefore there is no legitimate Christian responsibility to promote social reform (dispensational fundamentalism); 2) there *are* standards of social reform, but they are not uniquely biblical (liberalism, modernism); 3) there are standards of social reform, but we cannot turn to biblical law to find them, so we therefore should use biblical phrases to baptize numerous social reform programs that the humanist political liberals abandoned as unworkable or ineffective ten years ago ("trendier than thou" neo-evangelicalism, or what William White has dubbed "the Wheaton pox"). New York University psychology professor Paul Vitz was being overly generous when he wrote that "Somehow the Christian world is always buying into secular ideas at the top of their influence, and selling out Christian ideas just when they have no place to go but up."[2] Instead, neo-evangelicals consistently pay retail prices for dead secular ideas ten years after everyone else has sold them at a discount into the used fads market.

Fundamentalists enthusiastically stand up and sing the words of the hymn, "O, how love I thy law; it is my meditation all the day," and then sit down to delight in an hour-long sermon that rejects Old Testament law as legalistic. They dismiss the stoning of gluttonous, drunken, rebellious adult sons as barbaric and then are preached into a frenzy about the evils of "demon rum." For

---

2. Cited by Richard John Neuhaus, "Religion and Psychology," *National Review* (Feb. 19, 1988), p. 46.

over a century, American fundamentalists have had no influence on the social and political events of the day, save only for the ill-fated political experiment in the United States called Prohibition (1918-33). Prohibition's visible failure to keep people from drinking alcohol, and the voters' subsequent repeal of the Eighteenth Amendment, drove fundamentalists into the American political wilderness for two generations. How can people who prefer anything and anyone to Moses be expected to speak out effectively in the name of the Lord on social and cultural issues? They can't, they haven't, and they don't. They won't, either, until they rediscover and recommit to Exodus 21-23. It is here that we find the theological foundation for a thoroughly biblical reform of the criminal justice system, which today surely *is* criminal.

The Reform of the Criminal Justice System

What would be the marks of civil justice during an era of biblical justice? Victims would see the restoration of their stolen assets, while criminals would see their ill-gotten capital melt away because of the financial burden of making restitution payments. The dual sanctions of *curse and blessing* — part four of the biblical covenant model[3] — are invoked and imposed wherever the principle of restitution is honored in the courts, both civil and ecclesiastical. Restitution brings both *judgment and restoration*, which affect individual lives and social institutions.

There are limits to biblical restitution. First, the full value of whatever was stolen is returned by the thief to the original owner. Second, the thief makes an additional penalty payment equal to the value of the item stolen. To encourage criminals to admit their guilt and seek restoration before their crimes are discovered, the Bible imposes a reduced penalty of 20% on those who admit their guilt voluntarily (Lev. 6:2-5).

There are two explicit exceptions to the payment of double restitution. The law singles out oxen and sheep as deserving special protection in the form of five-fold and four-fold restitution in cases where the stolen animals are killed or sold. Because oxen

---

3. Ray R. Sutton, *That You May Prosper: Dominion By Covenant* (Tyler, Texas: Institute for Christian Economics, 1987), ch. 4.

and sheep are symbolic of helpless human beings, God's law in principle points to the need of protecting men from oppression and slavery. Man is given responsibility over oxen and sheep, implying that he is also given responsibility over other men in various circumstances. He employs them or makes lawful use of their services. To use illegal physical coercion to thwart another person's exercise of his lawful calling is a crime against that person's God-given position as dominion man, and is punishable by God. This is why kidnapping and murder are capital crimes. The five-fold and four-fold restitution payments for slaughtered or resold ox and sheep are symbolic of these two extremely serious crimes against people.

The Goals of Restitution

Economic. Proportional restitution is imposed by the civil government as God's lawful representative on earth. The three economic goals of proportional restitution are these: 1) restoring full value to the victim; 2) protecting future potential victims by means of the deterrence effect of the penalty payment (Deut. 13:11): a) animals, especially those symbolic of man's helplessness (sheep and oxen), and b) property owners; and 3) offsetting the lower economic risks of detection associated with certain kinds of theft — the slaughter or sale of specially protected edible animals. All of these are designed to protect the rights of victims. The innocent, not the guilty, are to be the recipients of protection from the civil government. The victim can agree to be lenient to the criminal by accepting a reduced restitution payment, but that decision is his, not the court's.

Civil. Biblical restitution also has at least three civil goals in addition to the three economic goals. The first civil goal of restitution is to make life easier for the law-abiding citizen by fostering external social conditions in which he can live in peace and safety. Peace and safety are the fully legitimate goals of all biblical justice, which God has promised to bring to pass in world history through His church during a future period of earthly millennial peace. The nations will come to God's church ("the mountain of the house of the LORD") in search of true justice (Mic. 4:1-5).

A second civil goal of biblical restitution is to make possible the full *judicial* restoration of the criminal to society after he has paid the victim what he owes him. The State is not to concern itself with the psychological restoration of the criminal, the victim, or society in general. The State's jurisdiction is strictly limited to the realm of the judicial: *restitution.* The psychological state of the criminal is between himself and God, as is the psychological state of the victim. Nevertheless, as in the case of the salvation of any individual by God's grace, judicial restoration is the first step toward psychological restoration.

The modern U.S. practice of never again allowing convicted felons to vote is clearly immoral. Under biblical law, a convicted criminal becomes a *former* convicted criminal when he has made full restitution to his victims. In this sense, he is "resurrected" judicially. After he has paid his debt to his victims, he must be restored to full political participation. To segregate the former convicted criminal from any area of civic authority or participation is to deny judicially that full civil restoration is made possible by means of God's civil law.

The third civil goal of biblical restitution is not intuitively obvious, but it may be the most important goal for the modern world. A system of biblical restitution is required in order to reduce the likelihood that citizens will come to view the civil government as an agency that lawfully initiates programs leading to personal or social transformation. The State's task is to assess the economic damage that was inflicted on the victim and then impose judgment on the convicted criminal that will reimburse the victim for his loss, plus a penalty payment. Normally, this means double restitution. *The State is not an agency of creative transformation. It is not to be regarded as a savior State. Men should not seek to make the State an agency of social salvation.* It is supposed to enforce biblical civil law – no more, no less. The State is not supposed to seek to make men righteous; its God-assigned task is to restrain certain specified acts of public evil. Theft is one of these acts.

Civil government is an agency of visible judgment in history. *Justice demands judgment.* The judgments handed down by civil government acknowledge the historic judgments of God, as well as point to the final judgment of God. The goal of civil justice is always restoration: restoration through restitution or restoration through execution. This two-fold system of civil judgment also characterizes God's judgments, which are equally judicial.

Judgment unto Restoration

When God deals with His people in a harsh way in history, it is a means of restoration: judgment unto restoration, not judgment unto destruction. The atoning work of Jesus Christ at Calvary points the way to a better world in history; restitution has been made to God by the only possible ethically acceptable representative of man, the Son of God. The Christian's expectation of better earthly times is therefore valid. Christ's restitution payment has been made, on earth and in history.

One thing which is needed to translate His atonement into social reality is the progressive transformation of the criminal justice system in terms of biblical law, something which cannot take place until the humanistic theology which undergirds the existing system of criminal justice is replaced by biblical orthodoxy. This means comprehensive revival. Anyone who denies that such a progressive transformation of the criminal justice system is possible in history is thereby also denying that the atoning work of Christ *can* be manifested progressively in history. Anyone who denies that such a progressive transformation of the criminal justice system will actually take place in history is thereby also denying that the atoning work of Christ *will* be actually manifested progressively in history. People should therefore consider carefully the economic, social, political, and ethical implications of their eschatological views. When they make eschatological pronouncements, they are inescapably also making implicit economic, social, political, and ethical pronouncements. Eschatology and ethics cannot be successfully separated.

Appendix

VIOLENT CRIME IN THE UNITED STATES, 1980

The Model Penal Code [of the American Law Institute, 1962] requires the judge to employ "generally accepted scientific methods." Until at least 1978, the consensus of the criminology establishment was that offenders could be rehabilitated in prisons and also in the community under the tutelage of probation officers. This opinion prevailed even though irrefutable statistics revealed that at least two thirds of all offenders upon release from prison or discharge from probation commit other offenses.

The goals and standards embodied in the Model Penal Code are really little more than vague concepts which at one time were found palatable by the criminology and jurisprudence establishments. They do not provide precise modalities of treatment or clear instructions to the sentencing judge. It is interesting and significant that the word "punishment" is not used nor is the concept of making whole the victims of crime any part of the purposes of sentencing. Indeed, the victim of crime is not even mentioned except in a passing reference in Section 7 that a fine should not be imposed if it would prevent restitution. Neither restitution nor reparation is included in the purposes of sentencing.[1]

This short appendix focuses on violent crime in the United States. Three observations are necessary. First, the year 1980 seems to have been a peak year for violent crime in the U.S. Subsequent data indicate that rates dropped in many areas. This

---

1. Lois G. Forer, *Criminals and Victims: A Trial Judge Reflects on Crime and Punishment* (New York: Norton, 1980), pp. 77-78.

may be due to the aging of the U.S. population, since young unmarried men commit the largest proportion of crimes. Second, the rates for murder began to rise in the mid-1980's, probably because of drug-related criminal behavior. Third, the growth in criminal activity is a Western phenomenon, not just national. In Canada between 1970 and 1974, the number of recorded crimes rose by over 30%. In England and Wales, crime also rose by 30 percent, 1974-78. Substantial increases also took place in France, Sweden, the Netherlands, West Germany, Denmark, Austria, and Italy.[2] This indicates the direction of the growth in the 1970's. Of great concern is the fact that actual crimes seem to have exceeded reported crimes by many times. In the U.S., actual crimes were as high as three times those reported; in England and Wales, it was closer to ten times higher.[3]

There is no doubt that there is a still major crime problem today in the U.S. Reports one article on the economics of prisons: "Every week, like clockwork, the total number of prison inmates in the U.S. grows by 1,000 people. That's two big prisons worth of lawbreakers, most of whom cost between $14,000 and $30,000 a year to feed, house and guard. With 605,000 men and women behind bars in state and federal prisons, the U.S. already has the highest incarceration rate in the Western world; about four times that of the U.K. or France on a per capita basis. And that's not even counting the 300,000 or so in county jails across America. . . . With 37 states under court orders to reduce overcrowding, the U.S. has embarked on a prison-building program unparalleled in history."[4] The primary response of the authorities to crime has been prison-building. The rate of incarceration has grown every year from 1972: from slightly under 100 per 100,000 population to over 220.[5] "Just as rehabilitation was the byword

---

2. David J. Pyle, *The Economics of Crime and Law Enforcement* (New York: St. Martin's, 1983), pp. 1-2.

3. *Ibid.*, p. 2; citing H. J. Schneider, "Crime and Criminal Policy in some Western European and North American Countries," *International Review of Criminal Policy*, (1979), pp. 55-65.

4. Katherine Barrett and Richard Greene, "Prisons: The Punishing Cost," *Financial World* (April 18, 1989), p. 18.

5. *Ibid.*, p. 21.

The Explosion in Crime, 1960-80

In the United States, from 1960 to 1980, reported violent crimes skyrocketed in the United States and Western Europe, although not in Japan.[7] The major increase in the United States took place in the periods 1964-73 and 1976-80. (Part of this reported increase in the 1960's was the result of improvements in the statistics of several large cities.)[8] Between 1963 and 1973, violent crimes rose 174 percent, while population increased by 11 percent, a 16-to-one ratio. Local public spending on police forces increased from less than $1 billion in 1964 — an incredibly low figure, given the enormous size of tax expenditures on public schools, welfare, streets, and buildings — to $7 billion in 1974.[9] In 1960, there were about 3.4 million serious crimes committed in the United States. By 1974, there were over 10 million.[10] Violent crimes increased by 47 percent, 1969-74, from 659,000 to 970,000.[11]

Scholars debate furiously as to the causes of crime, and why rates of violent crime change.[12] Such factors as urbanization, the growing proportion of young unmarried males in a society, and the absence of wars — outlets for violent behavior — have all been used to explain the increase. Since 1968, economists have entered the debate; they tend to focus on the costs and rewards of crime and crime prevention, on the assumption that crime is just an-

---

6. *Ibid.*, p. 18.

7. "Social Scientists Say U.S. Crime Has Leveled Off," *New York Times* (Feb. 2, 1982). On Japan, see "Tokyo, Where Law Means Order," *Wall Street Journal* (Nov. 29, 1973).

8. James Q. Wilson and Richard J. Hermstein, *Crime and Human Nature* (New York: Touchstone, 1985), p. 32.

9. U.S. News and World Report (June 10, 1974).

10. *Ibid.* (April 7, 1975).

11. *Ibid.* (Nov. 24, 1975).

12. One source of information on these scholarly debates is the University of Chicago publication, *Crime and Justice: An Annual Review of Research.*

other form of profit-seeking, risk-avoiding behavior.[13] One scholar even argues that on the whole, over the last seven centuries, homicides as a proportion of total population have declined by a factor of 10 in Britain.[14] But the American public is aware of the fact of violent crime, whatever the causes.[15] The March 23, 1981, issues of both *Time* and *Newsweek*, the two most widely read U.S. news magazines, ran articles on violent crime: "The Plague of Violent Crime" (*Newsweek*) and "The Curse of Violent Crime" (*Time*). (We might also consider conducting a research project on "spying and petty theft in the news magazine publishing industry.")

In the United States between the periods 1930-34 and 1975-79, population grew by 84 percent, 123 million to 226 million. Homicides went up by almost 600 percent, from 14,618 to 101,044. Homicides per 100,000 population climbed from 11.9 to 44.7. Interestingly, the number of civil executions per homicide dropped by over 99 percent, from one per 18.8 to one per 33,681. The growth in homicides was relatively low from the 1935-39 era until 1945-49. But the curious fact is that homicides per 100,000 of population dropped from 1946 until 1962, from 6.9 murders per 100,000 to 4.5. By 1972, it had climbed to 9.4.[16] Homicides went from 44,000 in 1960-64 to 101,000 in the 1975-79 period.[17] In Los Angeles, the increases were comparable: population increase was

---

13. Between 1968 and 1979, about 250 articles on crime by economists appeared; before that, there had been only a handful. D. J. Pyle, *The Economics of Crime and Law Enforcement: A Selected Bibliography* (New York: Rand Institute, 1979). Most economists believe that the key essay that launched the field was Gary Becker's "Crime and Punishment: an Economic Approach," *Journal of Political Economy*, LXXVI (1968), pp. 169-217; reprinted in Gary S. Becker and William M. Landes (eds.), *Essays in the Economics of Crime and Punishment* (New York: National Bureau of Economic Research, 1974), ch. 1.

14. Ted Robert Gurr, *Crime and Justice: An Annual Review of Research*, Vol. III.

15. On crime rates, see Donald J. Mulvihill and Melvin M. Tumin (eds.), *Crimes of Violence*, Vol. 11 of the staff report to the National Commission of the Causes and Prevention of Violence (Washington, D.C.: Government Printing Office, 1969), p. 54.

16. James Q. Wilson, *Thinking About Crime* (New York: Basic Books, 1975), pp. 5-6.

17. Statistics compiled by the staff of California State Senator H. L. Richardson, based on the Federal Bureau of Investigation's *Uniform Crime Reports* and the U.S. Department of Justice's *Sourcebook of Criminal Justice Statistics, 1979*.

142 percent, homicides were up 686 percent, and homicides per 100,000 of population tripled.

As evil as the crime of murder is, however, it must be understood that many of the victims are far from innocent victims. A study of murder victims in New York City made in 1977 found that half of 1,622 victims in 1976 had police records. Thirty-five had been arrested on murder charges themselves. Young men were the most vulnerable single group, constituting about a third of the victims. Youths between the ages of 16 and 20 accounted for over a quarter of those arrested for murder. Almost half of the victims were black, and 30 percent were hispanic. But 124 of the victims were elderly people who were probably killed during robberies.[18]

James Q. Wilson points out that the number of robberies per 100,000 dropped from 1946 until 1959. Then, in 1960, it increased sharply, remained stable for two years, and then jumped again in 1963, 1964, and 1965. In 1959, the rate had been 51.2 per 100,000; in 1968, it was 131. Auto theft had increased from 1949 until 1963, when it rose dramatically.[19] He writes, "It all began in about 1963. That was the year, to overdramatize a bit, that a decade began to fall apart."[20]

The 1970's brought no relief. The combined rate of three violent crimes — murder, rape, and robbery — in the United States increased from slightly over 350 per 100,000 of population in 1970 to just under 600 per 100,000 in 1979. The rate had peaked in 1975, dropped with the recession of 1975-76, and then began

---

18. *New York Times* (August 28, 1977).

19. Wilson, *Thinking About Crime*, p. 6.

20. *Ibid.*, p. 5. As I point out in my book, *Unholy Spirits: Occultism and New Age Humanism* (Ft. Worth, Texas: Dominion Press, 1986), the period beginning with the assassination of President John F. Kennedy brought radical changes to the culture of the West: a rise in revolutionary activity, beginning with the campus violence of the fall of 1964; the escalation of the Vietnam War and the protests against that war; a radical change in culture, especially music, beginning with the Beatles in late 1963 and 1964; and a tremendous shift in the theory of knowledge (epistemology) on the campus: from empiricism and liberalism's optimistic "can-do" pragmatism to subjectivism, relativism, and mysticism. This shift was accompanied by a huge increase in the use of drugs and hallucinogens, and also a tremendous increase in the extent of visible occult activity, especially among those who had received college educations.

increasing again during the Carter Administration.[21]

"Fear of Crime Leads in Survey on Reasons to Leave Big Cities" announced a *New York Times* headline (May 16, 1981). The poll was conducted by the Gallup organization. In the 1970's there was no prominent cause of the migration out of the cities. In cities of one million residents or more, half of those who left cited a high crime rate. The article goes on to say that the Federal Bureau of Investigation's *Uniform Crime Reports* on the number of crimes reported to the police show that violent crimes of murder, rape, robbery, and assault rose 31 percent from 1976-80, while crimes against property — larceny, burglary, and theft — rose by 16 percent in the same period. The biggest increase for both categories came in 1980. "For cities over one million population, violent crime was up 17 percent and property crime 13 percent. Also, suburban and rural crime have been increasing in all regions of the country at a rate not far behind that of the big cities."

Juvenile Crime

Juvenile crime has accelerated since the end of World War II. Arrests for violent crimes by juveniles increased by 98 percent from 1967-76, and arrests of those 18 and older increased by 65 percent.[22] A study released by the Ford Foundation in 1978, *Violent Delinquents*, reveals that a hard core of 3 percent to 5 percent of those arrested account for more than half of the violent crimes perpetrated by juveniles — in effect, a hard-core criminal class. According to Prof. Marvin Wolfgang of the University of Pennsylvania, who has conducted studies of delinquent youths in Philadelphia since 1945, over one-third of the youths are picked up by the police for something more serious than a traffic offense, but 46 percent of these delinquents had no further police contact

---

21. *Time* (March 23, 1981).

22. *U.S. News and World Report* (July 17, 1978). Wilson cites Prof. Norman Ryder, a demographer at Princeton University, concerning children: "There is a perennial invasion of barbarians who must somehow be civilized and turned into contributors to fulfillment of the various functions requisite to societal survival." Wilson, *Thinking About Crime*, p. 12. The increasing failure of humanist society to effect this transformation of its children is the source of endless crises. Wilson lays much of the blame for rising crime on family disorganization: p. 206.

after the first offense. Concludes Wilson: "Though a third started on crime, nearly half seemed to stop spontaneously. . . . Out of the ten thousand boys, however, there were six hundred twenty-seven — only 6 per cent — who committed five or more offenses before they were eighteen. Yet these few chronic offenders accounted for *over half* of all the recorded delinquencies and about *two-thirds* of all the violent crimes committed by the entire cohort."[23] Wolfgang's research also indicates that the degree of injury inflicted by youths on their victims has increased. "People are getting their heads bashed in and seriously hurt in ways that didn't happen before."[24]

A Loss of Confidence

The result of this visible failure of the criminal justice system has been a growing distrust of the police and the courts by the public. A poll taken by *Newsweek* magazine in 1981 and published in the March 23 issue asked: "How much confidence do you have in the *police* to protect you from violent crime?" The responses:

A great deal 15%
Quite a bit 34%
Not very much 42%
None at all 8%
Don't know 1%

Second question: "How much confidence do you have in the *courts* to sentence and convict criminals?" The responses:

A great deal 5%
Quite a bit 23%
Not very much 59%
None at all 11%
Don't know 2%

When 70 percent of those surveyed have very little or no confidence in the court system, there has been a massive failure on the part of those high officials who are entrusted with the

---

23. Wilson, *Thinking About Crime*, p. 200.
24. *New York Times* (Feb. 2, 1982).

responsibility of providing justice and safety for the public.

On Average, Crimes Pays

It is a well-known fact that very few crimes result in an arrest. This does not tell the whole story. Most crimes are committed by a handful of professional criminals. By arresting, convicting, and eliminating the activities of one burglar or rapist, the law-enforcement system drastically reduces crime on the streets. One estimate says that if all people convicted of a serious crime in New York State were given prison sentences of at least three years, the rate of serious crime would be reduced by two-thirds.[25]

The U.S. Department of Justice's National Institute of Justice in 1987 released the results of a study of 2,190 inmates in California, Michigan, and Texas. It concluded that when a repeat offender is released from prison, he commits an average of 187 crimes per year until he is again imprisoned. The cost to victims of crimes committed by these people is an estimated $430,000 per year. (Warning: this assumes that the 187 crimes a year are on average expensive crimes, rather than shoplifting, which involves large numbers of less expensive crimes. This does not appear to be the case. The reliability of the statistics have been challenged by academic professionals, as statistics so often are.)[26] The cost of building a new cell and maintaining it for a year is $25,000 per prisoner, the study estimated. (This can be seen in a different way: the construction cost is between $50,000 and $100,000 per bed, with the amortized cost at $25,000 a year per prisoner.[27] Actual operating costs run about $15,000 per prisoner.)[28] The study concluded that the $8.6 billion cost of operating the nation's prisons and jails was about one-tenth of the cost to society if the institutions were shut down.[29] This conclusion appears to be self-serving on the part of the corrections bureaucracy, but the public

---

25. Wilson, *Thinking About Crime*, p. 201.
26. Barrett and Greene, *op. cit.*, p. 19.
27. "Passing through for lack of cells," *Washington Times* (Jan. 27, 1989).
28. "The Success of Authority in Prison Management," *Insight* (Feb. 13, 1989), p. 15.
29. Associated Press story, *Dallas Times Herald* (July 4, 1988), p. A-3.

sees no other alternative.

In any case, it needs to be recognized that the total expenditures of civil government at all levels in the U.S. is today in the range of $1.5 trillion per year. Thus, the cost of prisons, or even the law enforcement system as a whole, is a tiny fraction of total government expenditures.

Arrest and Conviction

Nevertheless, the issue is not simply the cost of maintaining prisons. The issue is the effectiveness of this particular sanction. Does this threatened sanction reduce crime more effectively than some other sanction would? Are actual victims better off? Are potential victims more secure in the long run? The threat of imprisonment is no better than the likelihood of a sentence being imposed and carried out. The question must be asked: What is the relationship between arrest and conviction? According to the headline of a *New York Times* article (Jan. 4, 1981), "99% of Felony Arrests in the City Fail to Bring Terms in State Prison." About 80 percent are not even prosecuted as felons. About one in six serves time in a city jail for under one year. "At a time of rising concern about crime, the police, prosecutors, city officials and research specialists say that law enforcement officials have decided to treat all but the most serious offenses as misdemeanors, more often than not by a plea agreement reached during arraignment."

The process by which felonious crimes are dealt with in New York City – and, by implication and statistics, most other major American cities – is revealing. Consider statistics for 1979. Officially, 539,102 felonies were reported to the police. This, of course, is only a fraction of the felonies committed, although no one is sure just how large a fraction.[30] The police arrested 104,413 persons on felony charges. This cleared up about 63,000 of the reported crimes, or only about 12 percent. Grand juries charged 16,318 of these arrested people with felony crimes. The cases against the other 88,095 were dismissed by the district attorneys

---

30. Some national estimates of the ratio between crimes committed and crimes reported run as high as five to one: "Study Finds Crime Rates Far Higher than Reports," *New York Times* (April 27, 1973).

or treated as misdemeanors. Of the 16,318, 56 percent resulted in felony pleas by the defendants of guilty; 16 percent resulted in misdemeanor pleas; 13 percent in trials leading to a verdict; and 12 percent in dismissals.[31] In short, criminals are rarely sent to prison for any particular criminal act.

The criminals know for certain what the public suspects: crime *does* pay.[32] The risks of being caught for one crime are low. The risks of a repeater's being caught are high. The risks of being convicted and serving a lengthy period in prison are minimal. Prof. Walter Burns, a political scientist at the University of Toronto, has summarized the problem: "Between 1966 and 1971 the U.S. murder rate increased by 52%, and the crime rate as a whole rose by 74%, as reported in *Crime in the United States: Uniform Crime Reports, 1971*. Crimes of violence (murder, forcible rape, robbery and aggravated assault) went up 80%. In 1971 there were 5,995,200 index crimes (crimes catalogued by the FBI) reported to the police, and everyone knows that a large number of crimes are never reported to the police. The proportion of arrests to crimes reported was only 19%, persons charged 17%, persons convicted as charged 5%, and persons convicted of lesser offenses .9%. All of which means that punishment was meted out in only 5.7% of the *known* cases of crime. The conclusion is inescapable: *crime*

---

31. These statistics appear to be precise. This is an illusion. The confusion in New York City police and court records is legendary. See the article, "Police in New York City Turning to Computers to Untangle Records," *New York Times* (Feb. 27, 1982). For every arrest, 15 different forms have to be filled out, and paper work is scattered throughout the city. "According to the police, about 2,000 of the 100,000 or so persons arrested on felony charges last year will have been tried. They say they want to know what happened to the other 98,000 cases. . . ." This raises another problem: Who will have access to the computerized files? Will the security system resist intrusion? No such system has been devised so far.

32. Economists and economics-influenced legal scholars, especially those of the so-called "Chicago School," have used economic theory to produce some remarkable conclusions in this regard, especially Gary Becker, Richard Posner, and Gordon Tullock. For an introduction to this literature, see Posner's speech, *The Economic Approach to Law*, published in 1976 by the Law and Economics Center of the University of Miami, Coral Gables, Florida. Posner's textbook is also important, *Economic Aspects of Law* (Boston: Little, Brown, 1986). *The Journal of Law and Economics* and *The Journal of Legal Studies*, published by the University of Chicago, are important outlets for this research.

pays. Moreover, some authorities insist that most crimes are not reported to the police and that only 1½% of all crimes are punished, which is to say that 98½% of the crimes committed go unpunished."³³

Aging and Crime

The rate of crime began to drop in the early 1980's in the United States. The only reasonable hope that citizens of the United States seem to have for continuing this reduction in crime in the near future, apart from a religious revival, is that with a falling birth rate, the number of young men, especially unmarried young men, ages 18-24, as a percentage of population, will fall. Older men commit fewer crimes. They get married, and marriage reduces crime. Gilder points out that about 3 percent of criminals are women; only 33 percent are married men. "Although single men number 13 percent of the population over age fourteen, they comprise 60 percent of the criminals and commit 90 percent of major and violent crimes."³⁴ In short, there is little evidence that tinkering with the criminal-investigation system will bring relief to the victims. The causes of crime are too complex.

By the late 1980's, major U.S. cities began to experience a rapid escalation of violent crime, especially murder, as the drug culture began to be organized on a highly businesslike basis.³⁵ An estimated 50,000³⁶ to 80,000³⁷ youths in the Los Angeles area now belong to gangs. Homicides per year peaked in Los Angeles County at 350 in 1980, fell to about 200 in 1982, and then rose again, beginning in 1984, to about 400.³⁸

---

33. Walter Burns, "Justified Anger: Just Retribution," *Imprimis*, III (June 1974), published by Hillsdale College, Hillsdale, Michigan.

34. George Gilder, *Naked Nomads: Unmarried Men in America* (New York: Quadrangle/New York Times Book Co., 1974), p. 20.

35. "Dead Zones," *U.S. News & World Report* (April 10, 1989).

36. Los Angeles Seeks Ultimate Weapon in Gang War," *Wall Street Journal* (March 30, 1988).

37. "Turf Wars," *ibid.* (Dec. 29, 1988).

38. *Idem.*

Biblical Law and Social Order

Modern criminology is a recent and very inexact science. It has been dominated by the ideology of political liberalism, which in turn is deeply committed to environmental determinism. Criminologists have had very few scientific studies available to support their opinions concerning the relationship between poverty and crime, or overcrowded urban life and crime. As Harvard University political scientist James Q. Wilson has pointed out: "It was not until 1966, fifty years after criminology began as a discipline in this country and after seven editions of the leading text on crime had appeared, that there began to be a serious and sustained inquiry into the consequences for crime rates of differences in the certainty and severity of penalties. Now, to an increasing extent, that inquiry is being furthered by economists rather than sociologists."[39] It is not surprising that criminology has not been influenced much by the concept of biblical law.

The legal standards found in the Bible provide society with a means of establishing social order. Biblical law works because it is comprehensive, and it deals with men as they are, yet in terms of an ethical code that tells us what we should attempt to become. When those who would shatter the foundations of social order openly disrupt the lives of law-abiding citizens, then the civil government is required to step in and restore order. This may involve the permanent elimination of the criminal. Biblical law imposes conditions which make crime expensive.

Thus, biblical law imposes the death penalty for certain classes of crimes that involve an intolerable attack on the foundations of social order. The biblical social order must be preserved. Courts make mistakes, justice is not perfect, and the innocent defendant may sometimes see his hopes crushed by a miscarriage of justice. *But an occasional miscarriage of justice is preferable to the advent of a permanent criminal class.* There will always be miscarriages of justice; the question is: In what direction is the criminal code headed? Toward the Bible or toward humanism?

There is a slogan in American jurisprudence: "Better that a

---

39. Wilson, *Thinking About Crime*, pp. 54-55.

hundred guilty men go free than one innocent victim be punished." This implies that it is legitimate to require standards of evidence so rigorous that only criminals are ever convicted. But the price of earthly perfect justice is the destruction of the legal system which attempts to provide such justice, as Moses discovered (Ex. 18). Such a quest for perfect earthly justice would subject a law-abiding society to waves of criminals who could not be convicted in terms of the standards of the perfection-seeking criminal justice system. The justice system would bankrupt the treasury by attempting to deliver perfect justice. The delay in punishment would increase the likelihood of crimes committed by present-oriented criminals, who tend to ignore the long-run consequences of their acts. The courts would be jammed with appeals, delays, and unpunished criminals waiting to be sentenced. The judges would tend to issue milder sentences, in order to speed up the wheels of justice. Plea bargaining by lawyers would get sentences reduced by getting criminals to plead guilty to lesser crimes. "The bigger the backlog, the lighter the sentence."[40]

There will be no plea bargaining on the day of final judgment. Justice will be perfect then. We must content ourselves with imperfect justice until then.[41]

---

40. Former New York City District Attorney Robert Morgenthau; quoted by U.S. Senator James Buckley, "Foreword," to Frank Carrington, *The Victims* (New Rochelle, New York: Arlington House, 1975), p. xv.

41. Gary North, *Moses and Pharaoh: Dominion Religion vs. Power Religion* (Tyler, Texas: Institute for Christian Economics, 1985), ch. 19: "Imperfect Justice."

SCRIPTURE INDEX

OLD TESTAMENT

Genesis

1:26	144
1:26-28	24
1:27	66
2:17	230
3:5	23
3:8	27
3:15	274
3:17-19	236
3:18	9
3:21	25
4:10	185
4:15	255
9:1-17	245
9:2	142-43
9:4-6	139, 160
9:5	56, 185
9:6	66
38:26	39
46:33-36	198

Exodus

18	259, 297
20:20	226
21:6	38n
21:12	41, 61
21:14	51, 51n
21:15	15, 21, 42, 61
21:16	42, 61, 65, 217
21:17	15, 21-22, 42, 61
21:18-19	85, 91, 100
21:19	61
21:20-21	105n
21:22	131
21:22-25	90, 99, 103, 113
21:24-25	117
21:28	143, 147
21:28-30	160
21:28-31	137, 155
21:29-30	93, 116
21:31	151
21:32	71, 149
21:33-34	167
21:34	61
21:35	139, 147
21:36	147
22:1	66, 180, 189, 193, 204, 211, 220, 254
22:3	83
22:4	150, 180, 193, 204, 210, 220, 254, 238
22:5	246
22:5-6	242, 251
22:7	254
22:9	230
22:19	42
21:30	117, 131
31:14-15	42
31:15	61

Leviticus

1:10	244
3:17	90
6:1-7	59, 70, 233

6:2-5	212, 281	13:6-11	144
6:4-5	255	13:11	227, 282
13	159	14:21	170
19:15	262	15	40
19:20	39	16:19	44
20:2	61	17:6	24, 29, 148
20:9	61	17:6-7	18
20:10	42, 43, 44, 47, 61, 195	17:7	30, 64, 273
20:11	61-62	19:16-19	24
20:12	62	19:16-21	106, 210
20:13	62	19:19	64
20:15-16	42	20:10-11	81
20:16	62	20:14	81
20:27	42, 62	21:1-8	222
21:9	46	21:1-9	36, 146, 258
24:14	273	21:5-8	185
24:16	42, 62	21:18	272
24:17	62	21:18-21	105n, 273
24:18	117	21:20	22n
25:39-41	40	21:21	53, 64
25:47-49	226	22:8	171
27:3-7	71	22:21	64
		23:1	140
Numbers		23:15-16	83
15:35-36	273	24:7	64
22:31	143	24:16	152
26:65	62	25:1-3	272
29:12-32	239	25:3	39
29:36	239	25:4	193-94
35:16-18	62-63	25:12	39
35:16-27	184	28:1-14	110
35:20-21	63	28:15-68	9, 36, 110, 262
35:22-28	156	28:58-59	225-26
35:30-31	47	32:35	108
35:31	41, 63, 117, 160, 189	32:41-42	108
		32:43	108
Deuteronomy			
1:17	44	*Joshua*	
4:5-8	xi, 1, 55	4:7-8	274
5:32	253, 256, 278	5:12	63
8:19-20	5		
12:16	90	*Judges*	
13:1-5	25	1:6-7	113
13:6-9	25		

Scripture Index

I Samuel		119:1-6	178
12:14	3	139:7-8	138
17:34-37	196		
		Proverbs	
II Samuel		6:31	254
12:4	189	16:6	225
12:5-6	196		
12:13	189	*Isaiah*	
12:14-18	197	6:9-10	2
12:18	189	14:13-15	27
13:29	197	17:9-10	148
14:14	44		
18:14	197	*Jeremiah*	
		23:23-24	138
I Kings		50:17	195
2:24-25	197		
18:21	96	*Ezekiel*	
18:40	96	3:17-19	187
19	97	34:5	195
21:13	273		
		Micah	
Psalms		4:1-5	282
22:12-13	151		
23:1	195	*Zechariah*	
50:10	66	13:7	195
68:30	151		
73:3-5	109	*Malachi*	
73:17-19	109	1:14	244
83	101		
106:15	102		

NEW TESTAMENT

Matthew		12:30	11
1:19	47	12:36	137
5:14-15	1	13:15-16	2
5:16-20	1	16:23	26
5:28	76, 137-38	18:14	195
5:28-30	115	18:21-22	255
5:31-32	27	18:23-35	34, 265
7:13-14	253	19:7-9	20
10:6	195	20:13-15	259-60
10:28	226	21:43	60, 82

21:44	142	2:14-15	232
25:32	27	2:22	68
26:15	151	3:23	30
26:31	195	6:23	224
27:2-10	151	7:7-12	9
27:4	37	7:9-13	180
27:6	37	9	138
		11	32, 43
Luke		12:17-13:7	91
10:17-19	123	12:19	108, 224
12:46-48	63	13:1-7	30, 121
12:47-48	20, 75, 251, 262	13:4	238, 253
14:28-30	261	13:8	157n
21	47		
23:34	25, 34, 35, 43	*I Corinthians*	
		2:14	184
John		3:11-15	75
7:53-8:11	29	5:5	186-187
8	28-33	7:23	83
8:4	29	9:9	194
8:7-8	29	10:21	24
8:10-11	30	11:30	239
9:4	76		
10	198	*Galatians*	
10:4-5	199	5:1	83
10:11	195	6:7-8	136
14:15	10-11		
21:15-17	198	*Ephesians*	
		5:16	76
Acts			
5:1-10	244	*Philippians*	
5:5	58	2:12	66, 115
5:11	244	3:20	140
8	140		
10:34	44	*I Timothy*	
12:7	58	4:10	204
15:20	90	5:17-18	194
21:33	58		
25:11	120	*Hebrews*	
		2:14-18	244
Romans		8	204
1:20	15-16	9	239
1:22-23	5	9:12-14	244

10:30	108	*Jude*	
James		6	58
4:1	90	*Revelation*	
		1:18	90
I Peter		20:1-2	58
5:2	198	20:14	41
		20:14-15	7, 228
II Peter			
2:4	58		

GENERAL INDEX

abortion
  capital punishment, 105
  changing attitude, 100-1
  criminal act, 100
  nineteenth century, 100
  penalty, 116
  physicians, 100
  victim's rights, 102
Absalom, 197
accidents, 176
Adam, 18, 23-25, 27, 41, 204, 259
Adoni-bezek, 113-14
Adonijah, 197
adoption, 82-83
adultery
  capital crime, 30, 42-46
  David, 196
  mercy, 43-45
  woman taken in, 28-33
aging, 10
Albeck, Shalom, 168, 170
aliens, 183
Amnon, 197
Ananias, 244
anarchism, 278
animals
  pits, 169-70
  responsibility, 139, 142-47
  victims, 193-200
  wandering, 243-45
animism, 145
annihilationism, 229n
antinomianism, 3-5, 105, 280-81
antinomians, 21

appeals court (bottom-up), 18
arbitrariness, 19
assault, 65-66
atheists, 240
atomic bomb, 159
atonement, 51
auction, 125-29, 133-35
Augustine, 87-88
autonomy, 145, 186
axe head, 156

Bahnsen, Greg, 28
Banfield, Edward, 76-77
baptism, 140, 183
beast, 143, 146
  see also animal
Beckman, Petr, 164n
bicameralism, 152
blindness, 2
blueprints, 281
blood avenger (see kinsman redeemer)
boundaries, 81, 242
boxing, 91
Bucer, Martin, 4
Bukovsky, Vladimir, 275
bureaucracy, 18, 179, 259
buyer, 214

calling, 66, 77, 86
Calvinism, 184
Calvin, John, 4, 229n
capitalism, 243
capitalization, 207-9
capital punishment
  abortion, 101, 105

Adam, 18
adultery, 41-48
  barbaric?, 146
  critics of, 21
  divorce and, 28
  final judgment, 227
  God's court, 40-41, 51
  incorrigible criminals, 203
  justified, 65-66
  kidnapping, 66-68
  modern, 274
  murder, 47
  murder only?, 20, 21
  Noah's covenant, 53
  pleonasm, 19, 22, 50
  prostitution, 46
  rabbis vs., 51n
  rebellious son, 22
  rejection of, 275
  restitution to God, 189
  social benifits, 69
  time horizon, 77
  witnesses, 29
cash, 207
Cassuto, U., 206
chaos festivals, 88-89, 97
chaplain, 238n
chimney sweeps, 250
Christ (see Jesus)
church, 42, 157
  antinomian, 3
  discipline, 3n
  guardian, 239-40
  kingdom, 60
  oath, 139-40
  sins of, 2
  see also pleonasm
citizen's arrest, 37
citizenship, 140, 182, 184
citizen's patrol, 93n
city on a hill, 1, 2
civil justice, xi
clans, 97
class conflict, 123-24

coercion, 80
committee, 260
common grace, 204, 239
communion, 90
compassion, 104
complexity, 260
concentration camp, 268-69, 279
confession, 70-71, 211-16
conflict (costs of), 85-86
consumer sovereignty, 79
continuity, 77
corporation, 157
co-sign, 157n
cost, 172, 261
costs
  collective ownership, 252
  estimations, 132
  fire code, 248-50
  insurable, 246-47
  internal-external, 251
  omniscience &, 250-51
  property lines, 245
counter-offer, 129-30, 134-35
court, 237-38, 240
courts, 97, 261 (see also judges)
covenant
  adultery, 42
  broken, 42
  defined, 26
  eternal punishment, 229n
  execution, 28
  family, 45
  inescapable concept, 26
  legal claim, 36
  Noachic, 53-58
  oath, 45
  point two, 15
  representation, 16
  representatives, 96
  upholding, 59
covenant lawsuit
  Adam and Eve, 23-25
  authorized agent, 36
  husband, 43, 45

judges and, 17
murder, 184
prosecutor, 32, 35
sin and, 26
State, 50
State initials, 19, 65
victim initials, 16
witnesses, 18
covering, 25
cowardice, 93
creation, 16
crime
  against God, 8, 220, 224
  confession, 211-16
  convictions, 293-94
  debate, 287-88
  defined, 27
  demographics, 10
  deterrence, 69, 220-32, 282
  economics, 287-88
  habitual, 52
  increase, 7
  juvenile, 290-91
  Old Testament era, 20
  pays, 276, 292-95
  penalties in Bible, 59
  repeat, 285
  resurgence, 295
  sins, 225
  social atomism, 9
  statistics, 271, 285-91
  unsolved, 258
  victimless, 40, 50, 60, 81, 225-26, 231-32
criminal
  counter-offer, 122-23, 125-27
  incorrigible, 272
  insurance, 124-25
  restoration, 180-81
criminology, 296

Dallas, 276
damages, 251
Darwinism, 5

David, 3, 196
deafness, 2
debt, 40, 257
deeper pockets, 161
deterrence
  death penalty, 69
  final judgment, 228
  goals of, 282-84
  God's wrath, 220-21
  restitution, 201
De Tocqueville, 267
discount, 207-9
dismemberment, 115, 224n
dispensationalism, 3, 54, 101
division of labor, 80-81, 84, 242
divorce, 20, 27-28, 45-46, 60
Dobson, James, 105n
dominion (kidnapping), 66
dominion covenant, 255-56
donkeys, 199
drug laws, 80
drunk drivers, 176-77
duel, 90-93

earnest, 109
economic growth, 243
efficiency, 81, 84
Egyptians, 198
Elijah, 96
envy, 123
equality, 73-75, 83-84, 262
ethics, 56
eunuchs, 140
evangelism, 2, 3
exclusion, 217
execution (see capital punishment)
executions, 146
Exodus, 15
expiation, 146-47
ex post facto, 19
externalities, 167, 251
eye for eye (*lex talionis*)
  applications, 119-25
  auction, 125-29

brutal?, 113, 128
class differences, 118
economic interpretation, 118-19
Hayek, 258-63
limits state, 256
literal?, 114
nations, 262
paying back, 106, 263
predictability of law, 97-98
primitive?, 107
punishment fits crime, 135
restitution, 105, 116-17
Roman law, 106

fair fight, 91
fairness, 109, 119
family, 42, 45, 46
fear, 244
fence, 170, 216
fences, 245-46
final judgment, 5, 7, 227-30, 30, 274
fines
   denial of State's omniscience, 175-76, 179
   drunk drivers, 177
   gored ox, 151
   State's income, 121-22, 176
   victim's compensation, 257-58
Finkelstein, J. J., 143-47
fire, 246, 248-49
fire code, 179
flogging (see whipping)
forgiveness
   adultery, 43-45
   kidnapping, 70
   protection of victim, 48-49
   restitution, 205, 255
   victim's right, 34-35, 37-39, 59
Forer, Lois, 285
freedom, 261
free market, 80-81
French Revolution, 274
Fudge, Edward, 229n
Fuller, Lon, 188

fundamentalism, 4

games, 87-88
Getty, J. Paul, 72
God
   abominations, 48
   assault on, 65-66, 85
   court, 51
   covenant lawsuit, 24
   crimes against, 8
   deals, 123n
   decree, 138
   final judgment, 5
   harsh?, 3-5
   heavenly court, 236, 238-40
   holiness, 168
   judge, 40
   judgment of, 109
   knowledge of, 63
   lawgiver, 34
   mercy of, 265
   mistake?, 22
   murder of, 65-66
   owner, 242
   penal sanctions, 7
   perfect wrath, 228-29
   representative, 17, 42
   representatives, 16, 24, 36, 121
   restitution, 109
   restitution to, 225, 40
   restoration 181-82
   sanctions, 9
   striking, 15, 16
   torture, 5, 69n
   torturer, 21
   vengeance, 108-9
   victim, 16, 17, 24, 34, 36, 40, 180, 186, 224
   witness, 31
   wrath of, 2
grace, 25, 123, 239
guilt
   animal, 144
   collective, 185-86

General Index

covering, 25
objective, 144
ox, 140
removal, 181
sense of, 24, 37
witnesses and, 30

Hammer, Armand, 72n, 100n
Hammer, Julius, 100n
Hammurabi, 67, 68, 74, 106n, 151
harshness, 3-5, 51
Hayek, 225, 258-63
Hayek, F. A., 74-75
heaven, 6
heifer, 185
hell, 6, 266
heresy, 21
hierarchy, 15, 18, 26-27
highway safety, 174
Hirsch, S. R., 38, 50-51, 59, 70n, 117-18, 168-69
history, 76
Hittites, 206
Hobbes, Thomas, 56
homocides, 288-89
honor, 92
Horowitz, George, 51n
horses, 199
House, Wayne, 53-55, 56n
humanism, 8, 9, 11-12
husband, 42-43, 99
hypocrisy, 177-78

Ice, Thomas, 53-55, 56n
idolatry, 68
impersonalism, 274-75
incorrigible sons, 272
insurance, 124-25, 247
    automobile, 162
    economics, 161-62
    negligence, 160-61, 165
    nuclear power, 163
    screening risk, 165
intellectuals, 100-1

interest, 208
intolerance, 96
irresponsibility, 90
Islam, 114, 254
Israel
    conversion of, 43
    death penalty, 43
    history, 189
    kingdom, 60
    Rome and, 43

jail, 7
jealousy, 123n
Jesus
    antinomian?, 4
    atonement, 284
    city on a hill, 1
    covenant lawsuit, 184-85
    debtor's prison, 265
    gored slave price, 151
    grace, 25
    Jews and, 2
    jubilee laws, 82
    kinsman – redeemer, 184-85
    laws and, 1
    mercy of, 60
    restitution, 190, 204
    resurrection, 41
    sanctions fo God, 25
    Sermon on Mount, 1
    slave – sin, 150-51
    trial, 37
    victim, 35
    wages parable, 259-60
Jewish law, 168-69
Jews, 2
Jordan, 47
    Jesus as slave – son, 150-51
    stoning, 142
    unclean beast, 141-142
Jordan, James, 39n, 41, 106n
Joseph, 44, 47-48, 60
jubilee, 40
jubilee laws, 81-82

Judaism, 83-87, 189, 206
Judah, 38-39
Judas, 37
judges
    Adam and Eve, 24
    arbitrariness, 19
    authority, 130-33
    cost estimates, 247-48
    covenant lawsuit, 17
    discretion, 49-50
    discretion of, 39
    divorce, 45-46
    external evidence, 149
    lawless, 97
    leniency, 49
    limits on, 60
    profession of faith, 182
    representatives, 185
    respecting persons, 124
    setting penalties, 130-33, 133-35
    victim's agent, 122
    without sin?, 30
jury, 188
justice
    costs, 236
    demonic, x
    eternity, 236
    history, 237
    judgment &, 283-84

Kaiser, Walter, 205-6
Kelsen, Hans, 145
kidnapping
    adoption laws, 82-83
    calling, 66
    capital crime, 42
    capital punishment, 66-68
    pleonasm, 69-70
    ransom, 71-73
    risk to victim, 69-70
    selling animals, 230
    Talmud on, 51n
    theocentric principle, 65-66
Kingdom of God, 60, 82

kinsman redeemer, 184, 266
knowledge
    fines and, 175
    goring ox, 147-49,
    limited, 155, 179
    risks &, 159
Ku Klux Klan, 94-95

lashing, 39
law
    barbaric?, 105
    blessings, 278
    blueprints, 286
    boundaries, 81
    case, 223
    case laws, 13, 17, 22
    chains, 58
    civil and criminal, 221, 231
    class, 262
    clear, 253
    deterrence, 226
    equality, 75, 107, 262
    equality before, 74, 83-84
    evangelism tool, 2, 3
    ex post facto, 19
    goal, 180
    grace and, xi
    harsh?, 3, 6
    hatred of, 101, 278
    ignorance of, 25
    impersonalism, 274-75
    Jesus and, 1
    known, 259, 260
    limits, 180
    negative function, 9-11
    negative sanctions, 9-11
    new covenant era, 20
    Old Testament, 279-81
    outward confirmity, 183
    "package deal," 276
    predictable, 19
    procedure, 31
    rabbinic, 50-51
    resurrected, 55

General Index

rigor of, 22, 28
sanctions, 39
social order, 296-97
social order and, 2
Ten Commandments, 223
under, xi
universalized, 55
lawlessness, 271
legalism, 280
legal predictability, 93
legislation, 172, 178
legitimacy, 95, 101
leniency, 278-79
Levi, Edward, 202
Lewis, C. S., 121
lex talionis (see eye for eye)
liability, 147-49
　corporate law, 157-59
　church, 157
　knowledge and, 155, 159
　legislation and, 171-72
　limited, 155-66
limited liability, 138-39, 250
linear history, 114
Locke, John, 56
loopholes, 32

magic, 273
Maimonides, 87n, 142, 147, 189n, 195n, 210, 244n
manslaughter, 92
Manson, Charles, 270-71
Mardi Gras, 88
Marxism, 96
Masonic oaths, 111
Massachusetts, 152, 202-3, 249
measures, 186-87
mercy (see forgiveness)
Minnesota, 190, 201
monopoly, 81
murder, 7, 20, 21, 47
　capital punishment, 55n, 160
　covenant lawsuit, 184
　execution, 146

expiation, 185
God, 65-66
Massachusetts, 146
Noah's covenant, 53
no ransom, 117
State as agent, 40
trial of Jesus, 37
unsolved, 36, 185
Murray, John, 55n, 56n
mutilation, 134, 136, 255-56

Nachmanides, 117
National Victim Center, xi
nations, 54-55
natural law, 56
negative sanctions, 9
negligence
　costs &, 152-53
　externalities,
　insurance, 165
　knowledge &, 159-60
　pit, 167
neighbor, 231
neo-evangelicals, 280
neutrality, 10-11, 182, 245-46, 267
Newton, Isaac, 4
Noah's covenant, 53-58
"No Trespassing," 170, 174
nuclear power, 163

oath, 110-11, 239-40
omniscience, 18, 250-51, 260
ownership, 143, 167-68
　bundle of rights, 212, 216
　lawful title, 216-18
　legal immunities, 217
　right to exclude, 217
ox, 116, 131, 137, 139-40
　executed, 160
　owner's negligence, 152-54
　self-disciplined, 142
　stoning, 143-47
　training, 194

parents, 15, 18n

peace, 85, 97, 181
perfection, 108
perfect justice, 155-56
perjury, 24, 107
permission, 18
personalism, 138, 152
Pharisaism, 37
Philadelphia, 249
Phillips, Anthony, 222-24
physicians, 103
pickpocket, 254, 256
pietism, 101
pit, 167
plea bargaining, 215n, 218-19, 297
pleonasm
   adultery, 43, 45-47
   automatic execution? 34, 44
   cases, 42, 61-63
   deceased victim, 41-42
   emphasis, 48-49
   judges, 19, 60
   kidnapping, 69-70
   rebellious son, 22, 52-53
   reespect for persons, 43
   State, 65
pluralism, 95-96
pollution, 245
Posner, Richard, 77
precedent, 19
predictability, 261
price, 207, 210
prices, 218
price tag, 122-23
prison, 127, 257
   anti-history, 266
   brutality, 270
   bureaucracy, 271
   concentration camp, 268-69
   costs, 292
   debtor's, 265, 268
   doubts, 270
   guards, 275
   Israel, 266
   origin, 202

rehabilitation, 267
restitution and, 266
sanction, 276
prisons, 59, 286
Prohibition, 281
property, 168-69, 242-43
property rights, 167-68, 243, 252
prosecution, 17
prosperity, 110
prostitution, 46
Protestant ethic, 115
Puritans, 4, 56
purjury, 239

Quakers, 202

railing, 171
ransom, 71-73, 116
ransom insurance, 160-63
rebellious son, 21-23, 51-53, 272
redemption, 9
reform, 281-82
refrigerator door, 171
rehabilitation, 69, 188, 257, 267, 285, 286-87
rent, 207
repentance, 181-84, 226
representation
   Adam & Eve, 24
   covenant, 15-16, 96
   family, 42
   inescapable concept, 26
   sheep and oxen, 200
   super natural, 26-27
responsibility
   active, 169
   animals, 143
   complete, 137
   collective, 5
   duel, 91
   increases, 63
   knowledge and, 147-49
   limited, 138-39
   New Covenant, 20

General Index

ownership, 143, 167-68, 170
  personal, 179
  stewardship, 243
  upward and downward, 139-40
    (see also liability)
restitution
  best goods, 244
  bloody sacrifice, 186
  confession, 70
  defrauded buyer, 214-15
  deterrence, 201
  double, 231
  economics, 209-18
  experiments, 190-91, 201-2
  eye for eye, 105
  fines, 175-76
  fitting the crime, 205
  five-fold, 193-95, 200
  four-fold, 194
  goals, 282-84
  God and, 25
  hell, 266
  meaning, 8
  prison and, 266
  purposes, 180-81
  rehabilitation and, 9
  restoration, 181, 283
  "resurrection," 283
  Rushdoony, 210
  Rushdoony on, 205
  sacrilege, 68-69
  seven-fold, 254-55
  slavery, 276
  substitute, 204
  technology and, 128-29
  two-fold, 199
  vengeance, 109
  victim, 59
restoration, 180-81, 263, 283
resurrection, 41, 55
revolution, 65
rights (bundle), 212
risk
  calculating, 75-78

crime, 294-95
criminal, 69
detection, 230
drunk drivers, 177
insurable, 247
insurance costs, 162
kidnapper, 75-77
kidnap victim, 67-69
owner, 139-40
rich, 74
slave trade, 79
social, 157n
speeding, 258
transferring, 246-48
victims, 258
zero, 156-57, 172-73, 174-75
Rome, 87-88
rope, 156
Rothbard, M., 207-8
Rothman, David, 267-68
Rousseau, J. J., 56
Rushdoony, Rousas J.
  civil oath, 240
  eternity, 236
  divorce, 28
  eunuchs, 140
  incorrigible sons, 272
  juvenile delinquents, 52-53
  limited liability, 158n
  restitution, 205, 210
  sacrilege and theft, 68
  stealing freedom, 83
  victim's rights, 84

sabbath, 55n
sabbatical year, 40
sacrifice, 244
sacrifices, 239
sacrilege, 68
safety (see risk)
sanctions
  absence, 56
  collective, 220-21, 225-26
  criminal's right, 120

deserved, 119-20
deterrent, 201
dichotomy?, 56
fines, 121-22
husband, 99
inescapable concept, 10
maximum, 54, 119
national, 262
"needs of society," 121-22
negative, 3, 5, 6
Old Covenant, 39
penal, 7
specified in advance, 19
State, 57
substitute, 10
unequal results, 73-75
universalized, 55
victims decide, 257
whose?, 54
worldwide, 110
Sapphira, 244
Satan, 24, 123
Schaeffer, Francis, 12
seat belts, 178
self-government, 18, 95, 142
Sermon on the Mount, 1
sheep
  helpless, 195-96
  passive, 194
  selling, 213
  stupid, 198
  symbolic, 195, 198
  training?, 207
  two-fold restitution, 231
shepherd, 195, 197-98
silence, 213-15
sin, 26-27, 30
slave, 149-51
slavery, 40, 78, 81, 276
  abolition, 80, 84
  conversion, 83
  criminals, 127
  efficiency, 84
  efficiency of, 81

evangelism, 81-82
laws against, 80-81
representation, 127
war and, 81
slave trade, 19, 66, 78
slippery places, 109-10
smoke detectors, 173
social atomism, 9
Social Gospel, 12
socialism, 260, 278
social order, 2, 183, 191, 296-97
social theory, 5, 110
South, 92, 94
sparks, 246, 250
speed limits, 174-75, 258
Stalin, 268-69
State
  arbitrary, 19, 257, 270
  coercion, 80
  covenant lawsuit, 19
  divinized, 149, 240, 269
  fines, 175-76, 258
  fire codes, 248-49
  God's agent, 40
  insurance and, 162-65
  intolerant, 96
  liability insurance, 162-65
  limited, 253-54, 256
  limits on, 54, 120-21
  messianic, 19, 122, 188, 279
  monopoly agent, 37
  new sanctions?, 20
  nuclear power, 163
  oath, 240, 241
  omniscience, 156
  perfectionist standards, 155-56
  pleonasm, 48, 51, 65
  primary function, 221
  private ownership, 167-68
  prosecutor, 32, 35-41, 85
  represents God, 121-22
  restitution to God, 231
  restrained, 19
  restricted, 19, 36, 38

salvation, 283
sanctions, 57
slave monopoly, 127
subpoena, 23n
trustee, 176
unlimited power, 57
vengeance, 108, 111, 253
victim, 60, 70
stay of execution, 25
stewardship, 242
stolen goods, 216-18
stoning, 105n, 142, 143-47, 273
subpoena, 23n, 37
swimmers, 245
swimming pool, 171
Switzerland, 121
Sutton, Ray, 26, 27
symbolism, 199-200, 230

table tennis, 12-13
Tamar, 38-39
tattle tales, 18n
Ten Commandments, 223
Texas, ix
theft, 167
theocracy, 241
thief (silent), 213-15
thumb, 114n, 116
time, 76-77
title, 216-18
torture, 5, 7, 21, 69n
toxic waste, 159
treason, 144
trust funds, 175-76
Tyndale, William, 4
tyranny, 58

uncertainty, 208-9, 246
unclean beast, 141-42

value, 207
vengeance, 104, 108-9
　legitimate, 131
　price tag, 122
　public, 110

victim's, 122
victim
　covenant lawsuit, 16, 186, 237
　court's agent, 235
　estimating sanctions, 129-30
　forgiveness, 36, 37
　God, 16
　God's agent, 36
　God's representative, 16-17, 122, 186
　husband, 42-45
　innocent buyer, 211
　Jesus Christ, 35
　mercy by, 20
　prosecutor, 38
　protection, 48-49
　pursues justice, 236-37
　restitution, 109
　wife, 45-46
victimless crimes, 40, 50, 177
victims
　animals, 193-200
　"soft on," 6
　witnesses?, 36
victim's rights
　abortion, 102
　civil court, 237
　divorce, 27-28
　forgiveness, 34-35
　maximum sanctions, 57
　mercy, 59
　plea bargaining, 219
　protection of innocent, 46
　rebellious son, 22
　sanctions, 47
　specifies penalty, 211
　specifies sanctions, 122
vigilantes, 93-95
violence, 66, 85, 98

war, 81
Wenham, Gordon, 234
West
　future-oriented, 114-15
　impersonalism, 275

insurance, 166
technology, 128-29
torture, 7
Wheaton pox, 281
whipping, 274
Wilson, James Q., 8
witness, 118, 234, 237-38

witnesses
  Adam & Eve, 23-25,
  adulterous woman, 29-30, 32-33,
  covenant lawsuit, 36-37
  double, 148
  stoning, 273
wives as victims, 45-46

DISCARD